Bioterrorism

Bioterrorism

Confronting a Complex Threat

edited by
Andreas Wenger
Reto Wollenmann

LYNNE
RIENNER
PUBLISHERS

BOULDER
LONDON

Published in the United States of America in 2007 by
Lynne Rienner Publishers, Inc.
1800 30th Street, Boulder, Colorado 80301
www.rienner.com

and in the United Kingdom by
Lynne Rienner Publishers, Inc.
3 Henrietta Street, Covent Garden, London WC2E 8LU

Library of Congress Cataloging-in-Publication Data
Bioterrorism : confronting a complex threat / Andreas Wenger and
 Reto Wollenmann (eds.).
    p.   cm.
 Includes bibliographical references and index.
 ISBN-13: 978-1-58826-525-8 (hardcover : alk. paper)
1. Bioterrorism. 2. Bioterrorism—Prevention. I. Wenger, Andreas.
II. Wollenmann, Reto.
HV6433.3.B56   2007
363.325'3—dc22

                                                          2006033578

British Cataloguing in Publication Data
A Cataloguing in Publication record for this book
is available from the British Library.

Printed and bound in the United States of America

        The paper used in this publication meets the requirements
 ∞   of the American National Standard for Permanence of
        Paper for Printed Library Materials Z39.48-1992.

 5 4 3 2 1

Contents

Part 3 Managing the Threat: Policy Options

Part 4 Conclusion

Foreword

THE USE OF PATHOGENS AS WEAPONS OF WAR AND TERROR HAS A LONG HISTORY, but in recent years our focus on these risks has greatly intensified. Earlier, many policymakers thought of bioweapons as the stuff of antiquity (cadavers catapulted over walls to spread plague in medieval cities under siege, blankets infected with smallpox to decimate American Indians opposing the British in their American colonies) or eccentricity (a Rajneeshee cult spreading salmonella in salad bars to disable political opponents, Aum Shinrikyo attempting to obtain and work with anthrax before resorting to sarin in their efforts to trigger an apocalypse by attacking Tokyo subway passengers). Starting in 1989, however, Russian defectors triggered an appreciation of how heavily the Soviet Union had invested in this weaponry. More recently, the attacks of September 11, 2001, and the anthrax letters that were mailed to US senators and media figures immediately afterward focused attention on both bioweaponry and the imaginative malevolence of terrorist groups that might use it. Since that time, an order of magnitude more money, effort, and debate has gone into the subject.

The first response when confronting a newly perceived risk is to continue to do what was being done previously in other contexts, but to relabel it as relevant to the new threat. A second common reaction is to allocate much more money to the problem, permitting us to double, quadruple, or otherwise greatly multiply those preexisting efforts. A third response is to reorganize: forming committees, councils, commissions, divisions, and ultimately even departments bearing names that suggest they will solve, or at least address, the newly perceived problem.

Normally, it is only later that we start to do what we should have done first: debate the character of the new problem. How substantial is this risk? What are its special characteristics? Will the problem be the same in the next decades as at present? How might it manifest itself? What near-term capabilities might protect us? Are these capabilities the same as those we should be pursuing for the long term, or do our long-term and short-term strategies diverge? It is only when these and other fundamental questions are asked and answered that we can begin to choose wisely among existing efforts, detect the gaps in what we are doing, initiate relevant new efforts, and organize and invest to respond to our challenges.

It took us some years to develop new thinking in response to the realities of nuclear weapons. Bioterrorism is, if anything, a more complicated problem. It demands not only an understanding of both biology—a science that is changing faster than nuclear physics did after World War II—and terrorism, but also a grasp of such diverse topics as the physics of aerosols, our food distribution systems, agricultural and public health systems, mechanisms of decontamination, and systems of policing and interdiction.

Moreover, in one dimension bioterrorism is a security problem, related to foreign enemies. In another, it is a domestic problem, subject to exploitation by criminals and disaffected loners as in the model of the Unabomber. Viewed a third way, bioterrorism is intimately connected to natural challenges, particularly those of pandemic disease. From a fourth perspective, bio-challenges may occur from "bio-blunders," problems that arise neither naturally nor malevolently but from scientists who accidentally unleash new pathogens. Fifth, bioterrorism should not be considered in isolation, but instead in tandem with all other potential hazards.

It should not be surprising, then, that we are still in the midst of debate and at present have no consensus as to the problem, much less as to how to deal with it. It is the strength of this volume that it captures the range and richness of this debate. While we have no consensus, the way we will get there is through discussions like this.

—*Richard Danzig,*
Former Secretary of the US Navy (1998–2001)

Acknowledgments

THIS BOOK EVOLVED OUT OF AN ATTEMPT TO SHED NEW LIGHT ON THE BIOTERROR-
ism threat—a threat that became the subject of widespread media attention and political rhetoric in the aftermath of the 2001 anthrax letters.
It is the result of collaboration by an interdisciplinary group of colleagues in areas ranging from security policy and counterterrorism to
public health and the life sciences.

Along the way, we received the support and assistance of many people and in a variety of ways. We thank the authors of this book for their
patience with our comments and suggestions and for their willingness to
take into account new developments. A conference organized by ETH
Zürich (Swiss Federal Institute of Technology) was a crucial part of our
collaborative process, and we thank all the conference participants who
presented their views and shared their insights. In addition to the
authors of this volume, they are Ken Alibek, Janet Martha Blatny, Jürg
Balmer, Edward Borodzicz, Richard Danzig, Myriam Dunn, Gerald
Epstein, Ernst Felberbauer, John Gilbert, Frank Gottron, Gigi Kwik Grön-
vall, Jesper Grönvall, Michael Guery, Rohan Gunaratna, Stein Henriksen,
Melissa Hersh, David Heyman, David Humair, Frida Kuhlau, Ajey Lele,
Michael Mair, Mark Maskow, Victor Mauer, Michael Moodie, Eric K.
Noji, Anders Norqvist, Aleksandr Rabodzey, Klaus Riedmann, Martin
Schütz, Yoram Schweitzer, Ted Whiteside, and Doron Zimmermann.

We are delighted that our manuscript ended up in the capable hands
of Lynne Rienner and Lisa Tulchin, who have handled the review and
publication process with great skill. We wish to extend our thanks to
Isabelle Abele-Wigert and Martin Wählisch, and especially to Jennifer
Gassmann of the Center for Security Studies, for their outstanding work
in preparing and organizing the conference. We thank Michelle Norgate

and Christopher Findlay for their excellent editorial assistance. Finally, we owe a great debt to Susanne Schmid as a truly indispensable partner in our day-to-day work.

While we have greatly benefited from the comments, criticism, and encouragement of all those mentioned above, the final responsibility for any errors is of course ours alone.

—Andreas Wenger and Reto Wollenmann

Bioterrorism

1

Bioterrorism: A Complex Threat

ANDREAS WENGER AND RETO WOLLENMANN

BIOTERRORISM, A HIGHLY COMPLEX THREAT, IS THE CONCERN OF A WIDE RANGE of academic and political fields, including science, politics, law, and security. Soon after the terrorist attacks of 9/11, the 2001 anthrax letters and a worldwide series of related hoaxes alerted the world's media to the potential threat of bioterrorism and catapulted the issue onto the security policy agendas of the United States and many Western governments.

The debate about bioterrorism and biodefense is not entirely new in expert circles, and, given the difficulties in defining the extent and characteristics of the threat, it comes as no surprise that the many expert evaluations have often contradicted one another. However, the degree to which this debate has been—and will continue to be—shaped by US policies, on the one hand, and by a growing gap between the views held by the academic community and those held by the policymaking community, on the other, is indeed remarkable.

This book addresses two important topics: the nature and the relevance of the threat to our societies of the deliberate use of biological weapons, and the difficulties associated with designing the right policy mix to successfully manage a complex and still largely unsubstantiated threat. The better we understand the many challenges involved in the assessment of the threat—the persistence of political conflict and the changing nature of terrorist warfare, the present and future activities of state actors in bioweapons production and biodefense research, the rapid technological advances in the life sciences, the global spread of dual-use expertise and commercial biotechnological applications, and the risk of a rapid global spread of natural diseases—the better able we will be to deal with the problem.

1

An examination of bioterrorism elicits a host of complex questions: How urgent is the bioterrorism threat? Do we underestimate or overestimate bioterrorism, and what are the potential consequences of our estimates? What can we learn from bioterrorism events of the past? How will the rapid developments of technology and those in the life sciences affect the future threat? Who are the likely perpetrators of bioterrorism? How much of a threat are state actors, nonstate terrorist actors, and lonely insiders of growing governmental biodefense programs? What policy options are there for managing the bioterrorism threat? How do governments prioritize their policies for the prevention and management of natural diseases, on the one hand, and for the prevention and management of the malicious use of bioweapons on the other? To what degree is bioterrorism a security policy issue as opposed to one of health or other public policies? The authors of this book address these questions.

While not intended as the final word on bioterrorism, the present book offers the opportunity to compare a variety of views of experts from a wide range of professional and academic backgrounds. Most of the literature to date has focused either on the technical aspects of bioterrorism or, more generally, on the threat posed by weapons of mass destruction (WMD). Several recent books, for example, discuss technical issues related to a specific sector of bioterrorism, such as laboratory security, food safety, infectious agents, viral bioterrorism, and biodefense or syndromic surveillance.[1] Others track the evolution of the WMD threat.[2] This book, by contrast, focuses on bioterrorism in general and on the security policy aspects of the bioterrorism threat in particular.

The book consists of three sections. The first covers actors and capabilities; the second, threat perceptions; and the third, policy options. Part 1 deals with the legacy of the secret state biowarfare programs of the twentieth century, analyzing the factors that have influenced the historical evolution of state bioweapons capabilities. Aiming to provide a better understanding of the past, it also addresses the controversies surrounding the current threat by both state and nonstate actors. With a view to the future, it concludes with a discussion of the impact of scientific and technological change in biology and the associated life sciences on the potential malicious use of microorganisms by a wide range of actors.

Part 2 addresses the various, and sometimes contradictory, perceptions held by different communities about the nature of the biological weapons threat. It identifies a high level of uncertainty as a key characteristic of the bioterrorism threat and discusses a series of knowledge gaps about the scope and sophistication of existing biowarfare programs and past instances of biowarfare. Examining the literature and identifying uncertainty as the key determiner of such perceptions, it shows why experts make such very different policy prescriptions even though they usually work with the same historical data.

Part 3 highlights a set of policy challenges relating to bioterrorism and offers some solutions to them. It emphasizes the practical problems that policymakers face when making decisions about the trade-offs needed between investing resources in defense against bioterrorism and investing them in the prevention of natural diseases. Finally, it discusses endeavors for more security in the biosciences and in biodefense programs, and it calls for more transparency as a precondition for an informed public policy debate at the national and international levels.

Introducing Part 1, Jeanne Guillemin investigates the history of state biowarfare programs as a means of providing the reader with an assessment of the future likelihood of a bioweapons attack. Unlike chemical and nuclear weapons, biological weapons were rarely debated in public in the twentieth century. Secrecy, Guillemin shows, was the most important facilitator of the growth of the biological warfare programs of all major powers—whether democracies, republics, monarchies, totalitarian states, or military dictatorships—yet the extent of such programs remained largely unknown, even well into the twenty-first century. In addition to secrecy, scientific advocacy, an existing military-industrial infrastructure, the political perception of a dire threat to national survival, and the doctrine of total war, with its justification of using civilians as targets—all played an essential role in allowing for the creation of state biological programs.

The end of the Cold War brought about a new awareness of the dangers of biowarfare as the focus shifted to the potential diffusion of biological weapons to lesser states and nonstate terrorist actors. According to Guillemin, however, this diffusion is directly affected by the policies of advanced states in general and the United States in particular. Accelerated by the events of 9/11 and the subsequent Amerithrax[3] cases, US interest in—and consequently the research and funding of—biodefense increased dramatically. Dozens of counter-bioterrorism programs, most of them concealed from the public and not subject to congressional oversight, are now entrenched in a wide range of US federal agencies as a result of the shift in US policies toward defending all its citizens against germ attack. The emphasis of these programs, Guillemin points out, is on the development of new biodefense technologies, which has inadvertently led to a huge increase in the number of trained microbiologists who know how to grow and test lethal pathogens for warfare, exacerbating the danger of the diffusion of such expertise and technology to potential bioterrorists.

The US export of a narrow national security mission to its allies, Guillemin argues, undermines the long-term security interests of the United States. A strictly civil defense approach to bioterrorism, like that of the United States, ignores both the unstoppable global diffusion of biotechnologies and also the risk of an unusually deadly outbreak of an infectious disease. The spread of biotechnologies and natural epidemics can be effectively regulated and controlled only by multiple, coordinated international efforts. The alternative to transparency, institutional oversight, and organizational accountability at the national level, and to the criminalization of biological weapons at the international level, Guillemin concludes, is a disease catastrophe that will highlight the danger of government secrecy and the failures in international cooperation at the cost of lives and public trust.

Analyzing the current biological weapons threat from state and non-state actors, Milton Leitenberg takes issue with the claim of some experts that bioterrorism is the greatest existential threat of our age. Leitenberg shows that the number of state bioweapons programs has decreased markedly over the past few years. Various US authorities implicitly acknowledged the lessening threat of biowarfare when they dropped South Africa, Libya, Iraq, and Cuba from their intelligence assessments, and when they became more cautious after their intelligence failures in Iraq and qualified their assessments of several other national bioweapons programs, among them those of Iran, North Korea, and Syria. According to Leitenberg, no state is known to have assisted any nonstate or terrorist group in obtaining biological weapons.

Leitenberg goes on to show that there has been an extremely low incidence of real biological events in the past, in contrast to the large number of hoaxes spawned by political rhetoric and media attention. Aside from several right-wing groups in the United States and the Rajneesh group in The Dalles, Oregon, no terrorist group is known to have successfully cultured any pathogen. The most serious known attempt, Leitenberg notes, was Al-Qaida's efforts to develop bioweapons, which appear to have been at the early conceptual stage when the group's facility was overrun by US forces in Afghanistan and the individual who carried out the laboratory work was arrested. In fact, the production and distribution of anthrax powder in the United States in 2001 remains the most significant example of a nonstate biological weapons capability.

Since the mid-1990s, the risk and imminence of the use of biological agents by nonstate actors and terrorist organizations have been systematically and deliberately exaggerated and remain almost certainly

the single greatest factor in provoking Al-Qaida's interest in bioweapons, according to Leitenberg. He further points to increasing concerns about the risk of a natural flu pandemic, concurring with Guillemin that the current political rhetoric of the US government should be tempered in the face of the greater likelihood of a natural disease outbreak, and that the United States has been using an overwhelming proportion of its resources to prepare for the wrong contingency.

Focusing on the fields of biology and chemistry, which in recent years and through recent research breakthroughs have expanded into the fields of molecular biology and biochemistry, Malcolm Dando addresses the potential for the misuse of new and developing technologies. Dando first outlines the stages of development of these sciences in the twentieth century, moving on to show that the palette of agents now available to potential perpetrators has grown significantly as a result in particular of new manipulations of old viruses and bacteria. Of special concern is the fact that genetic engineering of traditional agents could increase the number of possible agents and the characteristics and uses of such agents to the extent that biodefense becomes unable to anticipate and protect against the threats.

In the not-too-distant future the rapidly expanding knowledge in biology could allow potential attackers to target any number of physiological processes in the human (or animal) body in many different ways. It took a hundred years, Dando points out, to achieve the ability to decode human DNA, and another fifty years to describe the DNA sequence of the human species. If developments in genetic science continue at the current pace, the ease with which various pathogens could be synthetically produced could well increase—and with it the diversity of pathogens and the means of delivering such pathogens. Thus, Dando argues, the future impact of the advances in biology has to be thoroughly investigated in order to curb the potential hostile use of life science research.

Dando draws the conclusion that we need a web of prevention, that is, a multilateral set of policies, including better intelligence on potential perpetrators, effective controls on exports of agents and equipment, and a strengthening of current public health and emergency planning procedures. This web of prevention, Dando argues, has to be bound together by the internationally accepted norm that modern life sciences must not be used for hostile purposes. The best way of achieving this, Dando suggests, is to ensure that the Biological and Toxin Weapons Convention (BTWC) is reassessed by the states parties to give the convention permanent organizational support and to ensure that strong measures are taken to strengthen the BTWC.

Introducing Part 2, Peter Lavoy addresses the contrast between, on the one hand, the extraordinary rhetoric of the United States and other governments in describing biowarfare and bioterrorism as one of the most frightening security threats and, on the other, the low level of preparedness of those governments, societies, and armed forces to deal with this threat. In explaining this contrast, Lavoy highlights two knowledge gaps, both linked to a lack of certainty about nearly every aspect of the threat. The first gap is the poor level of understanding about the scope and sophistication of the biological warfare programs that state and nonstate groups might currently possess. The second results from the technical, political, social, cultural, and other difficulties in identifying, characterizing, and attributing attacks involving biological weapons once they have occurred.

Discussing the biological weapons programs of the former Soviet Union, Iraq, and Al-Qaida, Lavoy points to the failure of the US intelligence community to adequately assess these programs at different points in time, when that community has either seriously underestimated the threat, as with the Soviet Union, or dramatically overestimated it, as with Iraq. Lavoy attributes these errors to a tendency of the US intelligence community to deal with a lack of reliable information by rallying behind one specific hypothesis to explain an adversary's conduct. Addressing a set of cases of alleged biowarfare by both superpowers and other states during the Cold War, Lavoy acknowledges the propaganda value of biological weapons while noting also the extreme difficulty in authoritatively validating their use or nonuse.

The two knowledge gaps addressed by Lavoy make it extremely difficult for governments to develop effective strategies and policies and to assign adequate resources to the management of potential biowarfare and bioterrorism. In order to ameliorate these policy problems, governments should try, Lavoy advises, to gain more information about the status of biowarfare programs and about the cases in which biological agents have been or may have been used. Since major information gaps will persist, Lavoy concludes, the military acquisition and war planning process should be based on planning scenarios that feature realistic biological weapons employment.

Marie Isabelle Chevrier addresses the widespread view that expert evaluations of bioterrorism appear to vary widely. She analyzes bioterrorism threat assessments by well-known experts, focusing particularly on the framing of the research question, the data considered, and the methods used. Chevrier finds similar arguments in the assessments, based on similar data, using similar reasoning, and evidencing little disagreement

about the likelihood of bioterrorism and the likely vulnerability of modern societies. Although the policy prescriptions of the experts vary considerably, the assessments themselves, Chevrier finds, mostly show that a successful bioterrorism event causing mass casualties is not likely to occur.

However, Chevrier demonstrates how the use of vague terminology makes it difficult to understand what experts mean when they describe the future likelihood of mass casualty bioterrorism as either "low," "not likely," "extremely unlikely," or "possible but not probable." Most experts fail to relate the likelihood of an event to a specific time frame (for example, "highly likely within the next five years"), and all find that there is insufficient historical data to predict with any certainty the likely occurrence of future bioterrorism events; consequently, most researchers have felt, Chevrier points out, that terrorist incidents involving chemical agents were appropriate cases from which to draw inferences about bioterrorism. However, given the differences in production and dissemination between chemical agents and biological agents, Chevrier notes, such analysis may overstate the estimated probability of a bioterrorism attack. The bottom line in most of the assessments is widespread agreement that any bioterrorism estimate is surrounded by a great deal of uncertainty.

Chevrier divides the assessments into two groups, those done before 2001 and those undertaken after the anthrax letters of 2001. She found that the assessments done after 9/11 and the Amerithrax cases represented some change, but not a substantial one. However, the gap between the academic and the policy communities has grown since 2001, driven by highly publicized exercises simulating worst-case scenarios. Most academic bioterrorism experts have been far more cautious and reserved in their assessments than those in the policy community. While the former often focus on the nexus between the terrorism threat and the biological weapons threat, the latter tend to see the bioterrorism threat in the larger context of the likelihood of deliberately caused disease.

Introducing Part 3, Anthony H. Cordesman notes that for policymakers there is no reliable way to establish the level of effort needed to deal with the biological weapons risk. Nonetheless, although there are grave uncertainties and extreme difficulties in tracking any form of biological warfare activity, governments cannot ignore the fact, Cordesman states, that Islamic terrorists have shown an interest in acquiring biological weapons. Further, the difficulties in manufacturing, weaponizing, and disseminating bioweapons are being steadily reduced by the spread of biological facilities, dual-use equipment, and technical skills. At the same time, Cordesman warns, governments should be extremely careful about crying wolf. The fact that a threat exists does not predetermine the kind of response that is needed; the priority the bioterrorism risk should be given in the context of other security policy and health risks; and the levels of investment in time, expertise, and money that are required.

According to Cordesman, most governments that have examined bioterrorism in terms of technological capability have acknowledged the possibility of a high-level attack. But dramatizing worst-case scenarios, he argues, should give way to real-world capability studies. Most bioterrorism events are likely to take the form of attacks where there is little real damage in terms of lethality, and where the main impact is most likely to be a mix of panic and political and economic effects. The level of uncertainty in the use of a bioagent and in terms of its potential lethality remains very high. The technical expertise is concentrated in official laboratories and research centers, but it is often lacking at the broader public policy level. As a result, Cordesman concludes, there is little transparency about the scale of national efforts that could shape an informed public policy debate or foster international cooperation at the operational level.

Addressing key policy challenges in the management of the biological risk, Cordesman points to the problems—with regard to both national policy and global cooperation—in determining the extent to which investments in the defense against and response to biological terrorism are competing with those in natural disease research, and also in defining possible synergies between the two. Even though there are practical limits to transparency and cooperation, he concludes, both are key to any effort to prevent bioterrorism, to deal with its political impact, and to create cost-effective programs. For if bioterrorism does become a serious reality, there will be an immediate need for large-scale cooperation—a fact that planning and preparation efforts should take into account.

Iris Hunger identifies a trend toward more secrecy in the biological field and argues that this trend has to be reversed in order to prevent an erosion of existing international norms against the use of biological agents as weapons. The rapid developments in the biosciences, together with the increasing civilian use of biotechnologies and the lack of national and international control measures, have resulted in a growing threat potential from bioweapons, from both states and terrorist groups. One reason why the threat is growing is the dual-use nature of many of the research, development, production, and testing activities in the biological field. Since it is often difficult to differentiate between peaceful and hostile activities, transparency, Hunger argues, must be the basis of such activities in the long run.

According to Hunger, two recent developments have increased the level of secrecy in scientific biodefense work in general, and in US efforts in particular. As a reaction to 9/11 and the Amerithrax events of 2001, governments have drastically limited their openness in the biosciences, while at the same time the scientific community has been imposing restrictions upon its own activities. In the United States, the reemergence of the category of "sensitive but unclassified" information, allowing restrictions on unclassified research, has occurred along with stricter controls on the transfer of knowledge to foreign nationals and, at the same time, the inclusion of prepublication review clauses into grants and contracts.

In addition, many states have created or enlarged their existing biodefense programs, a trend that is particularly pronounced in the United States. Not only has the US government not reported some of its secret biodefense programs to the member states of the BTWC, but it has also provided an enormous funding boost to bioweapons research, which in turn has dramatically increased the number of individuals who know how to deal with these agents, while funding for other diseases has been cut. Yet Western states have a chance to influence how biological research is conducted, Hunger asserts, since most of the sensitive research is still done in the West. Thus, they should lead by example and set legally binding standards by which biodefense programs that are close to the line between offensive and defensive activities can be identified and closely monitored.

This book makes apparent how difficult it is for governments to design sensible policies against bioterrorism. The threat of the malicious use of microorganisms or toxins by state and nonstate actors, along with the high level of uncertainty regarding both the intentions and capabilities of potential malevolent actors, defies traditional approaches to threat analysis. Consequently, if the aim is to secure our societies against the risk of bioterrorism, we must involve experts from a variety of academic and policy fields, including public and private actors at the local, national, and international levels.

Drawing on the findings of the chapters in this book, the concluding section discusses a series of key policy challenges in managing an elusive threat. Although the threat may be exaggerated and manipulated, it can neither be denied by experts nor ignored by policymakers. Formulating and implementing policy to protect a population against the threat of bioterrorism is a remarkably different challenge from formulating and implementing policy to secure a state against the threat of an armed attack by another state. With this difference in mind, the concluding section discusses the new policy challenges to both states and societies in their efforts to define countermeasures, assign responsibilities, and provide resources.

Notes

1. For example, see David McBride, *Bioterrorism: The History of a Crisis in American Society* (New York: Routledge, 2003); Barbara A. Rasco and Gleyn E. Bledsoe, *Bioterrorism and Food Safety* (Boca Raton, FL: CRC Press, 2005).

2. For example, see Jonathan B. Tucker, ed., *Toxic Terror: Assessing Terrorist Use of Chemical and Biological Weapons* (Cambridge, MA: MIT Press, 2000); Brad Roberts, ed., *Hype or Reality? The "New Terrorism" and Mass Casualty Attacks* (Alexandria, VA: Chemical and Biological Arms Control Institute, 2000).

3. The US Federal Bureau of Investigation dubbed the anthrax attacks "Amerithrax." It created a special website, which was given the same name, for the ongoing anthrax investigation.

Part 1

Understanding the Threat: Actors and Capabilities

2

The Legacy of Secret State Programs

JEANNE GUILLEMIN

A DEFINING CHARACTERISTIC OF THE TWENTIETH CENTURY WAS THE EXPLOITATION of the advanced sciences of chemistry, biology, and physics for military advantage in the realm of unconventional strategic weapons. Biological weapons were the least successful of this trio of weapons of mass destruction (WMD), in the sense that they were never fully assimilated by any state military. In the twentieth century, biological weapons were never used on a grand scale in battle the way chemicals were in World War I. Nor did they become a symbol of ultimate strategic military force, as nuclear weapons did after the 1945 US bombings of Japan. Instead, despite extensive development by the major powers (France, Japan, Britain, the United States, and the former Soviet Union), their history remained secret or ignored.[1] In the twenty-first century, though, biological weapons have assumed a new symbolic importance, greatly influenced by US policies, that links them to the potential exploitation of biotechnology by outlaw states and terrorists. Understanding the fundamental characteristics of the former programs can inform us about future prospects for biological weapons and restraints on them.

How the twentieth-century biological warfare ventures began is itself a historical conundrum. The literature on technological innovations in the modern military offers many examples of organizational resistance to the assimilation of new weapons.[2] Yet the major military powers of the twentieth century (with the notable exception of Germany) embarked on large antipersonnel germ weapons programs, despite admitted uncertainties about whether such weapons were technically possible or morally defensible. The potential of biological weapons to cause large-scale death and havoc accounts for the allure they had for certain advocates and also for the skepticism and even revulsion with which they were greeted by others within government. Biological weapons rely on living organisms that are inherently difficult to produce and standardize. They depend on the scientific ability to produce germs that kill or weaken important life-forms—humans, livestock, and crops. Their destructive effects might be delayed and uncertain; they might also (as with anthrax spores) result in prolonged environmental contamination, or they might (as with contagious diseases) infect friendly troops and civilians. Their main advantage—the element of surprise—could readily be subverted if an adversary were forewarned and protected with vaccines, antibiotics, masks, or other defensive technologies.

At present, most analysts presume that the advanced industrial powers are highly unlikely to resort to biological weapons given the end of the Cold War and the legal and moral norms against this category of arms. All but a few nations are party to the 1925 Geneva Protocol, which bans the use of both chemical and bacteriological weapons. The same is true for the 1972 Biological and Toxin Weapons Convention (BTWC), which bans bioweapons programs and the possession of such weapons. The intense secrecy necessary to hide a state program (to conceal its laboratories, production facilities, training and testing grounds, modes of transportation, and special troops) is generally uncharacteristic of advanced industrial states, and difficult for any country to sustain in a world of globalized commerce, travel, and communication. In addition, modern conventional and nuclear weapons have long fulfilled the requirements of national defense, including deterrence. Biological weapons have almost no place in modern state arsenals, nor do chemical weapons, which were banned by the 1993 Chemical Weapons Convention.

The end of the Cold War focused new attention on the potential diffusion of biological weapons to less politically powerful nations. The United States, in particular, has emphasized the danger that hostile "rogue states" and terrorists beyond the reach of political persuasion might acquire biological, chemical, or nuclear weapons. Still, as in the past, the policies of advanced industrialized nations directly affect the diffusion of the weapons they invent, including biological ones.[3] Now the world's preeminent power, the United States sets the standard for restraints against germ weapons programs and use. Since the mid-1990s, instead of engaging in broad international cooperation to reduce risks, the United States has emphasized limited national security goals. Following 9/11 and the 2001 anthrax postal attacks, this approach intensified as a part of new homeland security initiatives. The US "war on terror" has also entailed the engagement of US allies, particularly the North Atlantic Treaty Organization (NATO) and NATO-affiliated nations, in defensive exercises as well as in efforts to interdict traffic in materials relating to biological, chemical, and nuclear weapons. US preoccupation with bioterrorism has introduced a new integration of national security and the US biological sciences, ranked first in the world. The question is whether this approach can keep new biotechnologies and their inevitable global diffusion beyond Western industrialized nations for strictly beneficent rather than destructive purposes. A review of the political circumstances that fostered the former state programs suggests what the future threats of the hostile exploitation of the life sciences might be and what policies might reduce these threats.

Historical Background

A hundred years ago, the United States was neither the world's first military power nor its leader in the biological sciences. Rather, Germany and France emerged from the nineteenth century as dominant forces in both armaments and microbiology. In World War I, at Ypres in Belgium, Germany, then the leading nation in the chemical industry, launched the first mass chemical attack, provoking a chemical arms race that still has repercussions today. Also in World War I, the German army mounted a minor biological campaign against its enemies' pack animals, attempting to kill them with anthrax and glanders. After the war, partly in fear that a rearmed Germany might resort to germ air attacks, France and, soon after, the Soviet Union began their first forays into biological warfare programs. The militaries of both countries used their existing chemical programs as the basis for this new kind of indiscriminate weapon, anticipated for use in aerial bombing. After its 1931 military invasion of Manchuria, Japan (not a party to the 1925 Geneva Protocol) established a secret biological warfare program there, near the city of Harbin. In 1940, the Japanese Imperial Army began the only modern use of germ weapons in battle, attacking Chinese cities and towns with plague-infected fleas and poisoning food and wells. As part of its brutal retribution for the 1942 Doolittle Raid on Tokyo, the Japanese army attacked thousands of villagers southwest of Hankow with anthrax and glanders because they had aided or shown support for the US pilots.[4]

Britain's biological program, created in 1940 while it was under German air attack, had the most lasting consequence for sophisticated weapons development. The Soviet program was undermined by the 1937–1938 purges, and the French venture came to a halt with the Nazi occupation in 1940. After the US entrance into World War II in 1941, the United States took its cue from the British and in late 1942 instituted its program for developing virulent disease agents, aerosols, and bombs. After the war, British and US advocates of biological weapons argued that the lethal impact of their newly invented biological bombs, much lighter than chemical ones, might achieve the devastating capability of atomic weapons. They speculated that the Soviet Union, and later Communist China, could be subdued with disease agents such as anthrax, tularemia, and brucellosis, against which entire cities would be unprotected. During the Vietnam War, the US Army proceeded aggressively with biological attack simulations, achieving what it claimed was a new capability for regional dispersal of disease agents.

In the 1960s, the United Kingdom, armed with a nuclear weapons capability, retreated from its offensive biological programs and promoted legal restraints against biological weapons. France did the same, but more discreetly and slowly. In 1969, President Richard Nixon, concurring with the British, renounced biological weapons on behalf of the United States. Nixon's decision paved the way for the belated US ratification of the 1925 Geneva Protocol and the formulation of the 1972 BTWC. Thus, the military exploitation of new biotechnologies seemed to end. But by 1975, the Soviet Union was using a radical modernization of its biological sciences to mask a large biological warfare program. For nearly two decades, until its demise in 1991, the Soviet Union violated the 1972 BTWC, despite its having served as a depository nation for it, together with the United States and Britain.

Totalitarianism enhanced the bureaucratic secrecy that allowed the Soviet program to thrive. Yet the governments that sponsored biological warfare programs included representational democracies as well as totalitarian states and military dictatorships. Of the smaller states, apartheid South Africa and Saddam Hussein's Iraq were eventually known to be emulating the WMD programs of the major powers, while Israel has been strongly suspected of nuclear, chemical, and biological weapons programs, the latter as early as 1947.[5]

The Importance of Secrecy

Secrecy was the most essential factor in the growth of the biological weapons programs of the twentieth century. Closed-door decisions facilitated the creation of offensive programs and sheltered them from oversight and severe budget cuts, so that eventually they established secure organizational niches. The world learned a great deal about chemical weapons during World War I and a great deal about nuclear weapons at the end of World War II. In contrast, biological weapons were rarely discussed in public forums and never aroused the kind of international protest that brought about treaty and organizational restraints on chemical and nuclear weapons proliferation.[6]

The extent of the secrecy that enveloped each of the major biological warfare programs would be difficult to exaggerate. In open as well as closed societies, in war and in peace, the programs were often unknown to those in the other sectors of the military, and government leaders were often uninformed about or ignored the goals and achievements of their own biological weapons programs. In renouncing the US offensive biological weapons program, President Nixon accurately pointed to the fifteen years that had passed without the program's being subject to comprehensive review. During those years, a few congressional members had made sure that funding for the program was ample and secure. Later, in a much different context, the massive Soviet program was embedded in bureaucratic layers of secrecy until the 1990 defection to Britain of one of its leading scientists.[7]

Throughout the history of biological weapons, secret information was shared among allies, if not with the public. Soviet relations with satellite and client states likely included the sharing of information and perhaps of technology relevant to biological warfare. During World War II, Britain, Canada, and the United States shared personnel, research, and testing grounds; this tripartite arrangement continued after the war and later included Australia. In 1947, the US government secretly made a deal with Japanese bioweapons scientists to protect the Japanese from war crimes prosecutions in exchange for information on Japan's program and its use of germ weapons. In this way, evidence of the devastating impact of biological weapons on civilians, which otherwise would have been presented at the Tokyo war crimes tribunal (1946–1948), was suppressed.

Also during the history of secret biological weapons programs, governments encouraged disinformation to protect these ventures. When Japan attacked Chinese civilians with plague-infected fleas and with poisoned food and water, it masked its aggression by allowing these attacks to pass as naturally occurring epidemics. In the 1950s, the United States and Britain dismissed as propaganda reports about the December 1949 Soviet trial of Japanese germ warfare scientists its troops had captured in China in 1945. In other contexts, states exploited the public fear of and ignorance about diseases associated with biological weapons. In 1952, the Chinese and North Koreans accused the United States of using crude Japanese methods of attack in the Korean War, and they produced a huge compendium of largely concocted data to bolster their claims.[8] Following these accusations, the Chinese government instituted a nationwide anti-insect campaign, which it based on propaganda about US disease attacks.[9]

In the Soviet Union in the 1970s, two accidental outbreaks caused by the covert program were also explained as epidemics of natural occurrence. In the first, in 1972, several people were infected with smallpox in the Aral Sea test area. In the second, in 1979, sixty-eight people died from inhalational anthrax in the city of Sverdlovsk (present-day Yekaterinburg), in the Ural Mountains. An investigation of the latter showed the harmful effects of military secrecy: first, diagnosis was delayed, and second, the affected community was not alerted to the risks of exposure.[10] In the 1980s, the United States accelerated its defensive toxin projects and promoted chemical weapons innovation and production, while at the same time it accused the Soviet Union of assisting Laos and Vietnam with mycotoxin attacks on Hmong tribes and on Cambodians.[11] Cuba and the United States had long accused each other of making or using germ weapons, and they continued to do so after the Cold War had ended.[12]

Persuasive Scientific Experts

In addition to secrecy, four other factors allowed the major programs of the twentieth century to begin and to endure: scientific advocacy, established military-industrial resources, a perceived dire threat to national survival, and a total-war doctrine. Not all advanced industrial nations, even those capable of starting a biological program, chose to do so. Rather, key leaders, by interpreting national interests, determined whether and how research on this unusual weapon would commence.

Scientists played an essential role in laying the groundwork for state biological programs and in recruiting other scientific experts. In the interwar period, French, Soviet, and Japanese scientists were part of a general arms buildup. In France, Auguste Trillat started his career at the Institut Pasteur in Paris after obtaining his doctorate in chemistry in Munich. In World War I he was part of the French chemical corps. Then, in 1921, he became the first head of the French program, after reporting confidential information from a German source that Germany had begun its own biological weapons initiative. That information exaggerated Germany's activities, which centered on rearmament with conventional weapons and air power. Later, as the Nazis took power and Germany's belligerence intensified, Adolf Hitler's aversion to biological weapons restrained those German scientists who might have pursued such weapons programmatically.[13] Nonetheless, until the 1940 hiatus, the French program drew on the Institut Pasteur for resources and personnel.[14]

In the Soviet Union around 1925, military biologist Jacov Fishman started a biological weapons program as part of the modernization of the Soviet army promoted by General Mikhail Tukhachevsky.[15] That program was short-lived due to the 1937 Stalinist purges that led to the execution of Tukhachevsky and the incarceration of Fishman and many microbiologists from the fields of military and public health. In Japan, General Ishii Shiro, a military physician, spearheaded in 1931 the Japanese Imperial Army's offensive program, which lasted until 1945.[16]

The more technically sophisticated programs, which began with the United Kingdom and the United States in World War II, relied heavily on the talents of academic microbiologists. In 1939, in response to German military aggression, key civilian microbiologists in Canada, Britain, and the United States began to think like military strategists. In 1939, Nobel laureate Frederick Banting, the codiscoverer of insulin, urged the creation of a British offensive and defensive program and built his own research team in Toronto with funds from private donors.[17] Similarly, before becoming head of the British program at Porton Down in 1940, bacteriologist Paul Fildes advocated his country's need for a retaliatory and offensive capacity against Germany, and later he successfully argued this position at the highest levels.[18] In 1941, the United States began drawing on its many university scientists. Columbia University scientists Theodor Rosebury and Elvin Kabat wrote a comprehensive outline of select potential bioagents and a plan for a biological weapons program.[19] Rosebury went on to lead the important division that pioneered the study of aerobiology at Camp Detrick. After the war, as a civilian, he wrote openly against biological warfare programs.[20] Ira Baldwin, a University of Wisconsin expert on fermentation, became an important leader of the US wartime effort, in particular of the initiative to produce anthrax bombs.[21]

The role of civilian versus military scientists in the resurgence of the Soviet program in the 1970s is less well recorded. The well-known Soviet academician Yuriy Ovchinnikov is often portrayed as having persuaded the Kremlin to create Biopreparat, the state conglomerate that housed both commercial and secret research. At the same time, within the military, the older World War II veteran General Yefim Smirnov, former head of the Soviet public health ministry, was a powerful advocate for a biological warfare capability.[22]

The Existing Military-Industrial Infrastructure

The most advanced state biological programs (in France, Britain, the United States, and the former Soviet Union) were adjoined to the chemical weapons programs created during World War I. The use of chemical weapons in World War I established a precedent of indiscriminate attack employing the dispersal of toxic aerosols and mustard gas to break the impasse of trench warfare and claim broad terrain. In the interwar years, bomber aircraft presented even broader possibilities for strategic, long-range chemical attacks and, more theoretically, for biological attacks.

Adding early biological programs to established chemical ones brought considerable technical advantages. In the best of circumstances, the chemical programs had already developed effective bombs and spray generators, mastered aerosols, and conducted aerial tests. In the 1940s, the British biological warfare program, though small, benefited greatly from its physical proximity to the chemical program at Porton Down, where it was able to take advantage of its experts on aerodynamics and engineering. Its technical innovations were shared with the United States in 1942 and after. In the United States, the new biological program heralded an expansion of the militarily marginal chemical programs, with budget increases and enlarged testing sites and production facilities. The chemical program also had vociferous advocates in the military, industry, and among congressional officials who argued to government on behalf of both types of programs.

The move from laboratory research to volume production of disease agents, coupled with the mass production of suitable munitions for strategic attack, distinguished the two postwar superpower programs. The US program's accomplishments in these areas from World War II until 1969 brought biological weapons close to the early mass destruction capability envisioned by Banting, Fildes, and others. Before it ended, the Soviet program increased the scale of its endeavor, adding long-range missile capability and attempts to exploit the techniques of modern genetics.[23]

The Japanese program differed from programs in the West in that it was relatively isolated from Japan's chemical program. Although joint aerial chemical and biological exercises were occasionally conducted, the large central facility, Unit 731 near Harbin, was exclusively devoted to biological weapons research, as were subsidiary facilities. General Ishii, the creator of the Japanese program, was never able to devise a successful biological bomb, and the program's aerosolization techniques lagged significantly behind those of the Western allies. During World

War II, when the Japanese decided to retreat from chemical weapons, their biological program continued unaffected and unimproved.

Political Perceptions of a Dire Threat

A principal justification for offensive biological programs was the existence of a dire threat to national survival, a perception that bolstered the rationale for seeking an unconventional advantage over the enemy. By the early twentieth century, aided by increasingly destructive weapons, the military forces in Europe could threaten each other with extreme levels of physical destruction and human harm, and carried out those threats in two world wars. When the specific threat of biological weapons arose, though, it was usually ill-founded—a by-product of the larger conflict, but one with organizational repercussions.

In the 1920s, for example, the French suspected that their traditional enemy, Germany, would use its advanced microbiology and superior air power to invade and conquer France. Concerning German air power and intentions, the French assessments were accurate, but France was in error concerning its enemy's biological weapons. Although the German military had used anthrax and glanders in World War I, such use had proved to be of limited military value. As Germany began rearmament, French fears fueled its own pursuit of a biological weapons advantage. Later, Britain and the United States became similarly convinced of a biological threat from Nazi Germany. It was only in late 1944 that reliable Allied intelligence sources showed conclusively that Germany had no biological program.[24] By then, however, both the British and the US biological programs had become organizationally entrenched.

Japan's belligerence in the 1930s presented a different model of political motivation. In the 1930s, a militarized Japanese government had ambitions to make Japan the dominant force in Asia, replacing the British Empire. The dire threat to the nation, as Japan's leaders perceived it, was a lack of raw materials for industrial growth—an economic dilemma to which the solution was expansion into China.[25] In 1931, the Japanese forcibly occupied Manchuria and set up a puppet government under army control. In addition to building new cities and transportation systems, Japan located its secret biological warfare program there. Armed conflict with Soviet troops in the north, and then the war with China, troubled this territorial expansion. Years later, when asked to justify the program's secret horrors (which included human vivisection, the murder of Chinese research subjects, and attacks on civilians), one former Japanese biologist replied, "Because in a war, you have to win."[26]

Each government differed in the way authority was granted to its military to foster innovative biological programs. In 1940, with London under siege, a few key civil servants initiated the British program, placing it at Porton Down without the permission of the war cabinet or of the prime minister.[27] Later, Prime Minister Winston Churchill approved the program, although his advisers disagreed about the program's offensive goals. US president Franklin D. Roosevelt perhaps knew little about the US wartime biological program, which was orchestrated mainly by Secretary of War Henry Stimson. In imperial Japan, Emperor Hirohito, himself a biologist, likely approved the military program and authorized its expansion. Some believe that Soviet secretary-general Leonid Brezhnev personally gave the order to create Biopreperat, the conglomerate that housed both the secret biological weapons program and open biological research. Despite these variations, in each case civil authorities invariably made the crucial decision to start the program and then gave program officials extensive latitude to covertly pursue their objectives.

In the long Cold War era, dire threats to national survival were perceived both in terms of nuclear annihilation and mutual destruction. After World War II, the US and British offensive programs were revived in response to the perceived threat of Soviet aggression and the spread of Communism in Eastern Europe and China. Although military advocates argued that the Soviet Union would have biological weapons by the early 1950s, this estimate failed to take into account the war's severe toll on Soviet public health conditions and the retrograde impact of Stalinism on its biological sciences. As the Cold War commenced, US and British civil and military advocates spoke out in favor of the potential of germ weapons to rank with nuclear weapons in their destructive power.[28]

The United States, Britain, and France later abandoned germ weapons, in part because their nuclear and conventional weapons provided sufficient deterrence against the threat of aggression. Why the Soviet Union opted for biological weapons in the 1970s remains unexplained. Its nuclear arsenal was enormous, and its biological program was too secret to serve as a deterrent. Soviet leaders may have erroneously believed that the United States still secretly maintained its advanced program. As a monolithic garrison state, the Soviet Union may simply have been seeking to maximize all its military options.[29]

Cold War geopolitics spurred some diffusion of superpower biological programs to lesser states, but how much is uncertain. The best documented instances are the now defunct programs in apartheid South Africa and Saddam Hussein's Iraq, which were also fueled by perceptions of dire threats to national survival. Much more remains to be known about the extent to which other states under similar pressures and with sufficient resources—for instance, Israel, Cuba, Iran, Syria, Taiwan, and North Korea—secretly opted for biological weapons or, as in the case of Libya, rejected them.

Total War and Civilian Targets

The doctrine of total war, a response to the new scale of industrial-age warfare, included a justification for attacking civilians, who were integral to the production of weapons and the general sustenance of the armed forces.[30] By some reckonings, the destruction of a factory could weaken the enemy as much as a battlefield victory could. Frederick Banting wrote about the basis of the doctrine in his 1939 argument for a British biological weapons program:

> In the past, war was confined for the most part to men in uniform, but with increased mechanization of armies and the introduction of air forces, there is an increased dependence on the home country, and eight to ten people working at home are now required to keep one man in the fighting line. This state of affairs alters the complexion of war. It really amounts to one nation fighting another nation. This being so, it is just as effective to kill or disable ten unarmed workers at home as to put a soldier out of action, and if this can be done with less risk, then it would be advantageous to employ any mode of warfare to accomplish this.[31]

The total war doctrine signaled a striking moral regression. Industrialization had already produced the massification of the labor force that degraded individual autonomy and rights. The doctrine of total war went further by postulating that the deaths of enemy civilians en masse was a significant means to military victory as an end. Military air power became a vital part of this doctrine, inasmuch as aerial bombings promised unobstructed access behind enemy lines and the destruction of critical economic infrastructures, including factories and cities. Visions of biological bombs eradicating large populations with deadly diseases were part of a modernistic approach to warfare, which included chemical weapons as a theoretically quick way to shorten battles by overpowering the enemy with a single attack. Within the secret confines of the biological weapons programs, the total war doctrine gave militaries a license to target entire enemy populations with deadly or debilitating diseases.

An important supposition underpinning the total war doctrine was that a technological advantage would prevent the enemy from mounting an equally devastating retaliatory attack. During World War II, the Allied carpet bombing of enemy targets in Europe, and similar attacks on Japan, were conducted under the expectation that neither Germany nor Japan could counterattack with equal or greater force. The same rationale applied to the US decision to drop atomic bombs on Japan in 1945. During the Cold War, the nuclear arsenals of the United States and the Soviet Union pushed the total war doctrine to new limits in that they introduced the threat of mutually assured destruction to civilians on both sides of the conflict, "a stable, if grotesque, stalemate."[32]

With biological weapons, the expectation was that civilian targets were at a sufficient distance to avoid a risk of infection in the homeland. As for retaliation, each program proceeded as though it alone had the advantage of surprise, which, despite political perceptions of foreign threats, was generally true. Among major powers secretly developing biological weapons, the mass protection of civilians against exotic germ weapons was rarely proposed and never implemented. Soldiers and program researchers were, of course, vaccinated or otherwise protected, if possible, but public health systems operated separately from the secret military programs, although at the higher echelons in the United States and Soviet Union, not in total ignorance of them.

Present Threats

The trend in industrial societies has been toward an increase in technological risks, particularly the inescapable risk of transnational environmental damage caused by late industrial-age manufacture and energy use.[33] Similarly, the production of nuclear and chemical weapons by the two superpowers in the twentieth century has become recognized as a destabilizing global hazard in the twenty-first century. In contrast, biological weapons of the twentieth century have generated a different legacy, one of US scenarios of potential mass disease attacks that stir the public imagination, even though these predicted catastrophes have not occurred.

An important change in US policy occurred in the 1990s, when there was a shift toward defending all US citizens against germ attacks by foreign enemies, whether such attacks were against US military members stationed in the Middle East or Asia or against civilians in the home-land. This defensive position was in part a reaction to post–Cold War revelations about the Soviet biological program and, in 1992, that of Saddam Hussein, compounded by unprecedented acts of terrorism that, in method and scale, seemed to redefine US vulnerability to attack. This policy shift became embodied in legislation for "domestic prepared-ness" programs in 120 major cities and in presidential directives for antibiotic stockpiling and other measures to counter the threat of bioter-rorism, including a troubled universal anthrax vaccination program for the US military.[34] Although the United States was not at war, the nas-cent framework for domestic policies was national civil defense, a con-struct that found favor among Republicans who dominated Congress after 1994. Domestic preparedness was also generally supported by elected members of Congress on both sides of the aisle who sought a new source of funds for their states and districts.

The 11 September 2001 Al-Qaida attacks on the United States rein-forced this orientation toward civil defense, and the anthrax postal attacks that followed soon after guaranteed that bioterrorism would be a major national security issue. Washington's quick response was to demand in-creased regulation of any biological research involving disease agents that had been cultivated for biological weapons use and, subsequently, to ini-tiate an aggressive project to develop defensive technologies, with an emphasis on pharmaceutical innovations. The fright value of biological weapons also lent itself to political rhetoric and media exploitation.[35] In October 2001, the fictional bioterrorist scenario Dark Winter, created by a Washington think tank and exploited by the press and other mass media, caught the attention of Vice President Dick Cheney. Dark Winter depicted invading Iraqi terrorists infected with smallpox causing a US pandemic of catastrophic dimensions, based on facts that were later roundly criticized by medical experts.[36] Convinced by the scenario, Cheney immediately advised President George Bush to institute a national vaccination cam-paign. The president did so in late 2002, when the United States was bas-ing part of its case for the invasion of Iraq on the threat of Saddam Hus-sein's biological weapons. By that time, many US citizens had been persuaded that smallpox was an imminent threat to their health.[37] Partici-pation in the vaccination campaign faltered early on, after several older first responders died from coronary complications soon after being vacci-nated. Following the Iraq invasion, as it became evident that Saddam's biological program had been destroyed in the 1990s, US fears about small-pox sharply declined and with them the national vaccination campaign.

The smallpox vaccination campaign aside, the perceived threat of biological weapons has had lasting organizational effects. Dozens of federal counter-bioterrorism programs are entrenched in the Department of Homeland Security, the Department of Defense, the Department of Health and Human Services, the Department of Energy, the Department of Agriculture, the Federal Bureau of Investigation (FBI), the Central Intelligence Agency (CIA), and elsewhere. As part of the national security apparatus, many of the activities of these programs have been kept secret from the public and exempted from congressional or other government oversight. At the local level, state and city governments have been funded to intensify emergency response systems that adhere to the civil defense model, even as support for police, firefighters, and public health infrastructure diminishes. In this new era, a major emphasis has been placed on the invention of defensive pharmaceuticals (vaccines, antibiotics, serums, and antivirals) and of surveillance and detection technologies to counter the threat of bioterrorist attacks.

Scientific and Technical Resources and Weapons Capability

Sixty years ago, when the United States decided to continue its postwar biological warfare program, the numbers of expert microbiologists were relatively low and located in the West, and only a small number of states had built up the modern military organizations and arsenals that could potentially support a secret biological weapons venture. Today, thousands of microbiologists worldwide have skills comparable to those of scientists working in the old state programs. The military buildup in industrializing countries has also expanded, in organizational size and range of weapons. China, India, and Pakistan have acquired nuclear weapons, and others, including North Korea and Iran, may do the same.

Technologically, the contemporary threat of biological weapons diffusion exists on two levels, neither of which can be effectively controlled except by long-term international efforts. One threat can be called a "moderate capability," that is, proliferation that could arise from skills and technologies no more advanced than those used in the US and Soviet programs. These would include, for example, generic methods for increasing the virulence of pathogens, techniques for aerosolization, and the industrial-scale production of agents and munitions. As in the old programs, certain technical challenges would have to be met, such as the large-scale production of virulent agents and the building of effective mechanisms for agent dispersal. Compared to the proven military value of modern conventional weapons, even a moderate capability in biological weapons remains a luxury for small, economically disadvantaged states. Biological weapons could, however, appeal to more affluent states whose complex military-industrial bureaucracies might at least temporarily shelter covert programs. Some industrializing nations (for instance, China, India, Pakistan, and Brazil) now have the microbiological resources that could be exploited by their militaries should their governments feel compelled to seek a secret, illegal advantage. The major risk of a moderate capability in biological weapons is the onus of discovery, which would make a pariah of any nation known to violate existing treaties.

New biotechnologies that have "futuristic" weapons capabilities pose a second order of threat. These advances range from the cloning of higher mammals to new techniques for shaping human neurology and development.[38] Such innovations may sharpen the already considerable divide between the privileged who enjoy the benefits of modern medicine and those for whom they remain beyond reach. The science in Aldous Huxley's *Brave New World* is fanciful, but the use of technology to create a biologically determined social hierarchy may be a future hazard for humanity. US microbiology has had the edge in biotechnology so far, but the field is essentially international, and other centers of innovation, in Asia for example, are emerging.

The US biodefense initiative inaugurated in 2002 also poses some risks. The inadvertent consequences of biodefense technology—the unanticipated repercussions that can cascade into the future[39]—are a cause for concern. Lacking oversight and mechanisms for critical review, various biodefense projects could lead to the pioneering of new, more virulent select agents or futuristic technologies on the presumption, common in the old programs, that defensive research required offensive capability. In addition, by creating new environments for honing biological weapons skills, increased funding for biodefense research could have other unanticipated negative consequences. The biodefense project is predicated on having more high-containment laboratories (six or more at the maximum level four, plus eleven or more regional centers) and increased federal funding overall for select agent research in level-two and level-three laboratories. At the least, this multibillion-dollar enterprise will increase the absolute numbers of scientists familiar with the growing and testing of dangerous weapons agents.[40] Unlike those few government or military career scientists previously working on defenses against select agents, some thousands of new biodefense scientists, many affiliated with academic medical centers, must rely on federal grants and contracts. One problem will be whether they can survive shifting policy directives from Washington, which can produce boom or bust fluctuations in funding. Another will be the new impingement of secrecy on their scientific work and other challenges to publication and education.[41]

The Likely Perpetrators

What are the political opportunities that might engage today's many microbiologists in secret biological weapons programs? As in the past, the future of biological weapons depends on the intent of key authority figures, either heads of state or those in the higher echelons of decision-making, or, as another possibility, leaders of terrorist organizations. If the past is prologue, the states most likely to persist with or to initiate illegal biological programs are those whose centralized governments, existing military-industrial resources, and perception of dire political threats predispose them to seek unconventional weapons. Escalating border wars, internal conflict, or frustration with guerrilla warfare can lead to the choice of unconventional weapons; or militaristic economic national expansion might be used as justification, as with Japan in China. Eastern Europe—where the Soviet chemical weapons program was diffused to Bulgaria, Yugoslavia, Czechoslovakia, and Romania—has also been beset by conflict and political unrest. The United States itself is not immune to pressures to increase its options for unconventional weapons, especially when its military is engaged in ending insurgent and terrorist violence in Iraq and Afghanistan.

The past use of chemical weapons suggests models that could one day apply to biological warfare should the present implementation of treaty restraints prove insufficient. Following World War I and after the 1925 Geneva Protocol, chemical weapons were used in two different contexts. One was when an advanced industrial nation had the advantage of attack on foreign soil (Italy against Ethiopia in 1935–1936 and the US use of tear gas for lethal purposes in Vietnam); the other was when a relatively powerful developing nation sought to quell insurgents, civilian activists, or a relatively unprotected state adversary (for example, Egypt against Yemeni royalists in 1963–1967 and Saddam Hussein against Iran in the Iran-Iraq War and against Iraqi Kurds in 1988–1989). As a relevant example, apartheid South Africa employed small amounts of chemical and biological agents against insurgents within the state, in neighboring countries, and also in foreign sabotage.[42]

Generalized fears about the survival of their traditions and political influence might also influence nonstate actors to gain access to biological or chemical weapons. In two well-known, unusual cases involving religious cults, the choice of biological weapons paralleled in miniature the processes characteristic of state systems: scientists proposed the method, the leadership approved it, and resources were freed for laboratory research and experimental attacks. In 1989, the Rajneesh cult in Oregon spread nonlethal salmonella in restaurant salad bars and coffee stations in order to test a way to tilt voting participation in their favor. Some five hundred people fell ill, none fatally. As a second example, the Japanese cult Aum Shinrikyo was responsible for twelve deaths and dozens of injuries in the 1995 sarin nerve gas attacks on the Tokyo subway. Aum Shinrikyo included a number of scientists who also experimented with anthrax bacterium growth and dispersal.[43]

Fear and anger over violated traditions, worker deracination in the global economy, a distrust of government, military invasion and occupation, and ethnic enmity—the annals of terrorism include all these motivations. While Islamic extremists have come to represent fanatical resistance to Western influence, US militia groups and Christian fundamentalists have also been violently opposed to larger impersonal forces that they perceive as threats to individual freedom, their communities, or to family values. Timothy McVeigh was an out-of-work Gulf War veteran skilled with explosives who in 1995, influenced by the militia and the Christian Identity movement and enraged against the US government and society, blew up the Murrah Building in Oklahoma City, killing 168 people. Even suicide bombers, who appear insanely destructive, have also been analyzed as consistently motivated by altruistic resistance to foreign occupation.[44]

The motivations for terrorism are many, but thus far they have been only weakly linked to the means of bioterrorism. The 2001 anthrax postal attacks suggest that even a single disaffected scientist can cause havoc. For this reason alone, the expansion of the US biodefense project requires a prudent assessment of the risks of training a new generation of microbiologists to research, develop, and test select agents.

Civilians as Targets

The total war doctrine that justified attacks on enemy civilians during World War II was repudiated by the 1949 Geneva Convention, which affirmed protection of "the whole of the populations of the countries in conflict, without adverse distinction based, in particular, on race, nationality, religion or political opinion" (Section II, Article 13). The convention could not, however, prevent nuclear or biological weapons programs premised on mass civilian targeting, nor did the widespread killing of civilians in conflicts outside advanced industrialized nations cease.[45]

Contemporary terrorism after World War II, as it turned to civilian targets rather than political assassinations, has been characterized as an aftereffect of the war's violations of humane political codes and rule of law.[46] The tendency of contemporary terrorists to attack physical infrastructures such as subways and city centers appears to reenact total war strategies to disrupt technology "behind the lines." Civilians in democratic societies have become prime targets for terrorists, a liability that requires weighing the political infringements of antiterrorism projects against the preservation of individual privacy, group protest, political competition, and constitutional order.[47] In other states, such as Bosnia, Rwanda, and Sudan, the ultimate terrorism, genocide, has posed moral and political problems about mass civilian murder that the world believed ended in 1945.[48]

Biological weapons were created to target large numbers of civilians, and it is that aspect that warrants the most serious concern. What populations, then, are potentially most vulnerable to the impact of germ weapons? The level of risk from a naturally occurring disease varies by individual and group; in the same way, the risks of intentional epidemics vary, with some populations (for example, the very young and very old, pregnant women, those already sick or with compromised immune systems) more vulnerable to serious infection than others. Structural factors like social class also affect risk. Minorities and the poor can be disadvantaged in their general health status, education, and access to health care.

The literature suggests three different models of civilian vulnerability, involving terrorism, warfare, and accidental exposure, in which differential health risks can figure as variables. State-directed terrorist attacks invariably target marginal or low status groups (by ethnicity, religion, race, gender, or political beliefs) to coerce the wider society.[49] The same types of groups were targeted in twentieth-century cases of individual crimes in which disease agents (usually hoaxes) have been used.[50] It follows that, depending on the national context, populations against which animosities have already been expressed constitute the most likely future victims.

International conflict also presents a potential venue for disease attacks on civilians. Following World War II, after the advanced industrial nations ceased to make war against each other, the most vulnerable civilians in wars have been those in developing nations, where deaths due to direct violence have been augmented by preexisting poverty and disease, intensified by the privations of conflict. An attempt by a more powerful nation to disguise a hostile biological intervention in a subservient country would perhaps be less feasible now than when Japan was attacking China in 1940–1943, but it is not beyond the realm of possibility.

As a third model, the accidental release or spread of biological weapons agents highlights the health risks of the socially disadvantaged, who, like the working-class victims of the 1979 Sverdlovsk outbreak, would suffer disproportionately from an inadvertent exposure.[51] Although the mailing of the 2001 anthrax letters was intentional, the dispersal of spores in postal facilities was likely unforeseen by the perpetrator and had the effect of an accidental hazard. In the aftermath, federal officials in Washington proved more protective of predominantly white, middle-class Senate employees than of the black postal workers at the Brentwood postal facility, two of whom died after the alert about contamination in the building was withheld for four days.[52] The US expansion of the number of high containment facilities to research and test defenses against select agents has generated fears of similar differential risks based on social factors. In Boston, for example, local African American groups protested the location of a level four laboratory adjacent to their communities and demanded government oversight and regulation of research. While the new biodefense laboratories follow federal guidelines to prevent accidental releases or security breaches, no laboratory administrator or scientist can guarantee that accidents will never happen or that disease risks will be minor.

Secrecy, Transparency, and Biological Weapons

Government secrecy made past biological weapons proliferation possible, and it remains the greatest threat today. Even though the norms against biological weapons appear to be widely supported, secrecy can still provide a state with the necessary latitude to defy those norms, which increases the chances of nonstate actors' gaining access to biological weapons. The world remains full of highly centralized governments with military-industrial resources, where internal and external threats might be used to justify the secret exploitation of lethal and nonlethal biological weapons. Such threats from insurgents, enemies at the border, or ethnic or religious minorities might conceivably be employed to justify the eventual use of biological weapons masked as natural outbreaks

or accidents. All governments, as well as nongovernmental corpora-
tions, depend on "the secrets of the temple," that is, the information that
insiders keep from outsiders in order to safeguard institutional authority.[53] Thus, in many bureaucracies, transparency is interpreted as a
weakness within or incursion on the hierarchical structure, especially
in the military; or as an intolerable disruption of channels of communication, as in intelligence agencies; or as a threat to profit, as in industry.

In democratic societies, government institutions are charged with
serving the public, and they are obliged to be open, to allow citizens
and their elected representatives to exercise their authority. Regarding
disease threats, governments and other organizations, such as pharmaceutical companies, charged with mitigating risks are accountable for
providing the public with open, accurate, and timely communication, so
that the population at risk can make informed decisions. The possibility of a lethal outbreak from any source requires a responsive and open
government. Today, the way in which a state manages infectious disease
threats can be an indication of good governance—or bad.[54] The successful containment of an epidemic depends primarily on informed individual response on the part of the public, including the recognition of
symptoms and decisions about appropriate preventive interventions and
therapeutic approaches. A most successful scenario in this regard was
the 1947 New York City response to a potential smallpox outbreak, during which the coordinated cooperation of local health clinics, volunteer
civilians, the media, and an informed public allowed the orderly vaccination of 5 million people in two weeks—in an epoch when New York
could staff nearly 179 local clinical stations.[55]

Every instance of governments' withholding or distorting information about disease threats demonstrates the increased risks of delayed
diagnosis or misdiagnosis that secrecy imposes on the victims.[56] China's
six-week denial of the 2003 SARS (severe acute respiratory syndrome)
epidemic precipitated a global alert and the near catastrophe of international contagion, even as the crisis generated a rapid global public health
response. Secrecy was also a determining factor in the 1979 Sverdlovsk
anthrax outbreak, which was caused by an accidental emission of spores
from a military facility engaged in activities forbidden by the 1972
BTWC. The outbreak, the largest of its kind in history, was then exacerbated by continued government denials and disinformation regarding the
source.[57] The impeded flow of US government information in the course
of responses to the 2001 anthrax postal attacks presents another instance
of public endangerment, particularly for minority postal workers. Among
the worst effects of such secrecy is the breakdown of trust between

exposed communities and public health agencies, a trust vital to the containment of high-risk outbreaks. Currently, as the SARS epidemic demonstrated, it takes rapid international cooperation, including coordination with science and industry and the engagement of an informed public, to ensure protection against a dangerous emerging or unusual infectious disease. The same coordination of resources and information would be necessary in the event of a concerted bioterrorism attack.

For the same reasons, secrecy in biodefense research programs heightens civilian risk. A cloak of secrecy around laboratory research, for instance, forcibly narrows the critical review of laboratory techniques, objectives, and results and can easily lead to delayed or faulty solutions. Although rarely documented in the history of biological weapons, the organizational culture of classified government research can create closed systems within which political agendas trump quality science and groupthink overrides reflection on moral issues.[58] In addition to its negative impact on scientific credibility, secrecy undermines organizational accountability, so that errors tend to be excused or hidden and thereby perpetuated. Mistakes and delays also occur through "mission clash," when government agencies with different directives and standards of openness fail to cooperate. During the response to the 2001 anthrax postal attacks, turf wars between public health authorities, the FBI, the military, the CIA, and other agencies confused an anxious public and increased the risks of delayed or inappropriate medical response, and also impeded criminal investigation.

Given the risks of both moderate and futuristic biological capability, of chronic international tensions, and of the persistent social inequities in health risks, one must question why the current minimal restraints on biological weapons are tolerated. The BTWC remains as if still shackled by Cold War secrecy, when it could be forcefully updated to increase transparency in this new century. Even if international openness is imperfect, advanced industrial nations should seize the opportunity to offer developing nations new biotechnologies important to global health as an incentive for active treaty compliance. Present loopholes in the state-by-state enforcement of the BTWC make for erratic international security.[59] Equally serious is the lack of international law to criminalize the individual possession or use of biological and chemical weapons, which would ensure that no perpetrator of such crimes could find a state haven against prosecution.[60] The pharmaceutical industry is behind the curve in understanding its civic responsibility to support the BTWC. The US biodefense initiative also needs comprehensive evaluation and oversight, with a reduction of the scale of the project to less risky dimensions. If the biodefense initiative is sustained without accountability to the public, it could cause more health risks than it eliminates. Further, the US export of a narrow national security mission to its allies undermines long-term international security interests. Instead, the United States should use its primacy to address the policy deficits that compound the risks of destabilization and preventable human tragedy. Deadly infectious disease outbreaks from any source can have regional and global consequences, and therefore require innovative international approaches to solutions and sanctions. Since an intentional epidemic also demands a criminal investigation, it automatically requires an open, cooperative response, with no exceptions for the military, the intelligence community, private contractors, or industry.

The protection of civilians in the short and long term is the primary goal in countering the threat of biological weapons, and one on which everyone should agree. Such disagreement as exists is largely about which policies might best achieve that goal. A strictly civil defense approach to bioterrorism fails to reckon the unstoppable global diffusion of new biotechnologies and the pressures that might propel certain states toward biological weapons. Nor does civil defense protect citizens against the risks of an unusual deadly outbreak, whether natural, intentional, or accidental; by definition it does not promote the international coordination necessary to safeguard the public. The strengthening of existing treaties to promote transparency, increased oversight at national levels, and the international criminalization of biological weapons are all forward-looking policies that would keep the biological sciences active for beneficent rather than hostile purposes. The alternative is the risk of a disease catastrophe that underscores the danger of government secrecy and failed response, at the cost of lives and public trust.

Notes

1. For a historical overview, see Jeanne Guillemin, *Biological Weapons: From the Invention of State-Sponsored Programs to Contemporary Bioterrorism* (New York: Columbia University Press, 2005).

2. See Stephen Peter Rosen, *New Ways of War: Understanding Military Innovation* (Ithaca, NY: Cornell University Press, 1991).

3. Susan Wright, ed., *Biological Warfare and Disarmament: New Problems/New Perspectives* (New York: Rowman and Littlefield, 2002), pp. 3–24.

4. Li Xiofang, *Blood-Weeping Accusations: Records of Anthrax Victims* (Beijing: CCP Press, 2005).

5. Avner Cohen, "Israel and Chemical/Biological Weapons: History, Deterrence, and Arms Control," *Nonproliferation Review* 8, no. 3 (Fall/Winter 2001): 27–53.

6. Frederic J. Brown, *Chemical Warfare: A Study in Restraints* (New Brunswick, NJ: Transaction Publishers, 2005).

7. Simon Cooper, "Life in the Pursuit of Death," *Seed* 4 (January/February 2003): 68–72, 104–107.

8. Eric Croddy, "China's Role in the Chemical and Biological Disarmament Regimes," *Nonproliferation Review* 9, no. 91 (Spring 2002): 16–47.

9. Albert E. Cowdery, "'Germ Warfare' and Public Health in the Korean Conflict," *Journal of the History of Medicine and Allied Sciences* 39 (April 1984): 153–172.

10. Jeanne Guillemin, *Anthrax: The Investigation of a Deadly Outbreak* (Berkeley: University of California Press, 1999).

11. Julian Robinson, Jeanne Guillemin, and Matthew Meselson, "'Yellow Rain' in Southeast Asia: The Story Collapses," *Foreign Policy* 68 (Fall 1987): 108–112.

12. Guillemin, *Biological Weapons,* pp. 138–145.

13. Erhard Geissler, "Biological Weapons Activities in Germany, 1923–45," in *Biological and Toxin Weapons: Research, Development, and Use from the Middle Ages to 1945,* ed. Erhard Geissler and John Ellis van Courtland Moon, 102–104 (New York: Oxford University Press, 1999).

14. Olivier Lepick, "French Activities Related to Biological Warfare," in Geissler and Moon, *Biological and Toxin Weapons,* pp. 70–90.

15. Sally Stoecker, *Forging Stalin's Army: Marshal Tukhachevsky and the Politics of Military Innovation* (Boulder, CO: Westview Press, 1998), pp. 91–93.

16. "Summary of Information, Subject Ishii, Shiro, 10 January 1947," Document 41, US Army Intelligence and Security Command Archive, Fort Meade, MD.

17. John Bryden, *Deadly Allies: Canada's Secret War 1937–1947* (Toronto: McClelland and Stewart, 1989), pp. 34–57; Donald Avery, "Canadian Biological and Toxin Warfare," in Geissler and Moon, *Biological and Toxin Weapons,* pp. 190–214.

18. Brian Balmer, *Britain and Biological Warfare: Expert Advice and Science Policy, 1930–65* (London: Palgrave, 2001), p. 27.

19. Theodor Rosebury and Elvin A. Kabat, with the assistance of Martin H. Boldt, "Bacterial Warfare," *Journal of Immunology* 56, no. 1 (1947): 7–96.

20. Theodor Rosebury, *Peace or Pestilence? Biological Warfare and How to Avoid It* (New York: McGraw-Hill, 1949).

21. Bryden, *Deadly Allies,* pp. 118–119, 197–199.

22. Ken Alibek, with Stephen Handelman, *Biohazard: The Chilling True Story of the Largest Covert Biological Weapons Program in the World—Told from Inside by the Man Who Ran It* (New York: Random House, 1999), p. 37.

23. In addition to Alibek, *Biohazard,* see Igor V. Domaradskij and Wendy Orent, *Biowarrior: Inside the Soviet/Russian Biological War Machine* (Amherst, NY: Prometheus Books, 2003).

24. Geissler, "Biological Warfare Activities in Germany," pp. 91–126.

25. Louise Young, *Japan's Total Empire: Manchuria and the Culture of Wartime Imperialism* (Berkeley: University of California Press, 1998), pp. 55–114.

26. "Japan Confronting New Atrocity," *New York Times,* 17 March 1995.

27. Balmer, *Britain and Biological Warfare*, pp. 36–37.

28. Peter Hammond and Gradon Carter, *From Biological Warfare to Health-care: Porton Down, 1940–2000* (New York: Palgrave, 2002), pp. 102–104; Balmer, *Britain and Biological Warfare*, pp. 98–101; "Report by the Joint Strategic Plans Committee to the Joint Chiefs of Staff on Statements of Policy and Directives on Biological Warfare," JCS 1837/34, 11 June 1952.

29. Alibek, *Biohazard*, pp. 234–235; Raymond L. Garthoff, "Polyakov's Run," *Bulletin of the Atomic Scientists* 56, no. 5 (September/October 2000): 37–40.

30. Arthur Marwick, *Britain in the Century of Total War: War, Peace and Social Change* (Boston: Little, Brown, 1968).

31. Frederick O. Banting, "Memorandum on the Present Situation Regarding Bacterial Weapons," London: Public Record Office, WO188/653 10, n.d., p. 3. This statement was circulated by Banting in Britain in November-December 1939.

32. Graham Allison, *Nuclear Terror: The Ultimate Preventable Catastrophe* (New York: Holt, 2004), p. 129.

33. Ulrich Beck, *Risk Society: Towards a New Modernity,* trans. M. Ritter (London: Sage, 1992).

34. Jeanne Guillemin, "Inventing Bioterrorism" in *Making Threats: Biofears and Environmental Anxieties,* ed. Banu Subramaniam, Elizabeth Hartmann, and Charles Zerner, 197–216 (New York: Rowman and Littlefield, 2005).

35. See Zygmunt Bauman on "risk-fright" in *Postmodern Ethics* (Oxford: Blackwell, 1993), p. 204.

36. Martin I. Meltzer et al., "Modeling Potential Responses to Smallpox as a Bioterrorist Weapon," *Emerging Infectious Diseases* 7, no. 6 (November–December 2001): 959–969; Thomas Mack, "A Different View of Smallpox and Vaccination," *New England Journal of Medicine* 348, no. 5 (January 2003): 1–4; Raymond Gani and Steve Leach, "Transmission Potential of Smallpox in Contemporary Populations," *Nature* 414, no. 13 (December 2001): 748–751.

37. Robert J. Blendon et al., "The Public and the Smallpox Threat," *New England Journal of Medicine* 348, no. 5 (January 2003): 426–432; Tara O'Toole, Michael Mair, and Thomas V. Inglesby, "Shining Light on Dark Winter," *Clinical Infectious Diseases* 34 (April 2002): 972–983.

38. Matthew Meselson, "Bioterrorism: What Can Be Done?" in *Striking Terror: America's New War,* ed. Robert B. Silvers and Barbara Epstein, 257–276 (New York: New York Review Books, 2002).

39. Robert K. Merton, *Social Theory and Social Structure* (Glencoe, IL: Free Press, 1957), pp. 60–69.

40. Nicholas Schwellenbach, "Biodefense: A Plague of Scientists," *Bulletin of the Atomic Scientists* 61, no. 3 (May–June 2005): 14–16.

41. National Research Council Committee on Research Standards and Practices to Prevent the Destructive Application of Biotechnology, *Biotechnology in an Age of Terrorism: Confronting the Dual Use Dilemma* (Washington, DC: National Academy Press, 2003), p. 14.

42. Chandré Gould and Peter Folb, *Project Coast: Apartheid's Chemical and Biological Program* (Geneva: United Nations Institute for Disarmament Research, 2002).

43. David E. Kaplan and Andrew Marshall, *The Cult at the End of the World* (New York: Crown, 1996); W. Seth Carus, "The Rajneeshees," in *Toxic*

Terror: Assessing Terrorist Use of Chemical and Biological Weapons, ed. Jonathan B. Tucker, 115–137 (Cambridge, MA: MIT Press, 2000).

44. Robert A. Pape, *Dying to Win: The Strategic Logic of Suicide Terrorism* (New York: Random House, 2005); Mia Bloom, *Dying to Win: The Allure of Suicide Terror* (New York: Columbia University Press, 2005).

45. Irving Louis Horowitz, *Taking Lives: Genocide and State Power* (New Brunswick, NJ: Transaction Publishers, 2002), pp. 153–179; Benjamin A. Valentino, *Final Solutions: Mass Killing and Genocide in the Twentieth Century* (Ithaca, NY: Cornell University Press, 2004).

46. Michael Walzer, *Just and Unjust Wars: A Moral Argument with Historical Illustrations* (New York: Basic Books, 1980), pp. 197–204.

47. Horowitz, *Taking Lives,* p. 110.

48. Samantha Powers, *The Problem from Hell: America and the Age of Genocide* (New York: Basic Books, 2002).

49. E. V. Walter, *Terror and Resistance: A Study of Political Violence* (New York: Oxford University Press, 1969).

50. W. Seth Carus, *Bioterrorism and Biocrimes: The Illicit Use of Biological Agents Since 1900* (Washington, DC: Center for Counterproliferation Research, National Defense University, 2002).

51. Guillemin, *Anthrax,* pp. 207–239.

52. Jeanne Guillemin, "The Deliberate Release of Anthrax Spores Through the United States Postal System," in *Public Health Response to Biological and Chemical Weapons: WHO Guidance,* ed. Julian Perry Robinson, 98–108 (Geneva: World Health Organization, 2004).

53. Everett C. Hughes, *The Sociological Eye* (New Brunswick, NJ: Transaction Publishers, 1989).

54. David P. Sidler, "Germs, Governance, and Global Public Health in the Wake of SARS." *Journal of Clinical Investigation* 113 (March 2004): pp. 799–804.

55. Israel Weinstein, "An Outbreak of Smallpox in New York City," *American Journal of Public Health* 37 (November 1947): 1347–1384.

56. Jeanne Guillemin, "Bioterrorism and the Hazards of Secrecy: A History of Three Epidemic Cases," *Harvard Health Policy Review* 4, no. 1 (Spring 2003): 36–50.

57. Guillemin, *Anthrax,* pp. 188–206.

58. Diane Vaughan, *The Challenger Launch Decision: Risky Technology, Culture, and Desire at NASA* (New York: Oxford University Press, 1996); Hugh Gusterson, *Nuclear Rites: An Anthropologist Among Weapons Scientists* (Berkeley: University of California Press, 1996).

59 Nicholas A. Sims, "A Proposal for Putting the 26 March 2005 Anniversary to Best Use for the BWC," *CBW Conventions Bulletin* 62 (December 2003): 1–6; Angela Woodward, *Time to Lay Down the Law: National Legislation to Enforce the BWC* (London: Vertic, 2003).

60. Matthew Meselson and Julian Perry Robinson, "Draft Convention to Prohibit Biological and Chemical Weapons Under International Criminal Law," in *Treaty Enforcement and International Cooperation in Criminal Matters,* ed. Rodrigo Yepes-Enríquez and Lisa Tabassi, 457–469 (The Hague: OPCW, 2002).

3

Evolution of
the Current Threat

MILTON LEITENBERG

SPEAKING AT THE WORLD ECONOMIC FORUM IN DAVOS, SWITZERLAND, ON 27 January 2005, US Senate majority leader William Frist stated that "the greatest existential threat we have in the world today is biological." He added the prediction that "an inevitable bio-terror attack" would come "at some time in the next 10 years."[1] He was seconded by Tara O'Toole, head of the Center for Biosecurity at the University of Pittsburgh, who claimed bioterrorism "is one of the most pressing problems we have on the planet today."[2]

Are these statements realistic? Are they even proximately realistic? By way of the most cursory comparison, one can set potential bioterrorism against the following global issues:

- Global climate change could affect populations in every corner of the globe and alter the current growth cycles of food crops that have evolved over millennia, and consequently food production.[3]
- Ocean quality deterioration, deforestation, desertification, the depletion of freshwater aquifers—all these are also likely to have a global impact.[4]
- Another danger involves the complex of global population growth, food production demands, energy and other resource constraints, and the waste products—solid, liquid, and gaseous—produced by human society, and the impact of these factors on regional and global ecosystems.
- Between 224.5 million and 236 million people died in the twentieth century in wars and conflicts—say roughly 230 million.[5] At this point, it is impossible to say whether the numbers of conflict-related

39

deaths will be any different in the twenty-first century from what they were in the twentieth century.

- If we look only at the levels of international incidence of disease, we see that malaria, tuberculosis, HIV/AIDS (human immuno-deficiency virus/acquired immunodeficiency syndrome), measles, and diarrhea alone kill a total of some 9.5 million people per year worldwide. Smoking results in an additional 5 million deaths per year. Together these diseases kill 145 million people each decade.

- World Health Organization (WHO) officials have been warning for years of the imminence of a pandemic flu outbreak. Since the first appearance of H5N1 avian flu in 1997, the agent has been spreading to multiple migrating natural hosts, at the same time it has developed the ability to infect humans. The first cases of human-to-human transmission have now been recorded. Should a full-blown pandemic break out, varying estimates of global fatalities reach well over 100 million.[6]

No, it is absolutely clear that bioterrorism is not "the greatest existential threat we have in the world today" or "one of the most pressing problems we have on the planet today."

There were repeated statements in 1999, most prominently in the September 1999 US General Accountability Office (GAO) report *Combating Terrorism: Need for Comprehensive Threat and Risk Assessment of Chemical and Biological Attacks*, that no threat analysis of this subject—an examination of specific potential actors, their capabilities and intentions, and potential feasibilities—had ever been prepared inside the US government.[7] GAO reports for several years afterward indicated that this situation had not changed. The US Department of Homeland Security, established in 2003, is charged by law with preparing such a threat assessment, but it is not known what inputs will be used to make the assessment, and the results are not likely to be made public.

My aim in this chapter is to provide a brief evaluation of two subjects: the evolution of state biological weapons programs and the evolution of nonstate actors' ("terrorist") biological weapons capabilities.[8]

The Evolution of State Biological Weapons Programs

Information derived solely from official US, Russian, and British sources has been available since 1988, and it specifies how many and which nations have maintained offensive biological weapons programs.

Official US government statements repeated for many years that there were four nations in possession of offensive biological weapons programs in 1972, at the time of the signing of the Biological and Toxin Weapons Convention (BTWC), and that this number had increased to ten by 1989 (see Table 3.1). Then in November 1997, the director of the US Arms Control and Disarmament Agency (ACDA), during a statement to BTWC negotiating states in Geneva, increased the US estimate to twelve nations. The additional two states have never been identified by US officials. In July 2001, a US government official stated that thirteen countries had offensive bioweapons programs.[9]

There has been no equivalent statement or revised estimate since. All through the 1990s, it was common—in fact nearly universal—for commentators to depict the proliferation of state bioweapons programs as a constantly increasing trend. For example, Ambassador Donald Mahley, the senior US diplomat to all multilateral negotiations in Geneva concerning chemical and biological weapons, stated in an October 1996 Voice of America broadcast: "It is estimated that over the last several years, the number of countries suspected of having a biological weapons capability has risen."[10] However, it seems very possible that the number has been more or less stable since the mid-1980s. Moreover, there have been several notable reductions or deletions from the list since the mid-1990s. Since the overall total was not large to begin with, the shortening of the list represents a significant reduction:

- The bioweapons program of South Africa had been terminated by 1995.[11]
- On 1 November 2002, US undersecretary of state John Bolton stated that "Libya has an offensive BW program in the research and development stage, and it may currently be capable of producing small quantities of biological agent."[12] The statement was consistent with other US statements regarding Libya and bioweapons during the preceding decade. The phrasing in the 1993 report of the Russian Foreign Intelligence Service was substantially stronger: "There is information that Libya is engaged in initial testing in the area of biological weapons."[13] At the end of 2003, US and British government teams working in Libya ascertained that Libya had never had an offensive bioweapons program. In the words of a US administration briefer, "Libya acknowledged past intentions to acquire equipment and develop capabilities related to Biological Weapons." Libya had additionally "committed not to pursue a biological weapons program and to accept the

Table 3.1 Nations with Bioweapons Programs, According to Reports

	US Government Arms Control Compliance Reports to Congress (1993, 1995)	US Department of Defense Testimony to the Senate (1988, 1990, 1991); US Secretary of State Dick Cheney (1990)[a]	US, UK Governments (1995)	Russian Federation Intelligence Report (1993)[b]
Iraq	X	X		X
Libya	X	X		
Syria	X	X		X
Iran	X	X		
Egypt	X			
China	X	X		
North Korea		X		X
Taiwan	?			
India				?
South Korea				?
South Africa			X	
Russia[c]				

Notes: a. "Statement of Rear Admiral Thomas A. Brooks, USN, Director of Naval Intelligence, Before the Seapower, Strategic, and Critical Materials Subcommittee of the House Armed Services Committee on Intelligence Issues," 14 March 1990, p. 54; "Statement of Rear Admiral William O. Studeman, USN, Director of Naval Intelligence, Before the Seapower, Strategic, and Critical Materials Subcommittee of the House Armed Services Committee on Intelligence Issues," 1 March 1988, p. 48; "Statement of Admiral C.A.H. Trost, USN, Chief of Naval Operations Before the Senate Armed Services Committee on the Posture and Fiscal Year 1991 Budget of the United States Navy," 28 February 1990; "Remarks Prepared for Delivery by the Honorable Dick Cheney, Secretary of Defense, American Israel Public Affairs Committee, Washington, D.C., 11 June 1990," *News Release* 294-90, p. 4.

b. Russian Federation Foreign Intelligence Report, *Proliferation Issues: A New Challenge After the Cold War, Proliferation of Weapons of Mass Destruction* (in Russian), publication JPRS-TND-9-3-007 (5 March 1993).

c. There is uncertainty regarding the possible continuation of the offensive program initiated by the former Soviet Union.

necessary inspections and monitoring to verify that understanding."[14] Apparently, Libya may at some point have either procured or investigated the procurement of dual-use equipment that might have served such a program, and information about this was picked up by intelligence. This experience demonstrates a weakness of judgments based on procurement monitoring, which can be a useful indicator but cannot be considered definitive.[15]

- It is now clear that the bioweapons program of Iraq was disbanded between 1992 and 1995.[16] Unfortunately, the Iraqi program provided two other lessons. First, as shown by the period 1985–1990, an offensive bioweapons program can be hidden for quite a number of years, including during the period in which production is initiated. Second, precisely the opposite is demonstrated by the period 1998–2002: the most basic errors in judgment can be made by Western intelligence agencies.[17] In addition, public political manipulation of those mistaken judgments by political elites can take place.
- In 2004, the US administration withdrew the charge that Cuba was maintaining an offensive bioweapons program.[18]
- Given the Russian government's continued total rejection of international observers to the bioweapons facilities of the Russian Ministry of Defense (in Kirov, Sergiyev Posad, and Yekaterinburg), as well as continued impeded international access to relevant facilities of the Russian Ministry of Health, it is impossible to be certain of the status of bioweapons-related activities in Russia. Nevertheless, they are certainly greatly reduced from what they were up to the period 1991–1992.

This would mean an absolute reduction by four states—South Africa, Libya, Iraq, and Cuba—roughly one-third or one-fourth of the total number of states that, according to the US government, maintain offensive bioweapons programs.

In addition, the status of several other national bioweapons programs appears to be less certain than previously implied. A recent public Central Intelligence Agency (CIA) assessment of the bioweapons programs of Iran, North Korea, and Syria reads as follows:

- **Iran: Biological.** Even though Iran is part of the Biological Weapons Convention, Tehran probably maintained an offensive BW program. Iran continued to seek dual-use biotechnical materials, equipment, and expertise that could be used in Tehran's BW program. Iran probably has the capability to produce at least small quantities of BW agents.

- **North Korea: Biological.** North Korea has acceded to the Biological and Toxin Weapons Convention but nonetheless has pursued BW capabilities since the 1960s. Pyongyang acquired dual-use biotechnical equipment, supplies, and reagents that could be used to support North Korea's BW program. North Korea is believed to possess a munitions production infrastructure that would have allowed it to weaponize BW agents and may have some such weapons available for use.
- **Syria: Chemical and Biological.** Syria probably also continued to develop a BW capability.[19]

A statement on North Korea by CIA director Porter Goss on 17 March 2005 was somewhat stronger: "We believe North Korea has active CW and BW programs and probably has chemical and possibly biological weapons ready for use."[20]

By political agreement among the states parties to the BTWC, confidence-building measures were to be submitted annually beginning in 1987. Iran did not submit any until 1998 and 1999, and when it did, it conveniently "forgot" to submit perhaps the two most critical forms related to confidence-building measures of the eight required. They were the declarations that require the state to list national biological defense research and development programs (Form A2) and past activities in offensive and defensive biological research and development programs (Form F). In 2002, Iran declared that it "did not and does not have any national, subnational or individual programs/activities and/or facilities related to biological offensive purposes" and that it "did not and does not have any 'National Biological Defensive Program.' However the state has carried out some defensive studies on identification, decontamination, protection and treatment against some agents and toxins."[21]

From 2001 onward, official US statements regarding the Iranian bioweapons program reduced Iran's apparent status compared to that in assessments of the late 1990s. References to agent and weapon stocks disappeared. During US president George W. Bush's first term, the administration submitted only one arms control compliance report to Congress, although submission is intended by Congress to occur annually. The report was submitted during President Bush's first year in office,[22] and there has not been another one since. It therefore remains to be seen how the Iranian bioweapons program is described in any forthcoming report.

An unusual opportunity regarding Iran's bioweapons program arose in 2003 with the presentation in Washington, DC, of detailed allegations in connection with Iran's alleged bioweapons activities.[23] The information was provided by the National Council of Resistance of Iran, the same group that was in some cases the first to provide information on Iran's nuclear weapons complex, information that had not been publicly known nor apparently known by the International Atomic Energy Agency (IAEA) and that led to subsequent international action forcing Iranian government disclosures.

The bioweapons information was quite detailed, naming individuals, institutions, facilities, and locations. However, there has never been any comment on or corroboration of these allegations by the US government or by any other government or international agency. In November 2004, CIA director Goss reported to Congress that Iran continued "to vigorously pursue indigenous programs to produce nuclear, chemical and biological weapons." However, in March 2005, a special presidential panel decried the state of knowledge available to the US government regarding even Iran's nuclear weapons program.[24] The US Senate Select Committee on Intelligence was reviewing the information available to the administration regarding the nuclear, chemical, and biological programs of Iran and North Korea. It will be interesting to see if its report is made public, and, if so, what it will say with regard to the bioweapons programs of these two countries.

It is useful to recall a 1999 statement by John A. Lauder, former special assistant to the director of central intelligence for nonproliferation:

> Intelligence is all about ascertaining not only the capabilities, but also the intentions of one's adversaries. Because of the dual utility of the technology and expertise involved, the actual CBW threat is in fact directly tied to intentions.[25]

US government officials have never explained what the word "capability" means in such statements, that is, whether it means the procurement of dual-use biotechnology equipment, a national pharmaceutical production capacity, a dedicated defensive bioweapons research and development program, or the identification of dedicated infrastructure for offensive bioweapons research and development. It is clear, however, that after the Iraq weapons of mass destruction (WMD) intelligence failures, demonstrated by the reports of the Iraq Survey Group (ISG), the US administration decided to be much more cautious in the conclusions that it drew from perhaps rather ambiguous information.[26] Now and then during the 1990s, one occasionally overheard the comment by a government official or former government official that the evidence regarding country X or Y was ambiguous or weak, but the relevant evidence was never available for examination.[27] In 2003, a review of US assessments of WMD programs in various countries was initiated; the review on the proliferation of biological weapons was headed by Lawrence Gershwin, the National Intelligence Council's officer for science and technology. This review apparently led to the readjustment of some previous assessments.[28]

The CIA document containing the assessments of the Iranian, North Korean, and Syrian bioweapons programs quoted above is released twice a year. The analogous paragraphs for the half dozen or so years before 2003 have not been included here for comparison, but the above statements are all more low-key than statements made in earlier years in the biannual reports. The caveats are notable: "probably," "continued to seek," "the capability to," "would have allowed it to," "probably also continued to develop."[29] No definitive statements about the production, stockpiling, or nature of the munitions are included.

As always, there is no discussion of Israel's bioweapons capability or the status of its bioweapons program in any public US government report. It is interesting to note, with regard to the comments on proliferation that follow below, that in the only relevant data that appears to be available, Israel had the second largest number of visitors to the United States Army Medical Research Institute for Infectious Diseases (USAMRIID), following Britain, with which the United States shares bioweapons relevant information.[30]

We know that there has been an exaggeration of chemical weapons proliferation in the past, so this is not a unique experience. In 1990, Brad Roberts wrote, "We entered the 1980s with three, four or five chemically armed states; we will enter the 1990s with *upward of two dozen chemically armed states*" (emphasis added).[31] The estimate by the director of the ACDA was somewhat lower. It said that "at least 15 states possessed chemical weapons, with others attempting to acquire them." However, on 24 January 1989, the succeeding director, General William Burns, told the US Senate Foreign Relations Committee that only five or six of these countries actually possessed stockpiles of chemical weapons, in addition to the United States and the Soviet Union.[32]

The possibility of proliferation by three of the states with former or present programs—South Africa, Iraq, and Russia—has been raised at times by commentators. What is known is as follows:

- **South Africa:** The South African bioweapons program was minimal, and no more than a handful of researchers were involved.

Contrary to various media reports, the program did not include the genetic engineering of pathogens, nor—as far as is known—has there been any proliferation from the program whatsoever.[33]

- **Iraq:** There has been no known emigration of researchers from the former bioweapons program of Iraq. However, the addendum to the report of the ISG that was released in March 2005 states, "Migration of some WMD-associated program personnel to countries like Iran or Syria is possible." The phrasing is ambiguous in that it cannot be ascertained whether this is assumed to already have happened, or whether it is a generic statement suggesting that such migration could take place in the future. No disaggregation of WMD is provided. The report continues, "Since OIF [Operation Iraqi Freedom], the ISG is aware of only one scientist associated with Iraq's pre-1991 WMD program assisting terrorists or insurgents. However, there are multiple reports of Iraqis with general chemical or biological expertise helping insurgents produce chemical and biological agents."[34] Nothing further is said about these reports or about whether the ISG considered them credible or not. Much more significantly, the addendum then discusses a list of Iraqi bioweapons scientists that was prepared in early 2002 for possible transmission to Syria. However, it was not known if the list was ever transmitted to Syria, and the ISG did not discover any evidence of emigration of Iraqi bioweapons scientists to Syria. However, the *Twentieth Quarterly Report on the Activites of the United Nations Monitoring, Verification and Inspection Commission* (UNMOVIC) raises the possibility that some of the pathogen cultures used for Iraq's bioweapons production program may remain in Iraq, a consideration that was also raised in the report of the ISG.[35]

- **Russia:** Again, contrary to unsubstantiated hints that find their way into media reports, there is no known evidence of the transfer of pathogens from the former Soviet Union or from ongoing Russian programs to any other state, either before or since 1992. The emigration of Soviet scientists once engaged in bioweapons-related research to any proliferant state has been minimal. The one known case is the move of ten to twelve researchers to Iran, largely from the institutes belonging to the Russian Academy of Sciences rather than from former bioweapons institutes. There continue to be statements, particularly by D. A. Henderson and the Pittsburgh group, that say the locations of Soviet bioweapons "stockpiles"—not culture collections—produced in the Soviet

Union prior to 1990 are not known. US intelligence and defense agencies have believed for over a decade that those "stockpiles" were destroyed by the Soviet Union roughly between 1988 and 1990, and there are no indications that these agencies have ever altered that judgment. Contrary statements appear to be deliberately misleading.

As late as June 2005, at a seminar at the Council on Foreign Relations in New York City, Henderson said with reference to the possible dispersion of smallpox from the former Soviet Union or the Russian Federation:

> There have been economic problems in the Soviet Union, or now Russia. Many of the scientists have left the laboratories. They've gone all over the world, different places, some in the United States, Europe, some have gone to North Korea, Iraq, Iran. So that [is what] the problem is, there is just no way of knowing who has what and where, and that's the concern, that there may be others with the virus, but we just can't find out about it.[36]

No Soviet or Russian scientists are known by the US intelligence community to have gone to North Korea or to Iraq. Those few Russian scientists who went to Iran did not come from institutes that worked with smallpox. The US intelligence community does not believe that the smallpox virus has been transferred from the former Soviet Union or the Russian Federation to any other state.

The Evolution of Nonstate Actor and Terrorist Biological Weapons Capabilities

Five extensive database studies were published in the 1990s covering nearly the entire twentieth century, and several of them have been updated since.[37] It is extremely important to distinguish between the eight different categories of bioweapons-related events that these studies cover: hoaxes, threats, the consideration or discussion of use, product tampering, the purchase of materials, attacks on facilities, attempts to produce biological agents or to use them, and actual use.[38]

The conclusions of these independent studies were uniform and mutually reinforcing. First, there has been an extremely low incidence of real biological (or chemical) events, in contrast to the number of hoaxes, the latter spawned by hype from the US administration and the media since 1996 that exaggerates the prospective likelihood and dangers of such events. A massive second wave of hoaxes followed the anthrax incidents in the United States in October and November 2001, running into total global costs of tens of thousands of dollars. It is extremely important that analysts who produce tables of real biological events do not count hoaxes as real events. A hoax is not a biological event; nor is writing the word "anthrax" on a slip of paper the same thing as anthrax, a pathogen, or a "demonstration of threat"—all of which labels various analysts and even government advisory groups have applied to hoaxes on one occasion or another.[39]

In addition, events that were actual examples of use were overwhelmingly chemical, and even these involved the use of easily available off-the-shelf, nonsynthesized industrial products. Many of these events were instances of individual murder and not attempts to cause mass casualties. The compilation by Jonathan B. Tucker and Amy Sands from the Center for Nonproliferation in Monterey indicates that exactly one person was killed in the United States in the one hundred years between 1900 and 2000 as a result of an act of biological or chemical terrorism.

Excluding the preparation of ricin, a plant toxin that is relatively easy to prepare, there are only a few recorded instances in the years from 1900 to 2000 of the preparation of biological pathogens in a private laboratory by a nonstate actor. The significant events to date are as follows:

- 1984: The Rajneesh group in The Dalles, Oregon, used salmonella on food.
- 1990–1994: The Japanese Aum Shinrikyo group unsuccessfully attempted to procure, produce, and disperse anthrax and botulinum toxin.[40] The group was able to obtain only the Sterne vaccine strain of anthrax, which is nonpathogenic under any conditions, and it was apparently also unsuccessful in working with even that properly. And it is now known that the group did not have any strain of *Clostridium botulinum* at all to work with and so of course was unable to produce botulinum toxin.[41]
- 1999–November 2001: Al-Qaida undertook unsuccessful early efforts to obtain anthrax and to prepare a facility in which to do microbiological work.
- October–November 2001: In the Amerithrax case, a high-quality dry powder preparation of anthrax spores that had been prepared within the preceding twenty-four months was distributed.

Before discussing the Amerithrax and Al-Qaida cases in more detail, it would be useful to mention two books, one published and one forthcoming. They are particularly important as collections of case studies containing detailed reviews of virtually all the groups or individuals who have—or who have been alleged to have—prepared or used chemical or biological agents. The first of the books is *Toxic Terror*, edited by Jonathan Tucker,[42] and the second is *Motives, Means, and Mayhem: Terrorist Acquisition and Use of Unconventional Weapons*, edited by John Parachini.[43] Together, these two books report on twenty-eight case studies. They demonstrate that several right-wing groups in the United States have produced ricin by extraction from mashed castor bean pulp, and that the Rajneesh group did culture the salmonella that it had obtained. However, there is apparently no other "terrorist" group that is known to have successfully cultured any pathogen. It is precisely because of the exceptional nature of the Amerithrax case that it is crucial to identify the person or persons who made the US anthrax preparation and to determine whether it was the same individual or individuals who prepared and mailed the letters.

In advance of the publication of his book, Parachini summarized in an article the conclusions from those studies that "provide an empirical foundation to assess the motivations, behavior, and patterns related to terrorist interest, or alleged interest, in unconventional weapons."[44] Parachini states in his article that perhaps the most important discovery from Tucker's book was that "upon rigorous inspection, several of the empirical cases frequently cited in the media and scholarly literature proved to be apocryphal." Parachini then discusses several factors that appear to be most significant in understanding the case studies. He finds the mind-set of the group leaders of an organization, the exogenous and internal constraints, and a combination of opportunity and the technical capacity of the group to be the factors that "most significantly influence a group's propensity to seek to acquire and to use unconventional weapons."[45] These conclusions are consistent with those made by another highly experienced terrorism specialist, Yoram Schweitzer of the Jaffee Center for Strategic Studies, Tel Aviv University. In a conference presentation in 2005, Schweitzer enumerated four factors that he felt served as inhibitors to terrorist organizations' considering use of biological weapons: (1) state dependency, (2) requirements of their local constituency, (3) requirements of the international constituency, and (4) group survival.[46]

If the leaders of a particular terrorist organization do not need to consider these factors, they may contemplate the use of biological agents more seriously. This may explain why the Rajneesh, Aum Shinrikyo, and Al-Qaida groups followed a path different from that of other terrorist groups. Similar conceptions were explored as far back as 1989 in a Rand study authored by Jeffrey Simon.[47] This sort of analysis of real cases of the behavior of real terrorist groups carried out by experienced terrorism analysts, when it is not disregarded entirely, is frequently met with disdain by the proselytizers of "the bioterrorist threat," as the example below shows.

The extremely brief reference to terrorist groups and their biological and chemical warfare capabilities in the December 2004 report of the US National Intelligence Council was minimalist in its description:

> Developments in CW and BW agents and the proliferation of related expertise will pose a substantial threat, particularly from terrorists, as we have noted.
>
> Given the goal of some terrorist groups to use weapons that can be employed surreptitiously and generate dramatic impact, we expect to see terrorist use of some readily available biological and chemical weapons.[48]

Since this report was looking ahead to the period between 2005 and 2020—the next fifteen years—the reference to "readily available" materials is particularly notable. It harks back to the conclusions of the database studies on events in the twentieth century and certainly does not seem to anticipate efforts at synthesis, genetic engineering, or more than the most elementary products.

Stephen Morse predicted much the same when speaking at a conference convened by the US National Academy of Sciences in January 2003. Morse had previously served at the Defense Advanced Research Projects Agency in the US Department of Defense and is currently director of the Center for Public Health Preparedness at Columbia University's School of Public Health. In answering his question "What sources would terrorists use?" he stated, "Most are likely to use easily obtained materials," and "state-sponsored [terrorists] might use 'classical BW.'"[49]

The latest US government intelligence estimates of the bioweapons capabilities of terrorist and nonstate actor groups became available in February and March 2005. They first appeared in three presentations to the US Senate Select Committee on Intelligence on 16 February 2005:

- Porter Goss, director of central intelligence, said, "It may be only a matter of time before al-Qa'ida or another group attempts to use chemical, biological, radiological, and nuclear weapons (CBRN)."

- Robert Mueller, director of the FBI, stated, "We are concerned that they are seeking weapons of mass destruction including chemical weapons, so-called 'dirty bombs' or some type of biological agent such as anthrax . . . I am also very concerned with the growing body of sensitive reporting that continues to show al-Qa'ida's clear intention to obtain and ultimately use some form of chemical, biological, nuclear or high-energy explosives (CBRNE) material in its attacks against America."
- Jim Loy, deputy secretary of the US Department of Homeland Security, made the following statements: "The most severe threats revolve around al-Qaida and its affiliates' long-standing intention to develop, procure, or acquire chemical, biological, radiological, and even nuclear, weapons for mass-casualty attacks. Al-Qaida and affiliated elements currently have the capability to produce small amounts of crude biological toxins and toxic chemical materials, and may have acquired small amounts of radioactive materials."[50]

On 17 March 2005, Vice Admiral Jacoby, director of the US Defense Intelligence Agency (DIA), said in a presentation to the US Senate Armed Services Committee:

We judge terrorist groups, particularly al-Qaida, [to] remain interested in Chemical, Biological, Radiological and Nuclear (CBRN) weapons. Al Qaida's stated intention to conduct an attack exceeding the destruction of 9/11 raises the possibility that planned attacks may involve unconventional weapons. There is little doubt it has contemplated using radiological or nuclear material. The question is whether al-Qaida has the capability. Because [biological agents] are easier to employ, we believe terrorists are more likely to use biological agents such as ricin or botulinum toxin or toxic industrial chemicals to cause casualties and attack the psyche of the targeted populations.[51]

CIA director Goss gave a presentation to the committee as well, and repeated verbatim his remarks of 16 February 2005 quoted above.

These rather similar extracts are the only references to nonstate actor interest or capability in the chemical and biological weapons area in all the presentations. They are significant for several reasons:

- No group other than Al-Qaida was mentioned.
- All of the statements are less specific, more general, and more low-key than those made in the preceding years, when George J. Tenet was director of the CIA.

- In two of the three statements, bioweapons are grouped together with chemical, radiological, and nuclear weapons, and in one even with high-energy explosives, making it impossible for someone without prior knowledge to know whether there is a specific basis for including bioweapons.
- One of the statements refers to "small amounts of crude biological toxins," which undoubtedly means ricin and not just any pathogen.
- It has been known at least since November 2001, when US and British military forces occupied Afghanistan, that Al-Qaida had been "seeking . . . anthrax" for two or three years before that date. The information therefore concerns Al-Qaida activities before the fall of Afghanistan, and there is no publicly available information to indicate that the group has been able to continue its efforts since the end of 2001.

Anthrax is endemic in Afghanistan, and a limited domestic animal vaccination program existed in the country at the time of the occupation. Nevertheless, there were undoubtedly some cases of the disease in animals each year. However, Al-Qaida apparently never obtained a pathogenic strain.

In addition, all of the four specific references to Al-Qaida–affiliated groups and ricin in 2003 turned out to be spurious. First, after the Ansar al-Islam camp in Kermal, northeast Iraq, was overrun by US military forces, sampling showed no presence whatsoever of ricin, nor of materials for its preparation. (In fact, the camp lacked running water.) Before the Iraq invasion, there had been several statements by US government and military officials that Al-Qaida was preparing ricin at the camp. As late as the vice presidential debate on 5 October 2004, US vice president Cheney, referring to Abu Musab al-Zarqawi, said, "He set up shop in Baghdad, where he oversaw the poisons facility up at Kermal, where the terrorists were developing ricin and other deadly substances to use."[52] As this remark was made long after the US government knew that the camp had contained no ricin, Cheney's statement has to be considered one of either ignorance or fabrication. There is no mention whatsoever of the Ansar al-Islam camp in the 2004 ISG report.

Second, during the ricin event in France in 2003, individuals were arrested by the French police after storing substances at the train station of Gare de Lyon in Paris. Those individuals arrested did not have any ricin, nor had they prepared any; they had only "planned to" produce ricin. The "chemicals" that the group had were apparently sodium cyanide.

Third, the "plots" in the spring of 2003 by a group associated with al-Zarqawi in Jordan reportedly involved sodium cyanide, not ricin.

(Jordanian authorities have referred to the planned use of 20 tons of high explosives in the planned event, and there is every reason to assume that the cyanide would have been destroyed in any such massive blast.)

Fourth, the premises of a group arrested in London in January 2003 were first reported to have shown "traces of ricin." Tests carried out at the British Defense Science and Technology Laboratory, Porton Down, demonstrated that "the traces were false positive field tests." The group was in possession of twenty-two castor bean seeds. Their equipment was a coffee grinder "with a brown residue" (probably coffee), a mortar and pestle, and a handwritten recipe taken from the Internet at an Internet café and transcribed into Arabic. The recipe was a derivative of the Maxwell Hutchkinson recipe in the notorious *Poisoner's Handbook*, which sold thousands of copies at US gun shows, a recipe that would very likely not produce ricin or extremely little of it.[53]

As for the "Encyclopedia of Jihad," in which such rudimentary and often inadequate recipes are supposedly located, it is not clear when it was composed. One suggestion is that its origin goes back to the 1978–1988 period of Afghan resistance to the former Soviet Union, which would be as much as ten years before Al-Qaida came into existence. A second suggestion is that it is an agglomeration that grew over the years, with material successively added to it and materials on toxin production added in later years. Although the encyclopedia is routinely attributed to Al-Qaida, it may, rather, have been inherited or adopted by the group.

Al-Qaida's Bioweapons Efforts in Afghanistan: From 1997–1998 to 2001

When we move to the Al-Qaida group in Afghanistan, the picture rapidly becomes much more serious, and all the preceding semifarcical events can be seen as inconsequential trivia. The first significant and meaningful information on what Al-Qaida may at some point have hoped to achieve in the area of bioweapons appeared on a single page in the journal *Science* in mid-December 2003,[54] and then in declassified documents that were obtained in the last week of March 2004. Appended to the single page in *Science* via an Internet address was a list of thirty-two items: eleven books and twenty-one professional journal papers nearly all dating from the 1950s and 1960s and dealing with pathogens or bioweapons. They were found in an Al-Qaida training camp near Kandahar, Afghanistan, in December 2001.[55] Half of the books dealt with historical or general aspects of bioweapons and would be of little practical use in an effort to produce bioweapons agents. However, at least some of the journal papers and the remaining half of the books might have been useful in such an effort. They were found only a few kilometers from the site near the Kandahar airport that contained the rudimentary equipment also procured by Al-Qaida.

Most important of all, the documents indicated that "al-Qaida's BW initiative included recruitment of individuals with Ph.D.-level expertise who supported planning and acquisition efforts by their familiarity with the scientific community." The journal papers concerned *Bacillus anthracis* and *Clostridium botulinum*, but also *Yersinia pestis* (plague) and hepatitis A and C. Fragments of two of the classified materials were included in the *Science* article as photocopies of handwritten letters. The letterhead of one of them read "Society for Applied Microbiology." The second item reported that the writer was unable to obtain a pathogenic culture of anthrax, and that "the culture available in [deleted] is non-pathogenic." The website of the Society for Applied Microbiology advertises that organization as "the UK's oldest microbiological society." Another snippet from the handwritten letter, which explained that its author would "require at least the air ticket expenses," indicated that the person was flying either to or from Britain. The letter fragment also said, "The money with me is only for the purpose to buy strains or vaccines."

When the classified documents were obtained, it turned out that nearly all of the pages consisted of the journal articles themselves, as well as medical handbook excerpts on anthrax, plague, botulinum, and other pathogens.[56] There were also many additional pages of references to books and journals, including many standard reference works such as the SIPRI volumes on *The Problems of Chemical and Biological Warfare* and the 1969 UN study on chemical and biological weapons. It was the remaining ten pages that were of importance. They consisted of two three-page letters and accompanying handwritten notes suggesting the layout of a laboratory and the equipment recommended to outfit it, as well as "program requirements," including the time needed to train whoever was going to work in the laboratory and that person's assistants.

The author of the letters was a Pakistani microbiologist. There is reason to believe that he was writing to Ayman al-Zawahiri, the Egyptian who is Osama bin Laden's deputy. The writer reported visiting a biosafety level three facility in Britain, where he was shown a pathogen collection. He was not only trying to obtain and export pathogen cultures, but he was also seeking to buy vaccines for protecting personnel against anthrax infection. He was being supplied by Al-Qaida with funds with which to buy equipment and materials, which he itemized. He had also attended various European conferences dealing with pathogens—or had obtained their proceedings—including a conference on anthrax. The most recent had been in July and September 1999. He had signed his letters, named the laboratory that he had visited and its director, and identified one or two other individuals by name. All these identifications were deleted in the declassified materials.

The documents demonstrate that an individual with Ph.D.-level training who understood the professional microbiology literature and professional procedures for purchasing pathogen cultures was willing to trade on the access provided by his status while concealing the true purpose of his activities, which was to provide Al-Qaida with the means to attempt to develop its first real bioweapons production capability. However, he was not prepared to do any of the laboratory work himself. There is no evidence in any of the declassified pages that any bacterial cultures had been obtained, that any had been shipped to Afghanistan or Pakistan, or that any work had begun. In fact, all the phrasing on these pages suggests that none of these things had yet occurred. There is also no mention of the procurement of bacterial culture media, which would be necessary before any work could begin.

These materials were commented on by various senior US officials in 2002 and 2003. On 25 February 2002, General Tommy R. Franks, the commander of US military forces in Afghanistan, reported that after the examination of over 110 sites in Afghanistan,

> the United States has yet to find evidence that Al Qaeda was able to create a chemical or biological weapon at any of its camps, command centers, or caves in Afghanistan . . . We have seen evidence that Al Qaeda had a desire to weaponize chemical and biological capability, but we have not yet found evidence that indicates that they were able to do so.[57]

Similarly in February 2002, CIA director Tenet stated the following:

> We know that Al Qaeda was working to acquire some of the most dangerous chemical agents and toxins. Documents recovered from Al Qaeda facilities in Afghanistan show that Bin Laden was pursuing a sophisticated biological weapons research program.[58]

A note in the *Science* paper identified the documents referred to by Tenet as those just described. In his analogous assessment in 2003, Tenet told the US Senate Committee on Armed Services:

I told you last year . . . that bin Laden has a sophisticated biological weapons capability . . . In Afghanistan, al Qaeda succeeded in acquiring both the expertise and equipment needed to grow biological agents, including a dedicated laboratory in an isolated compound in Kandahar.[59]

The use of the words "pursuing" and "research program" in 2002 arguably makes the statement factually correct. Saying that Al-Qaida was "pursuing" a program is not the same as saying that Al-Qaida had produced any usable product. However, Tenet's language in 2003 is substantially different and implies much more, stating that Al-Qaida "has a sophisticated biological weapons capability." Nevertheless, these declassified papers permitted some proper understanding, for the first time, of the basis of statements made by US government officials that the status of Al-Qaida's bioweapons program might be more advanced than had previously been believed.

The relevant passages in the annual CIA and DIA threat assessment presentations to the US Senate in February 2004 also very likely reflected judgments based on the materials described above. The director of the DIA, Lowell E. Jacoby, said,

Al-Qaida and other terrorist groups remain interested in acquiring Chemical, Biological, Radiological and Nuclear (CBRN) weapons. We remain concerned about rogue scientists and the potential that state actors are providing, or will provide, technological assistance to terrorist organizations . . . While we have no intelligence suggesting states are planning to give terrorist groups these weapons, we remain concerned about, and alert to, the possibility.[60]

And the CIA director, George J. Tenet, stated,

I have consistently warned this committee of al-QA'ida's interest in chemical, biological, radiological and nuclear weapons. Acquiring these remains a "religious obligation" in Bin Ladin's eyes, and al-QA'ida and more than two dozen other terrorist groups are pursuing CBRN materials . . . Although gaps in our understanding remain, we see al-QA'ida's program to produce anthrax as one of the most immediate terrorist CBRN threats we are likely to face.[61]

The report of the US 9-11 Commission includes a bare few lines on the single individual identified to date, a Malaysian who was said to have carried out Al-Qaida's laboratory work:

In 2001, [Yazid] Sufaat would spend several months attempting to cultivate anthrax for al Qaeda in a laboratory he helped set up near the Kandahar airport . . . Sufaat did not start on the al Qaeda biological weapons program until after the JI's [Jemaah Islamiyah] December 2000 church bombings in Indonesia, in which he was involved.[62]

Sufaat was arrested in Malaysia in December 2001. Publicly available information about him has come from two important Al-Qaida sources. The first is Khaled Shaikh Mohammed, who was arrested on 1 March 2003 in Rawalpindi, Pakistan, at the home of a fugitive Pakistani bacteriologist, Abdul Quddus Khan. Handwritten notes and computer hard drives were seized in the home, showing, according to a reporter's description, that Al-Qaida had "completed plans and obtained the materials required to manufacture two biological toxins—botulinum and salmonella—and the chemical poison cyanide."[63] Cyanide would not be "manufactured," and it is unclear whether the "materials required" were the pathogen cultures, the bacterial growth media, equipment needed, or which of the above. The reference to "plans" does not indicate that any production took place. The press report of these discoveries was contradictory in places but claimed that in the materials seized, the recruitment of named scientists was discussed, production steps were outlined, and equipment, such as that found in Afghanistan, was described. Among items found was "a direction to purchase" *Bacillus anthracis*. Nothing translated so far has indicated that Al-Qaida had access to more dangerous microbial strains or to any advanced processing or delivery methods.

Mohammed also told his interrogators that Sufaat "took the lead in developing biological weapons for al Qaeda until he was arrested by Malaysian authorities."[64] Sufaat reportedly obtained a bachelor's degree in "biological sciences," with a "clinical laboratory concentration" from California State University in Sacramento in 1987. He then served as a laboratory technician in the Malaysian military, and in 1993 established a company in Malaysia "to test the blood and urine of foreign workers and state employees for drug use."[65] In the course of recent years, his company, and possibly another owned by his wife, appear to have been involved in financial transfers and the purchase of ammonium nitrate for producing explosives on behalf of groups affiliated with Al-Qaida operating in Indonesia, Malaysia, and the Philippines. The indication that Sufaat was not able to procure an appropriate strain of anthrax for use as a pathogen demonstrates the same difficulty faced by the Aum Shinrikyo group in Japan, which was only able to obtain the veterinary vaccine strain of anthrax. This appears to have been corroborated by reports in October 2003.[66] A photograph taken at an internationally supported animal vaccine production facility outside Kabul by an Associated Press photographer in November 2001 showed a large glass carboy jar labeled "anthrax spore concentration." It almost certainly contained Sterne strain anthrax vaccine. While this is suggestive of Al-Qaida's eventual intentions, all information to date indicates that Al-Qaida could not possibly have been responsible for the anthrax attacks in the United States in 2001.

Additional reports about Yazid Sufaat came from Riduan "Hambali" Isamuddin, the Indonesian operative of the Al-Qaida–affiliated organization Jemaah Islamiyah, which was responsible for the Bali bombing attack in August 2003. After his capture, Hambali told his interrogators that he had earlier been collaborating with Sufaat, that he had been "trying to open an Al Qaeda bio-weapons branch plant," and that Sufaat had been "working on an Al Qaeda anthrax program in Kandahar," in Afghanistan, but that after the US attack on the Taliban, they had planned to move the "program" to Indonesia. However, Sufaat had been unable to obtain a pathogenic strain of anthrax.[67] In another report, US and Malaysian security officials more accurately described the Al-Qaida program to develop biological and chemical weapons as having been "in the early 'conceptual stage' when it was cut short by the US invasion of Afghanistan."[68] In early October 2003, CBS nevertheless reported, "Al Qaeda may be hard at work trying to produce weaponized anthrax and other biological weapons."[69] Two weeks later, rumors that Jemaah Islamiyah branches in the Philippines were producing biological or chemical agents were quickly proved to be spurious.[70]

An important question relates to how much and what kind of actual laboratory work Sufaat may have been able to achieve in the "several months" available to him at the Kandahar site. Sufaat and Hambali apparently made four trips between Kandahar and Karachi to purchase materials.[71] The thousand-plus kilometers each way mean that these trips would have been by air, but together they could nevertheless have required several weeks to a month. Other lower-ranking Al-Qaida members also made purchasing trips to Pakistan. As far as is known, the Kandahar site appears not to have yet been functioning and reportedly contained little equipment aside from an autoclave.

In addition to the documents found in Kandahar and the information obtained through the interrogations of Mohammed, Hambali, and possibly some others at Guantanamo, there was yet one more source of information from within Al-Qaida regarding its interest in biological weapons. Additional fragments of information found at the end of 2001 on computer disks that appear to have belonged to Ayman al-Zawahiri provide little confidence in the competence of the Al-Qaida group to carry out either chemical or biological agent production. If anything, the disks cast doubt on assumptions of capability, although they apparently date from early in their efforts. The initial program investment was either US\$2,000 or US\$2,000–US\$4,000, and after several months, al-Zawahiri considered it to have been "wasted effort and money." The group at that time seemed quite constrained in economic resources, as well as in applicable talent, and did not at all appear to have the kinds of financial resources as those available to the Japanese Aum Shinrikyo group. This early effort appears to have been intended to produce a "nerve gas" from a commercial agricultural insecticide. Perhaps the most important information, in an al-Zawahiri memorandum of 15 April 1999, is contained in the following sentences:

> We only became aware of them [biological weapons] when the enemy drew our attention to them by repeatedly expressing concerns that they can be produced simply with easily available materials . . .
>   I would like to emphasize what we previously discussed—that looking for a specialist is the fastest, safest and cheapest way [to embark on a biological and chemical weapons program].[72]

Other information indicates that al-Zawahiri's remark that "the enemy drew our attention to them" refers to the greatly exaggerated prediction, made by US secretary of defense William Cohen on national television in November 1997, of what his five-pound bag of sugar, if it were anthrax, could achieve if it were dispersed over Washington, DC.[73]

Early in March 2005, a press item returned to the material found on the computer disk when Mohammed was captured and to the sentence quoted above from the 2003 *Washington Post* story. On 9 March 2005, the *Daily Times* wrote, "[Al-Qaida] obtained the materials required to manufacture two biological toxins—botulinum and salmonella—and the chemical poison cyanide. They are also close to a feasible production plan for anthrax."[74] This information was attributed to "US intelligence services quoted in the US media." No such published information has been located in US media materials. The cyanide information dates back to 1998. The phrase "obtained the materials required to manufacture" does not indicate that anything was made, or even that *all* materials necessary—such as the pathogen—had been obtained. The very next day, an editorial in the *Washington Post* stated, "This country has already experienced one anthrax attack. Security officials have repeatedly stated their belief that al Qaeda and others continue to search for more lethal bioweapons."[75] The US intelligence testimony of 2004 did not mention any "others": the sole group mentioned was Al-Qaida. And there are no identifiable public statements by US "security officials" saying that "al Qaeda and others" were searching "for more lethal bioweapons" than anthrax. It is possible that the "security officials" that the *Washington Post* editors had in mind were those referred to in another press comment during a 1 March 2005 Interpol conference: "Security officials have long worried of the risk of an al Qaeda attack using biological weapons such as anthrax, ricin, botulinum toxin, smallpox, plague or Ebola."[76] There are no identifiable statements by any "security official" warning of the potential use by Al-Qaida of smallpox or Ebola, and the suggestion is ridiculous.

On 31 March 2005, the *Report of the Commission on the Intelligence Capabilities of the United States Regarding Weapons of Mass Destruction* became available. The information that it contained concerning the status of Al-Qaida and bioweapons was vastly different from the brief paragraph in the report of the 9-11 Commission. The March 2005 report concluded that when the war in Afghanistan began, Al-Qaida's biological weapons program was both more advanced and more sophisticated than analysts had previously believed:

> Al-Qa'ida's biological program was further along, particularly with regard to Agent X, than pre-war intelligence indicated. The program was extensive, well-organized, and operated for two years before September 11, but intelligence insights into the program were limited. The program involved several sites in Afghanistan. Two of these sites contained commercial equipment and were operated by individuals with special training. Documents found indicated that while al-Qa'ida's primary interest was Agent X, the group had considered acquiring a variety of other biological agents. The documents obtained at the training camp included scientific articles and handwritten notes pertaining to Agent X.
>
> Reporting supports the hypothesis that al-Qa'ida had acquired several biological agents possibly as early as 1999, and had the necessary equipment to enable limited, basic production of Agent X. Other reporting indicates that al-Qa'ida had succeeded in isolating cultures of Agent X. Nevertheless, outstanding questions remain about the extent of biological research and development in pre-war Afghanistan, including about the reliability of the reporting described above.[77]

The sources of the commission's remarks all refer to classified reports. The two presidential commissions appear to have used different procedures to obtain documents for examination, and one suggestion is that as a result they did not in all cases obtain the same documentation for review.[78] Of course, if the hard information regarding Al-Qaida and bioweapons prior to the coalition invasion of Afghanistan was nil, then Al-Qaida's efforts would certainly have appeared more advanced and more sophisticated than had previously been believed once the actual information described in the preceding pages had become available. Is it possible to make any further guesses regarding the substance of the commission's phrasing?

The information in the "documents obtained at the training camp" and "the handwritten notes" are explained in detail above and concern anthrax, botulinum toxin, plague, and hepatitis A and C. Hepatitis viruses are extremely difficult to work with, even for professional virologists. They require cell culture technology but could, in theory, be used to contaminate food and water. The 2004/2005 US intelligence statements quoted above refer more often to botulinum toxin than they do to anthrax. Nevertheless, "Agent X" almost certainly refers to anthrax, with botulinum toxin the most plausible second guess. The key question regarding the information quoted above is whether there is additional documentary or material evidence to support it beyond that already obtained in the papers found in November 2001 and the locations occupied at that time.[79] Those did not indicate success "in isolating cultures of Agent X." And only the Sterne vaccine strain had been available to the group in Afghanistan. The statement that much of the commission's brief summation was a "hypothesis" dependent on "reporting," at the same time as there remained "outstanding questions . . . including about the reliability of the reporting described above" seems to leave much of it an open question and possibly adds nothing of substance to what was already known from the declassified documents.[80] Nevertheless, the reference to two sites containing "commercial equipment" may suggest additional Al-Qaida efforts beyond those disclosed in the declassified documents and other information so far available to this author. (See Table 3.2.)

A member of the WMD commission was asked if he thought that one should be any less skeptical about the intelligence concerning Al-Qaida's bioweapons activities in Afghanistan than about the allegations made by the US administration regarding the status of Iraq's bioweapons program between 1995 and 2002. He replied that one should not be any less skeptical about the intelligence on Al-Qaida's bioweapons capabilities.[81]

Pakistani press reports indicate that the Pakistani microbiologist who assisted Al-Qaida in information gathering, as well as an alleged

Table 3.2 Comparison of Bioweapons Efforts by Aum Shinrikyo and Al-Qaida

	Aum Shinrikyo	Al-Qaida
Number of professionally trained individuals	2–3	1 or 2 (?) plus consultants, purchasing assistants; the possibility of others is uncertain
Total number of individuals	10–12	Unknown
Duration of effort and status of program	1990–1994, including laboratory work	1998 (?) to 2001; laboratory work had apparently not yet begun
Access to pathogens	None; attempt to obtain failed	Apparently none; attempt to obtain anthrax reportedly failed
Acquisition of equipment	Adequate	Minimal, but precise dimensions unknown
Acquisition of information	300 books	12 books, 20 academic journal papers, additional references
Funds expended	Estimate of US$10–20 million	Unknown

"Yemeni . . . studying microbiology at the University of Karachi," were arrested in October 2001. If this is the case—with the facility overrun by US forces in December 2001, Sufaat also arrested in December 2001, and the two above individuals arrested in October 2001, even before US and British forces had found the documentation in Kandahar—it would appear that the Al-Qaida bioweapons program may have been dismantled at the end of 2001. The location of Abdul Khan, in whose home Mohammed was captured, is known to the Pakistani government. He is incapacitated and therefore reportedly not a factor of concern. Whether other dispersed individuals of the group have any available work sites for microbiology at any other location is unknown. The statement by French interior minister Dominique de Villepin at Interpol's First World Conference on Bioterrorism in Lyon, France, on 2 March 2005 claimed that "after al Qaeda groups were smashed in Afghanistan, international terrorist groups were still working on chemical and germ weapons in Georgia's Pankisi Gorge," but this seems highly implausible insofar as it refers to "germ weapons."[82] Al-Qaida elements in the Pankisi Gorge had reportedly been killed, captured, or dispersed by a joint US-Georgian special operation in 2002. In contrast to the French statement, Major General Eric Olson, the second ranking US military officer in Afghanistan, told the Associated Press on 25 February 2005 that he had no indications that Al-Qaida was attempting to obtain nuclear or biological weapons and that there was "no evidence that they're trying to acquire a terrorist weapon of that type."[83]

The three terrorist groups that have been innovative in their methods have one aspect in common: Tamil Eelam in Sri Lanka, the Japanese group Aum Shinrikyo, and Al-Qaida have all actively recruited educated college graduates and have specifically sought individuals with particular knowledge and training. (Tamil Eelam has shown no interest in bioweapons, and they used industrial canisters of chlorine gas in only one anomalous incident.) Mohammed completed a degree at a US college, as did Sufaat. An unclassified summary of information on detainees at Guantanamo states that "more than 10 percent of the detainees possess college degrees or obtained other higher education, often at Western colleges, many in the United States. Among these educated detainees are medical doctors, airplane pilots, aviation specialists, engineers, divers, translators, and lawyers."[84] At least one holds a degree in electrical engineering, another holds a graduate degree in aviation management, and a third a master's degree in petroleum engineering. Such recruiting patterns do not automatically translate into either an interest or capability in bioweapons, but they would be a key advantage should the interests of such a group turn in that direction, as al-Zawahiri's memorandum quoted above suggests they may.

The reports of the United Nations Special Commission (UNSCOM) and the report of the ISG provide valuable insights into what one might expect of the initial efforts by a terrorist group. The ISG report describes the early failures of the Iraqi national chemical weapons program to produce a chemical weapon between 1971 and 1978.[85] The information provided does not clarify whether the impediments were in the industrial synthesis of chemical agents or in their weaponization. Nevertheless, the efforts involved a state program, state resources, and a period of eight years. It was previously known from UNSCOM reports that the same failure had occurred in the Iraqi bioweapons program in the early 1970s, and again between 1974 and 1978. The ISG report also provides information on two efforts—in the period 2002–2003—made by insurgent groups inside Iraq to produce very basic chemical weapons agents. Although the services of several chemists were obtained to produce the agents, both efforts failed.[86] It is uniformly assumed that the production of classical chemical weapons agents, as well as their dissemination, is simpler than that of classical biological weapons agents.

This explains the crucial significance of establishing precisely who the perpetrator of the 2001 anthrax incidents in the United States was and how and where the anthrax preparation was produced. It is the sole outlier event. Without this event, and except for the Rajneesh salmonella incident, there would still be no evidence of the capability of a nonstate actor to produce a biological agent. There has also been no evidence uncovered to date of state assistance to a nonstate actor to produce biological agents.[87] If it should turn out, as is currently assumed, that the Amerithrax perpetrator came from within the US government's own biodefense program, with access to strains, laboratories, people, and knowledge, then all previous conceptions about the significance of the events would be substantially altered. It would *not* alter the fact that it can be done and that the preparation could have been dispersed in a much more harmful way. But it would affect the crucial question of "by whom?"—and the projections imputed to traditional "terrorist" groups.[88] With the exception of the Amerithrax attacks, all attempts by other groups have either failed or have been limited to relatively low levels of competence. Reports in 2002 and again in mid-2004 indicated that the investigations into the source of the anthrax used in the US events were yielding results.[89] The investigations had apparently reached the stage that suggested which US laboratory was the source of the strain used. Nevertheless, there has been no identification of the perpetrator or resolution of the case. In the words of former deputy assistant to the secretary of defense for chemical and biological defense, Anna Johnson-Winegar,

> We do not know who was responsible. We do not know the source of the anthrax spores (i.e. were they produced, stolen, or purchased?). We do not know the motive for the attacks. And, therefore, we are unable to make intelligent assessments about the likelihood of similar attacks in the future.[90]

Conclusion

A summary of the material presented in this chapter produces the following conclusions:

1. "Bioterrorism" may or may not develop into a serious concern in the future, but it is not "one of the most pressing problems that we have on the planet today."[91]

2. With regard to the evolution of state biological weapons programs, the number of state bioweapons programs has apparently been

reduced by one-third or one-fourth since 1988. The remaining number of countries with such programs appears to be stable; no correlative rise in offensive state bioweapons programs has been identified. In addition, the US government—which has almost without exception in past decades been the only country to publicly identify WMD proliferants—appears in its most recent statements to be qualifying the status of states with presumed offensive bioweapons programs. To date, no state is known to have assisted any nonstate or terrorist group to obtain biological weapons.

3. With regard to the evolution of nonstate and terrorist biological weapons capabilities, the production and distribution of a dry powder anthrax product in the United States in 2001 is the most significant event. However, understanding the degree to which such competence is relevant to "traditional" terrorist groups is impossible until the perpetrator or perpetrators of the anthrax events are identified. If the attacks were done with the assistance, materials, knowledge, and access of the US biodefense program, the implications would change entirely.

The Rajneesh group succeeded in 1984 in culturing salmonella. The Japanese Aum Shinrikyo group failed to obtain, produce, or disperse anthrax and botulinum toxin. The steps taken by the Al-Qaida group in efforts to develop a bioweapons program were more advanced than the United States had believed before its occupation of Afghanistan in November 2001. Nevertheless, as far as is publicly known, including the ambiguous information that appeared in the 31 March 2005 report of the Commission on Intelligence Capabilities, the group failed to obtain and work with pathogens. Should additional information become available regarding the extent to which Al-Qaida's bioweapons effort had progressed, that assessment might have to be changed.

Scenarios of national bioweapons exercises that place various bioweapons agents in advanced states of preparation into the hands of terrorist groups simply disregard the knowledge and experience that such groups would need to have in order to work with pathogens. Unfortunately, ten years of widely broadcast public discussion have provided such groups, at least on a general level, with suggestions as to what paths to follow. If and when a nonstate terrorist group does successfully reach the stage of working with pathogens, there is every reason to believe that such action will involve classical agents, without any molecular genetic modifications. Preparing a dry powder preparation is likely to prove difficult, and its dispersal to produce mass casualties equally so. Making predictions on the basis of what competent professionals may find "easy to do" has been a common error and continues to be so. The utilization of molecular genetic technology by such groups is still a long way off.

A note on the framing of "the threat" and the setting of the agenda of public perceptions and policy prescriptions: Since the mid-1990s, the risk and imminence of the use of biological agents by nonstate actors and terrorist organizations—or bioterrorism—have been systematically and deliberately exaggerated. The exaggeration increased after the combination of the 9/11 events and the subsequent October–November 2001 anthrax distribution in the United States. US government officials worked hard to spread their view to other countries. Myriad institutes, programs, conferences, and publicists have emerged that continue the exaggeration and fearmongering. A small group of vociferous proponents of "the bioterrorism threat" has obtained allies at the most senior levels of the executive branch and in Congress. After 2003, the drumbeat picked up. Beginning in the second half of 2005, however, a moderation has perhaps emerged based on the more realistic likelihood of a natural flu pandemic and the accompanying realization that the US government has been using an overwhelming proportion of its resources to prepare for the wrong contingency.

Others see such exaggeration as necessary in order to prompt preparation. They acknowledge that the issue has been exaggerated but argue that political action—the expenditure of public funds for bioterrorism prevention and response programs—will not occur without it. Bioterrorism may come someday, if societies survive all other impending crises. However, the persistent exaggeration is not benign: it is almost certainly the single greatest factor in provoking interest in bioweapons among terrorist groups, to the degree that it is to blame if a bioweapons interest currently exists, for example, in the Al-Qaida organization.

Notes

1. Agence France-Presse, "US Senate Leader Urges 'Manhattan Project' Against Bio-Terror Threat," 27 January 2005. See also http://www.state.gov/t/us/rm/31029.htm (accessed 18 September 2006). It is clear from other statements Senator Frist made roughly at the same time that his reference in January 2005 to "biological" referred to "bioterrorism" and not to any other biological problem or context. Senator Richard Lugar had previously said that terrorists armed with weapons of mass destruction presented an "existential" threat to the United States, and Senator Frist presumably adopted that word to deal with bioterrorism alone. Very similar phrasing to Senator Lugar's was also used by

President Bush in an address at the National Defense University on 11 February 2004 (except that he expanded the threat from the United States to "humanity"): "The greatest threat before humanity today is the possibility of secret and sudden attack with chemical, or biological, or nuclear weapons."

2. Ibid.

3. On 15 March 2005, Britain's finance minister, Gordon Brown, stated that "human-made climate change is the most far-reaching and almost certainly the most threatening of all the environmental challenges facing us. Problems from soil erosion to the depletion of marine stocks threaten future economic activity and growth." Heather Timmons, "Climate Change Is Called Economic Threat at Talks," *New York Times*, 15 March 2005. See also Jeremy Lovell, "Photos Show Climate Change: Ministers Meet in UK," Reuters, 14 March 2005. A report released on 14 March 2005 referred to greatly increased glacial melting in the Himalayas. This will introduce an additional regional aspect: increased flooding and then decades of drought as traditional agricultural water sources disappear, which will severely reduce food crop production for hundreds of millions of people. See World Wildlife Fund, *An Overview of Glaciers: Glacier Retreat and Subsequent Impacts in Nepal, India, and China*, WWF Nepal Region, http://assets.panda.org, March 2005.

One of the most useful general surveys remains US Council on Environmental Quality and US Department of State, *The Global 2000 Report to the President,* vol. 1, *Entering the Twenty-First Century*, vol. 2, *The Technical Report* (Washington, DC: US Government Printing Office, 1980).

In addition, the annual *State of the World* volumes produced by the Worldwatch Institute and published by W. W. Norton are an invaluable resource.

4. See the 2005 Millennium Ecosystem Assessment. A brief press summary appears in Shankar Vedantam, "Report on Global Ecosystems Calls for Radical Changes," *Washington Post*, 30 March 2005.

5. Milton Leitenberg, *Deaths in Wars and Conflicts Between 1945 and 2000*, Occasional Paper, no. 29 (Ithaca, NY: Peace Studies Program, Cornell University, 2003). A revised second edition of the monograph is available on the website of the Cornell University Peace Studies Program, http://www.einaudi.cornell.edu/peaceprogram/publications/occasional.asp (accessed 31 October 2005).

These sums of the total aggregation of mortality include mass domestic slaughters and politically determined starvation in the absence of civil war, as occurred in the former Soviet Union and in China during the twentieth century.

6. Elisabeth Rosenthal, "Human-to-Human Infection by Bird Flu Virus Is Confirmed," *New York Times*, 23 June 2006, p. 8.

7. Government Accountability Office, *Combating Terrorism: Need for Comprehensive Threat and Risk Assessment of Chemical and Biological Attacks*, GAO/NSIAD-99-163 (Washington, DC: US Government Accountability Office, 7 September 1999).

8. The original version of this study included two additional and equally long sections that discussed two sets of circumstances that are not usually considered in an evaluation of the biological weapons threat but that directly influence the evolution of such a threat. The first of these is the manner in which the threat

of bioterrorism is publicly portrayed. The second is the driving force of the massive US investment in biodefense-related research since 2001 and the relation of at least some of that research to the prohibitions set by the Biological and Toxin Weapons Convention. It was necessary to omit these sections here, but for a more detailed and documented version of this introduction, see Milton Leitenberg, *Assessing the Biological Weapons and Bioterrorism Threat* (Carlisle, PA: Strategic Studies Institute, US Army War College, 2005).

9. See Milton Leitenberg, *The Problem of Biological Weapons* (Stockholm: Swedish National Defence College, 2004), p. 13.

10. Voice of America, "Biological Weapons Inspections," October 1996. As noted elsewhere, exactly what the words "capability" and "capacity" mean in this context in US government statements is never clearly defined.

11. Chandré Gould and Peter Folb, *Project Coast: Apartheid's Chemical and Biological Warfare Programme* (Geneva: United Nations Institute for Disarmament Research, 2002).

12. "Remarks by John R. Bolton, Undersecretary of State for Arms Control and International Security, to the Second Global Conference on Nuclear, Bio/Chem Terrorism: Mitigation and Response," 1 November 2002.

13. For earlier examples of US assessments of the status of Libya's bioweapons program, see Milton Leitenberg, "Biological Weapons and Arms Control," *Contemporary Security Policy* 17, no. 1 (April 1996): 1–78, particularly p. 38. The Russian statement appears in *Proliferation Issues: Russian Foreign Intelligence Service Report*, Joint Publications Research Service JPRS-TND-93-007 (4 May 1993), p. 24.

14. White House Office of the Press Secretary, "Press Background Briefing by Senior Administration Officials," 19 December 2003. Also, personal briefings by a US National Security Council official, 15 April 2004, and a US Department of State official, May 2004.

15. Methods of weapons of mass destruction (WMD) intelligence include overhead reconnaissance of several different kinds (photo, measurement and signature intelligence), electronic intercepts, procurement monitoring, and human intelligence. The Iraq experience has demonstrated that the last of these—human intelligence—could be catastrophically compromised by concocted information deliberately passed to multiple Western intelligence agencies by politically motivated opposition groups. Precisely that occurred to both US and British intelligence agencies.

16. The official title of the final report of the Iraq Survey Group is Iraq Survey Group, *Comprehensive Report of the Special Advisor to the DCI on Iraq's WMD* (Washington, DC: 30 September 2004), https://www.cia.gov/cia/reports/iraq_wmd_2004 (accessed 18 September 2006).

17. The reports of the 9-11 Commission, the US Senate Select Committee on Intelligence, and the Presidential Commission on Intelligence Capabilities all demonstrate a literally unbelievable mishandling by members of the intelligence community of the testimony of the Iraqi defector code-named Curveball, to the point of outright lying by agency staff. Contrary and more accurate assessments by other sectors of the intelligence community were routinely rejected.

18. For a detailed discussion of the charges against Cuba and of Cuba's actual capabilities, see Leitenberg, *Problem of Biological Weapons,* pp. 160–163, 169.

19. US Central Intelligence Agency, Unclassified Report to Congress on the Acquisition of Technology Relating to Weapons of Mass Destruction and Advanced Conventional Munitions, 1 July Through 31 December 2003. Available at http://www.cia.gov/cia/reports/721_reports/july_dec2003.htm.

The statement in the same document for Libya reads as follows: "Biological. Libya disclosed past intentions to acquire equipment and develop capabilities related to biological warfare, but it remains unclear if these activities were offensive or defensive in nature. At the team's request, Libya took us to a number of civilian medical-, biotechnical- and agricultural-related research centers that have a 'dual-use' potential to support BW-related work. The team was given access to scientists at these facilities."

A useful recent review of the North Korean bioweapons program appears in International Institute for Strategic Studies (IISS), *North Korea's Weapons Programmes: A Net Assessment,* IISS Strategic Dossier, 21 January 2004. Available online: http://www.iiss.org/publications/strategic-dossiers/north-korean-dossier/north-koreas-weapons-programmes-a-net-asses/north-koreas-chemical-and-weapons-cbw-prog#measures. A similar International Institute of Strategic Studies volume on Iran contains a section on the Iranian bioweapons program. IISS, *Iran's Strategic Weapons Programmes—A Net Assessment,* IISS Strategic Dossier, 6 September 2006.

20. "Testimony of CIA Director Porter Goss to the Senate Armed Services Committee Hearing on Future Threats to US National Security," Washington, DC, 17 March 2005.

21. Iranian confidence-building measures submission to the BTWC, 2002.

22. US Department of State, Bureau of Verification, Adherence to and Compliance with Arms Control Agreements and Nonproliferation Agreements and Commitments (Washington, DC: US Department of State, n.d.); available at: http://www.state.gov/documents/organization/22466.pdf.

23. National Council of Resistance of Iran Press Briefing, "Subject: Iranian Regime's Programs for Biological and Microbial Weapons; Alireza Jafarzadeh and Soona Samsani," Washington, DC, 15 May 2003; and Joby Warrick, "Iran Said to Be Producing Bioweapons," *Washington Post,* 15 May 2003, available at: http://nucnews.net/nucnews/2003nn/0305nn/030515nn.htm#310.

24. Douglas Jehl and Eric Schmitt, "Data Is Lacking on Iran's Arms, US Panel Says," *Washington Post,* 9 March 2005. Goss had testified before the US Senate Select Committee on Intelligence on 18 November 2004.

25. John A. Lauder, "Unclassified Statement for the Record on the Worldwide WMD Threat to the Commission to Assess the Organization of the Federal Government to Combat Proliferation of Weapons of Mass Destruction, as Prepared for Delivery on 29 April 1999," http://www.nti.org/db/china/engdocs/laud0499.htm.

26. Iraq Survey Group, *Comprehensive Report.*

27. Only in the case of Cuba has it been possible to obtain several examples of defector information that was presumably also reaching US intelligence

agencies. In several instances, these were forwarded to the author by the *Miami Herald*, in another case by the former director of Radio Martí. Some information also appears in the book by the most senior political defector from Cuba, José Luis Llovio-Menéndez, *Insider: My Hidden Life as a Revolutionary in Cuba* (New York: Bantam Books, 1988).

28. Douglas Jehl, "US Intelligence Review Is Softening Some Judgments About Illicit Arms Abroad," *New York Times,* 18 November 2003.

29. See Leitenberg, *Problem of Biological Weapons*, pp. 160–163, 169.

30. General Accounting Office, "Foreign Visitor Documentation That GAO Reviewed (June 1989 Through June 1990)," App. 3 in *Defense Research: Protecting Sensitive Data and Materials at 10 Chemical and Biological Laboratories*, GAO/NSIAD-91-57 (Washington, DC: US General Accountability Office, 1991), p. 21. For the two-year period covered, there were thirty-three visitors from Britain, followed by twenty-eight from Israel. The next highest numbers of visitors from any one country were eleven, ten, and eight. Efforts made in 1994 and 1995 to obtain additional data from the USAMRIID for the years that followed proved unsuccessful.

31. Brad Roberts, "The Outpacing of Negotiations by Circumstance," in *Is It Feasible to Negotiate Chemical and Biological Weapons Control?* ed. K. M. Jensen and David Wurmser (Washington, DC: United States Institute of Peace, 1990), p. 46; see also pp. 45–50. For years during the 1990s, Roberts repeatedly disregarded official US government estimates and exaggerated the number of states that had offensive biological weapons programs.

32. Testimony of Elisa Harris before the US Senate Permanent Subcommittee on Investigations of the Committee on Governmental Affairs, *Global Spread of Chemical and Biological Weapons* (9 February 1989), Senate hearing #101-744 (Washington, DC: US Government Printing Office, 1989), pp. 55–59, 267–281, 605–629. See also Leitenberg, *Problem of Biological Weapons*, p. 13.

33. Gould and Folb, *Project Coast.*

34. Iraq Survey Group, *Addendums to the Comprehensive Report of the Special Advisor to the DCI on Iraq's WMD* (Washington, DC, March 2005), p. 3; see also pp. 2, 36. There is reported to be information available regarding the move of some Iraqi chemical weapons scientists to Syria in 1994, and perhaps further details regarding this may appear in the future.

35. United Nations Security Council, *Twentieth Quarterly Report on the Activities of the United Nations Monitoring, Verification and Inspection Commission* in Accordance with Paragraph 12 of Security Council Resolution 1284 (1999), S/2005/129 (New York: United Nations, 28 February 2005), pp. 4–5, http://www.un.org/depts/unmovic/new/documents/quarterly_reports/s-2005-129.pdf.

36. D. A. Henderson, "Transcript of Screening and Discussion of the Atlantic Storm War Game: Lessons for Smallpox and Influenza" (New York: Council on Foreign Relations, 7 June 2005), http://www.cfr.org/publication/8190/screening_and_discussion_of_the_atlantic_storm_war_game.html. Henderson's remarks are typical of his loose style of delivery.

37. (1) Harvey J. McGeorge, *Chemical and Biological Terrorism,* Briefing Document, Public Safety Group (Woodbridge, VA, April 1996) (covers 1945–

1994). See also Harvey J. McGeorge, "Chemical and Biological Terrorism: Analyzing the Problem," *ASA Newsletter* 42, no. 1 (16 June 1994): 13–14. At a conference in Croatia in 2001, McGeorge reported on an updated compendium of 404 incidents involving either "chemical or biological agents." However, this group also included "threatened use," without any indications of whether real chemical or biological agents were in the possession of those making the threats. (2) Ron Purver, *Chemical and Biological Terrorism: The Threat According to the Open Literature* (Ottawa, ON: Canadian Security Intelligence Service, June 1995) (covers 1945–1995). (3) Bruce Hoffman, "The Debate over the Future Terrorist Use of Chemical, Biological, Radiological, and Nuclear Weapons," in *Hype or Reality? The "New Terrorism" and Mass Casualty Attacks*, ed. Brad Roberts (Alexandria, VA: Chemical and Biological Arms Control Institute, 2000), pp. 207–224 (covers 1900–1998). (4) W. Seth Carus, *Bioterrorism and Bio-crimes: The Illicit Use of Biological Agents in the 20th Century* (Washington, DC: National Defense University, August 1998) (covers 1900–1999; updated to February 2001). (5) Jonathan B. Tucker and Amy Sands, "An Unlikely Threat," *Bulletin of the Atomic Scientists* 55, no. 4 (July–August 1999): 46–52 (covers 1900–1999; updated since), http://www.thebulletin.org/article.php?art_ofn=ja99 tucker.

38. A more detailed discussion for the early portions of this section is to be found in Leitenberg, *Problem of Biological Weapons*, pt. 1, sect. 3, "The Experience of the Use of Biological Weapons by Non State Groups," pp. 25–35.

39. For example, a US Defense Science Board Summer Study in 1997 referred to a particular hoax that had taken place in Washington, DC, as a demonstration of the "breadth of the weaponry" available to terrorist groups. *The Defense Science Board 1997 Summer Study Task Force on DOD Response to Transnational Threats*, vol. 1, *Final Report* (Washington, DC, October 1997), p. 13.

40. See Leitenberg, *Problem of Biological Weapons*, pp. 27–29. A more detailed description of the efforts of the Aum Shinrikyo group to produce biological agents is now available in three publications by Milton Leitenberg: "The Experience of the Japanese Aum Shinrikyo Group and Biological Agents," in Roberts, *Hype or Reality*, pp. 159–172; "Aum Shinrikyo's Efforts to Produce Biological Weapons: A Case Study in the Serial Propagation of Misinformation," in *The Future of Terrorism*, ed. Max Taylor and John Horgan (London: Cass, 2000), pp. 149–158.

41. Milton Leitenberg, "Botulinum Toxin: The Linkage with Bioterrorism" (paper presented at the National Academy of Sciences, Washington, DC, 25 October 2005), p. 9; available at http://www.iom.edu/file.asp?id=30831 (accessed 28 November 2005).

42. Jonathan B. Tucker, ed., *Toxic Terror: Assessing Terrorist Use of Chemical and Biological Weapons* (Cambridge, MA: MIT Press, 2000).

43. John Parachini, ed., *Motives, Means, and Mayhem: Terrorist Acquisition and Use of Unconventional Weapons* (Santa Monica, CA: Rand Corporation, 2006). Groups that were surveyed in this second set of case studies include Tamil Eelam (Sri Lanka), the Revolutionary Armed Forces of Colombia (FARC), the Irish Republican Army (IRA, Northern Ireland), Hamas (West

Bank), the AIG (Kashmir), and several others. Some preliminary judgments from the case studies appear in John Parachini, "Putting WMD Terrorism into Perspective," *Washington Quarterly* 26, no. 4 (Autumn 2003): 37–50.

44. Parachini, "Putting WMD Terrorism into Perspective," p. 42.

45. Ibid.

46. Yoram Schweitzer, "Al Qaida, 9/11 and Unconventional Means: Changes in Terrorists' Mindsets and Effects on Their Modus Operandi" (paper presented at the conference "Meeting the Challenges of Bioterrorism: Assessing the Threat and Designing Biodefense Strategies," Fürigen, Switzerland, 22–23 April 2005).

47. Jeffrey D. Simon, *Terrorists and the Potential Use of Biological Weapons: A Discussion of Possibilities*, Rand Paper R-3771-AFMIC (Santa Monica, CA: Rand Corporation, 1989), http://www.rand.org/pubs/reports/2005/R3771.pdf.

48. National Intelligence Council, *Mapping the Global Future: Report of the National Intelligence Council's 2020 Project*, NIC 2004-13 (Washington, DC: GPO, 2004), http://www.dni.gov/nic/NIC_globaltrend2020.html.

49. Stephen S. Morse, "Bioterror R&D: Assessing the Threat" (paper presented at the National Academy of Sciences, Washington, DC, 9 January 2003).

50. All three presentations were made on 16 February 2005 at a hearing on the "World Wide Threat" before the US Senate Select Committee on Intelligence. The individual presentations are available at the committee's website, http://intelligence.senate.gov/index.htm, and the quoted sentences appear there in Goss, p. 2, Mueller, pp. 3–4, and Loy, p. 3.

51. Vice Admiral Lowell E. Jacoby, *Current and Projected National Security Threats to the United States*, testimony before the US Senate Committee on Armed Services, *Hearing on Future Threats to US National Security*, 17 March 2005.

52. Don Van Natta Jr., "Who Is Abu Musab al-Zarqawi," *New York Times*, 10 October 2004.

53. George Smith, "More UK Terror Trial: Evil Foiled or More Mendacity," *National Security Notes*, 13 April 2005, http://www.globalsecurity.org/org/nsn/nsn-050413.htm; and George Smith, "Playtime Recipes for Poisons: The Bourgass Notes of Mass Exaggeration," *National Security Notes,* 18 April 2005, http://www.globalsecurity.org/org/nsn/nsn-050418.htm.

54. James B. Petro and David A. Relman, "Understanding Threats to Scientific Openness," *Science* 302 (December 2003): 1898. Also available online at http://www.sciencemag.org/cgi/reprint/302/5652/1898.pdf. At the time Petro was a member of the Defense Intelligence Agency, and Relman is at Stanford University.

55. "Operation Enduring Freedom: Afghanistan," *Global Secruity,* http://www.globalsecurity.org/military/ops/enduring-freedom.htm; and "Taliban Surrender Last Stronghold," *BBC World,* 7 December 2001, http://news.bbc.co.uk/1/hi/world/south_asia/1696811.stm.

It appears that Ayman al-Zawahiri drew up a list of publications that he wanted to read after reading a book about bioweapons, and it seems possible that the book was one of the Stockholm International Peace Research Institute (SIPRI) chemical and biological warfare volumes, probably *The Problem of*

Chemical and Biological Warfare, vol. 2, *CB Weapons Today* (Stockholm: Almqvist and Wiksell, 1973). On 15 April 1999, al-Zawahiri suggested to Muhammad Atef, the third-ranking official in Al-Qaida, "Perhaps you can find someone to obtain them."

56. A facilitated declassification request was made on 23 February 2004, and the declassification letter from the Defense Intelligence Agency to the author was dated 25 March 2004.

57. Tom Shanker, "US Analysts Find No Sign That Bin Laden Had Nuclear Arms," *New York Times,* 26 February 2002.

58. George J. Tenet, *Worldwide Threat: Converging Dangers in a Post 9/11 World,* testimony before the US Senate Committee on Armed Services, *The Worldwide Threat to United States Interest,* 107th Cong., 2nd sess., 19 March 2002, p. 10. An assessment such as this is presented annually to the US Senate Select Committee on Intelligence.

59. George J. Tenet, *Current and Future Worldwide Threats to the National Security of the United States: Hearing Before the US Senate Committee on Armed Services,* 108th Cong., 1st sess., 12 February 2003, pp. 7, 13.

60. Jacoby, "Current and Projected National Security Threats," pp. 3, 8.

61. George J. Tenet, *The Worldwide Threat 2004: Challenges in a Changing Global Context: Hearing Before the Senate Select Committee on Intelligence,* 108th Cong., 2nd sess., 24 February 2004, p. 4.

62. *The 9/11 Commission Report,* 17 June 2004, p. 151 and n. 23.

63. Barton Gellman, "Al Qaeda Near Biological, Chemical Arms Production," *Washington Post,* 23 March 2003.

64. Susan Schmidt and Ellen Nakashima, "Moussaoui Said Not to Be Part of 9/11 Plot," *Washington Post,* 28 March 2003.

65. Mark Fineman and Bob Drogin, "Terror: In Malaysia a Jailed Cal State Graduate Helps Unravel Al Qaeda's Southeast Asia Network," *Los Angeles Times,* 2 February 2002; and Jack Kelley, "Malaysia Site of September 11 Plotting, FBI Report Says," *USA Today,* 30 January 2002.

66 "Al-Qaeda Agents Reveal Their Hunt for Anthrax," *Straits Times* (Singapore), 13 October and 14 October 2003. The reports were aired by CBS and CNN.

67. "Is Al Qaeda Making Anthrax?" *CBS News,* 9 October 2003, http://www.cbsnews.com/stories/2003/10/09/eveningnews/main577395.shtml (accessed 24 September 2005); Maria Ressa, "Al Qaeda Operative Sought Anthrax," *CNN,* 10 October 2003; "Qaeda Man Discloses Anthrax Plan," *New York Post,* 10 October 2003; Lincoln Wright, "Hambali's Taunt: We'll Kill Again," *Herald Sun* (Melbourne), 12 October 2003.

68. Rohan Sullivan, "Afghan War Curbs al-Qaida Arms Program," Associated Press, 26 January 2004; and Cam Simpson, "US Seeks Access to Al Qaeda Suspect," *Chicago Tribune,* 7 December 2003.

69. "Is Al Qaeda Making Anthrax?" (see n. 67).

70. Luz Baguioro, "Raid on Hideout Raises Fears of JI Bio-terror Plans," *Straits Times* (Singapore), 20 October 2003; Luz Baguioro, "Manila Quells Bio-Weapons Fears: Residues in JI Hideout Were for Bombs," *Straits Times*

(Singapore), 21 October 2003; "Philippines Says No Bio-Chem Traces at JI Hideout," *AlertNet,* 22 October 2003.

71. Personal communication to author, 2 May 2005.

72. Alan Cullison, "Inside Al-Qaeda's Hard Drive," *Atlantic Monthly* 294, no. 2 (2004); see Alan Cullison and Andrew Higgins, "Forgotten Computer Reveals Thinking Behind Four Years of Al Qaeda Doings," *Wall Street Journal,* 31 December 2001; Andrew Higgins and Alan Cullison, "Terrorist's Odyssey: Saga of Dr. Zawahiri Illuminates Roots of Al Qaeda Terror," *Wall Street Journal,* 2 July 2002.

73. Personal communication to author. See also, Leitenberg, *Problem of Biological Weapons,* p. 41.

74. "Madrid International Terrorism Conference: Matter of Time Before Chemical Weapons Are Used," *Daily Times* (Lahore), 9 March 2005.

75. "An Acidic Message," *Washington Post,* 10 March 2005, http://www.washingtonpost.com/wp-dyn/articles/A22101-2005Mar9.html.

76. Mark Trevelyan, "France Calls for Global Watchdog on Bio-Warfare Risk," Reuters, 1 March 2005.

77. *Report of the Commission on the Intelligence Capabilities of the United States Regarding Weapons of Mass Destruction,* Report to the President of the United States, 31 March 2005, pp. 269–270, http://www.gpoaccess.gov/wmd/pdf/full_wmd_report.pdf.

78. Personal communication to author.

79. Personal communication to author.

80. This may be justified by the fact that the declassified documents were never discussed in the report of the 9-11 Commission. On the other hand, the report of this presidential commission fiercely attacks the intelligence process for relying on unreliable informants, while all the *new* information provided in the paragraph quoted seems to depend on uncorroborated interrogation reports.

81. Personal communication to author, May 2005.

82. "French Interior Minister: Chemical and Germ Weapons Developed in Pankisi Gorge, Georgia," *Pravda*/Interfax, 4 March 2005.

83. Paul Haven, "Agents Say al-Qaida's Ability Diminishing," Associated Press, 13 March 2005.

84. Joint Task Force Guantanamo, *Information on Detainees.*

85. Iraq Survey Group, *Comprehensive Report of the Special Advisor to the DCI on Iraq's WMD,* vol. 3 (Washington, DC, 30 September 2004). See the chemical weapons section of the report, pp. 5–6, 58, 61–62. Page 6 of the section on bioweapons also contains a statement on the initial Iraqi bioweapons failure.

86. Ibid.; see pp. 9–95 in the annex of the section on chemical weapons.

87. Leitenberg, *Problem of Biological Weapons,* pp. 23–24.

88. Ibid., pp. 137–154.

89. See Timothy D. Read et al., "Comparative Genome Sequencing for Discovery of Novel Polymorphisms in *Bacillus anthracis,*" Science 296 (14 June 2002): pp. 2028–2033, http://www.sciencemag.org/cgi/content/short/296/5575/2028 (accessed 29 September 2005); Scott Shane, "Distinct Signature Found in '01 Anthrax," *Baltimore Sun,* 4 July 2004.

90. "Appendix B: Anna Johnson-Winegar Review," in *Bayes, Bugs, and Bioterrorists: Lessons Learned from the Anthrax Attacks,* ed. Kimberly M. Thompson, Robert E. Armstrong, and Donald F. Thompson, Defense and Technology Papers 14 (Washington, DC: Center for Technology and National Security Policy, National Defense University, April 2005), p. 58; available at http://www.ndu.edu/ctnsp/Def_Tech/DTP14%20Bayes%20Bugs%20Bioterrorists.pdf.

91. See n. 1 for statement by Senator William Frist.

4

The Impact of Scientific and Technological Change

Malcolm Dando

PEOPLE INTERESTED IN SECURITY ISSUES CAN HARDLY HAVE FAILED TO NOTICE THE increasing signs of concern among public officials in many countries and in international organizations over the possible use of chemical and biological weapons. Yet this is not an easy issue to assess. Most people interested in security issues are not chemists or biologists, and few chemists or biologists have any interest in security issues. Thus, most of us lack the knowledge and expertise needed to see the problem from every angle and the means to find commentators who can provide the kind of informed analysis we would like to see in a public debate about a potentially extremely serious threat.

Compounding the difficulties is the widespread feeling that the threat of terrorism—including chemical and biological terrorism—is being hyped for political reasons. There is also the difficulty, for nonscientists, of making sense of a field of research that is quite clearly changing at an incredibly rapid rate. It is hardly overstating the case to say that the recent completion of the Human Genome Project (HGP)—in which the hereditary material (DNA) of humans was decoded—has enormous significance. This significance flows from what that decoding portends for the science and technology of the twenty-first century and from the fact that the success resulted from the joint efforts of international consortia spending billions of dollars. In other words, the HGP was definitely a case of "big science" as opposed to the more fragmentary and lower cost chemical and biological research that was more characteristic of the twentieth century.

My aim in this chapter is to give a straightforward account of the problem of chemical and biological warfare and chemical and biological terrorism that we face today and will face almost certainly in the coming decades. The concentration here is therefore on the implications of the ongoing revolution in biology and the associated life sciences. In that context, having attempted to define the problem, I also ask what needs to be done to further minimize the possibilities of misuse of the modern life sciences, and, by way of conclusion, I review briefly how well we are doing in that critical task. It is necessary, however, to begin by setting the problem in its historical context.

Biological Warfare in the Twentieth Century

Today we talk less of chemistry and biology as separate subjects and more often of molecular biology and biochemistry. This is surely a correct appreciation, because as we understand more and more of the functions of living organisms at the molecular level, the distinction between chemistry and biology has little significance. Thus, it is necessary to think not of separate chemical and biological threats but of a chemical and biological threat spectrum. This spectrum ranges from classical lethal chemical weapons agents, such as nerve agents, through midspectrum agents, such as toxins and bioregulators, to traditional biological agents, such as anthrax and genetically modified biological agents.

Most of us know of the original use of chemical weapons on a large scale in World War I, which became possible as the science of chemistry developed, and of the other uses of chemical weapons in the twentieth century, such as their employment by Iraq in its war with Iran in the 1980s. Less well known is the series of offensive biological weapons programs carried out by major states during the twentieth century that followed from the elucidation at the end of the nineteenth century of the microbial nature of the pathogens that cause infectious diseases.[1]

During World War I, both sides are known to have used biological agents in attempts to attack the valuable draft animal stocks of the other. In the interwar years, a number of states, such as France, Hungary, and the Soviet Union, had offensive biological weapons programs. Perhaps the most important interwar program was in Japan. It led to many gruesome experiments carried out on people in China in the late 1930s and early 1940s, and to large-scale field trials of the use of biological agents there. The Japanese program was not very scientific, however, and it was the British, fearing a biological attack by Germany, who first developed effective biological weapons. Five million cattle cakes were impregnated with anthrax spores as an interim deterrent to destroy the German livestock industry if that became necessary. It was subsequently demonstrated in the British program that the best way to attack people and animals was to spread the biological agent on the wind in a form that lodged in the victims' lungs and grew there.

This "advance" was to form the basis of antipersonnel biological warfare for the rest of the century. After World War II, all the major victors appear to have considered biological weapons to be as serious a threat as nuclear weapons. There were major offensive programs in Britain, the Soviet Union, France, and particularly the United States (which was also extensively linked in work with its British and Canadian allies). Later, during the Cold War period, there are thought to have been a number of other state-level offensive programs. At present, we know for certain that there were programs in Iraq, South Africa, and the former Soviet Union. The Soviet program, which was greatly—and illegally—expanded after the United States closed down its offensive program and after the Biological and Toxin Weapons Convention (BTWC) came into force in 1975, was on a very large scale. It was also important because it involved the first applications of the new genetic engineering technologies to "improve" the biological agents.

Compared with this long history of interest from major states in biological warfare, there is very little evidence of bioterrorism by non-state actors in the twentieth century. The use of biological agents by a religious sect in Oregon in the 1980s and the attempted use of biological agents—and successful use of chemical agents—by another sect in Japan in the 1990s stand out as the exceptions rather than the rule. What changed after 9/11 was first of all the realization that some terrorists might consider it useful to kill very large numbers of people. Previously, though terrorists were known to think it worthwhile to kill *some* innocent people, they were also thought to believe that mass killing was counterproductive to their political objectives. Should they attempt to kill large numbers of people, they would necessarily be interested in the possible use of weapons of mass destruction (WMD)—including biological weapons.

In this context, it should be understood that although chemical weapons are generally classed with nuclear and biological weapons in a separate category, as WMD, this classification does not really stand up to analysis. Nuclear and biological weapons have potential effects that put them in a different class. It really would take very large amounts of the classical chemical weapons to be delivered in order to achieve the same effects. Here, therefore, I shall concentrate on biological weapons, with the proviso that as midspectrum agents could be delivered by replicating biological agents, we need to pay some attention to current interest in so-called nonlethal chemical agents.

Though biological agents might be easier to obtain than nuclear material, the evidence from the state programs of the twentieth century suggests that it was far from easy to weaponize these agents for the purpose of killing large numbers of people. A change at the turn of the millennium was the fact that the growth and spread of the new biology and the associated biotechnology industry might greatly simplify the problem for a substate group. So while our major problem remains that of preventing states from making the decision to initiate and maintain offensive biological weapons programs, there is an increasing danger of terrorists' being interested in, and capable of, bioterrorism.

What Kinds of Attack?

The key point we need to understand about bioterrorism and biowarfare attacks is that there are many different possibilities. For a start, evolution has produced a wide variety of pathogens, both bacteria, such as anthrax (*Bacillus anthracis*), and viruses, such as smallpox (*Variola major*). There are also, of course, an enormous number of toxins and bioregulators (communication chemicals of living systems) that could be misused. Second, while the target for an attack using biological agents might be humans, agriculture could also be attacked. Fungi are effective pathogens against crops (think of the Irish Potato Famine), and animal viruses can be particularly virulent (as in the major natural outbreak of foot-and-mouth disease in Britain just after the turn of the twenty-first century).

We obviously have to consider, too, that an attacker could be a state or a substate group or even an individual. An attacker might use biological agents for a single assassination (remember the Bulgarian dissident Georgi Markov's death in London during the Cold War period when a small amount of ricin toxin was injected into his body in a deliberate attempt to kill him) or to contaminate the food or water supply and cause moderate casualties. A perpetrator might also attempt to kill enormous numbers of people—civilian or military—in a WMD-scale attack. Finally, it must be understood that different pathogens are likely to cause different levels of incapacitation and death, which could be significantly affected by the precautions and treatment available to the victims of the attack.

The differences in possible lethality are reflected in the attempt made in the United States to classify the most likely antipersonnel agents into category A (the most dangerous) and categories B and C (less dangerous). As might be expected, the category A listing includes anthrax, smallpox, plague, botulinum toxin, tularemia, and viral hemorrhagic fevers like Ebola and Marburg. The B and C categories include agents that have been weaponized in the past, like brucellosis, Q fever, Venezuelan equine encephalitis, and staphylococcus enterotoxin type B. Similarly, chemical agents can range from the highly lethal nerve agents to the kind of chemical incapacitants (thought to be derived from fentanyl) used to break the Moscow theater hostage crisis in 2002.

The states parties to the BTWC began to recognize the potential impact of the advances in biology at their Second Review Conference in 1986. It was clear by that time that a gene for a toxin could be introduced into the genome of a bacterium, and that organism could then be grown in large quantities. This development made it much easier to obtain larger quantities of a toxin. The prohibitions of the BTWC prevent the hostile development, production, stockpiling, acquisition, and retention of agents. To make clear the new dangers, the states parties declared that

> the Convention unequivocally applies to all natural or artificially created microbial or other biological agents or toxins whatever their origin or method of production.

They went on to agree that

> consequently, toxins (both proteinaceous and non-proteinaceous) of a microbial, animal or vegetable nature and their synthetically produced analogues are covered.[2]

By 1991 the states parties also agreed that the BTWC covered "all microbial or other biological agents or toxins, naturally or artificially created *or altered, as well as their components*" (emphasis added), thereby recognizing the increasing manipulative possibilities open to biologists.

In the mid-1990s, the US Department of Defense publicly set out some of the concerns it had about genetic engineering of the traditional biological agents. It suggested that we could be faced with a variety of manipulations:

- Benign microorganisms genetically altered to produce a toxin, venom, or bioregulator

- Microorganisms resistant to antibiotics, standard vaccines, and therapeutics
- Microorganisms with enhanced aerosol and environmental stability
- Immunologically altered microorganisms able to defeat standard identification, detection, and diagnostic methods
- Combinations of the above four types with improved delivery systems[3]

There thus appeared the prospect that if the biodefense capabilities of civilized societies were improved to cope with attacks using the traditional agents, the offense could still present a major threat through the manipulation of the agents used. Further analysis suggested that the situation for defense might actually get much worse in future decades.[4] If it is assumed that there are a limited number of possible agents and a limited number of agent manipulations, then—theoretically at least—it would eventually be possible to counter such manipulations. Unfortunately, it is likely that our knowledge of biology will be such as to allow the attacker to target any number of physiological processes in the body in many different ways. Think, for example, of the way in which HIV (human immunodeficiency virus) produces AIDS (acquired immunodeficiency syndrome) by attacking the body's immune system, leaving it open to opportunistic attack from many different pathogens. In such a situation it is difficult to see how defensive capability could catch up with the capabilities for attack. Clearly, the future impact of the advances in biology has to be thoroughly investigated in order to understand the looming threat and what might be done about it.

The Future Impact of Biotechnology

In the atmosphere following the 9/11 attacks, the sending of anthrax-impregnated letters in the United States caused consternation in the security community. Of particular concern was the fact that at least some of the anthrax had been treated in the manner used for successful weaponization. Naturally, therefore, the security community became more interested in what was happening in the life sciences.

There had already been cause for concern as what the Soviet Union had done in the Cold War era with genetic engineering had begun to leak out, and in early 2001 a lot of attention was paid to the mousepox experiment in Australia.[5] Scientists there were trying to find a way of dealing with plagues of mice. They incorporated the gene for a mouse egg protein into the genome of a mousepox virus. They reasoned that infected mice would have an antibody response to the protein and would therefore reject their own eggs. This would stop the increase in the mouse population.

The experiment was successful in producing an antibody response, but the response was not strong. The scientists then added the gene for a cytokine (IL-4) to the mousepox genome, thinking this would boost the antibody response. This shut down the cell-killing arm of the immune response. The virus was thus able to multiply without hindrance. The modified mousepox was highly lethal to mice normally genetically resistant to mousepox, and it even killed a large percentage of mice that had previously been immunized against the virus. It did not take long for people to ask whether this showed the way for those with hostile intentions to create a smallpox virus that could even overcome the protection offered by vaccination.

In the following year, 2002, another publication caused equal concern. In this case the scientists had bought stretches of DNA from companies advertising such products. The lengths of DNA chosen were from the known sequence of polio virus. The scientists then joined these pieces together to obtain a full-length sequence of DNA complementary (cDNA) to that of the RNA sequence of the virus. They then proceeded to assemble the viable virus synthetically: "The synthetic polio virus cDNA was transcribed by RNA polymerase into viral RNA, which translated and replicated in a cell-free extract, resulting in the de novo synthesis of infectious polio virus."[6]

While it had long been known that such an experiment was theoretically possible for a relatively simple virus like polio, this experiment raised the question of whether more complex viruses—say Ebola—might eventually also be constructed in the laboratory by some person with malign intent.

Also in 2002, there was another publication concerning the smallpox virus that raised similar concerns. Our immune system is divided into two parts. There is an ancient innate immune subsystem and a more recent adaptive immune subsystem. While it is much less flexible than the evolutionarily recent subsystem, the innate subsystem is the body's first line of defense and key also to activating the adaptive subsystem. Scientists discovered that the vaccine strain of smallpox has a protein that interferes with the operation of the innate immune subsystem. They then scanned the databases on the smallpox genome sequence, which are available on the Internet, and discovered that real smallpox has a similar sequence. The vaccine strain protein is called vaccinia virus complement control protein (VCP), and the analogous real smallpox protein is called smallpox inhibitor of complement enzymes (SPICE). They then found that "SPICE is nearly 100-fold more potent than VCP" in inhibiting a key element of the innate subsystem.[7] Naturally, this raised the question of whether the difference in potency between SPICE and the VCP was one of the reasons why smallpox was so virulent and the vaccine strain was not. It also raised the question of whether the VCP might be replaced by SPICE by someone with hostile intentions.

While concerns began with such individual experiments, it did not take long for bigger issues to be raised. The mousepox experiment was followed by similar experiments on rabbitpox and cowpox (which can jump species), and there were rumors of the experiment being carried out on monkeypox. Questions arose as to where all of this might lead. Should we not be concerned about the whole program of research and not just about the individual experiments?

This issue came spectacularly to the fore with a sequence of work that began in the mid-1990s. The most devastating epidemic to hit the human species is generally agreed to be the 1918 Spanish influenza, thought to have killed between 20 and 40 million people. Worried about the possible reoccurrence of such an influenza, scientists began to try to recover some of the viral genetic material, for example from post-mortem tissues of those who had died, and to sequence the material they were able to recover. They then began to reinsert synthesized parts of the viral genome into other influenza strains to see if they could discover why the 1918 version had been so lethal. As one review pointed out: "Sequencing the genome of the 1918 Spanish influenza is nearly complete; once it is published, unscrupulous scientists could presumably utilize . . . virulence sequences."[8] And sure enough in 2005 the whole sequence was published.[9]

Nevertheless, if we think about the possible offense-defense interaction that could take place in the future, such a concentration on the possible agents by the security community is perhaps misplaced. Perhaps we need to think more widely about what is happening in the life sciences and where that might eventually lead us. One person who has strongly argued this point is George Poste. He has urged us to think "beyond bugs" and suggests that

> as we begin to understand the exquisite molecular mechanisms that regulate this remarkable structure called the human body . . . the ability to understand those [brain] circuits means that simultaneously we gain the capacity to scramble them . . . So that means that you can engineer a series, a complete spectrum of activity from transient immobilization . . . to catastrophic effects which can be acute or chronic.[10]

If we grasp the implications of our new knowledge of signaling chemicals in the body (bioregulators) of the immune system, like IL-4 or the chemical neurotransmitters of the brain, we can see why Poste insists that just thinking about pathogens is far too narrow a perspective. Indeed, if the HGP is the most significant event to date, we should surely ask where that research program is heading.

At the Core of Biology

The fundamental mechanisms of evolution—variation and selection—were elucidated one hundred fifty years ago. One hundred years later, James Watson and Francis Crick were able to understand the structure of the DNA code in our hereditary material, and fifty years after that the DNA sequence of the human species was described in the HGP. In that project there was a rapid and systematic acceleration of the speed of sequencing and a lowering of the unit costs of the sequencing.

Now biologists want to be able to synthesize long lengths of genetic material. The polio virus genome has some seventy-five hundred nucleotides and had to be put together from synthesized pieces. What biologists want now is to be able to go far beyond that and to have the capability to produce much longer strands with few errors and at lower and lower unit costs. New methods of fabricating DNA, for example, on microchips[11] and of reducing error are consequently being developed and published.[12] Other techniques for the manipulation of DNA, such as accelerated evolution through DNA shuffling[13] and silencing of genes through RNA interference (RNAi),[14] are rapidly developing as well. It can be confidently expected that DNA synthetic capabilities will come to parallel those of DNA sequencing.

Biologists want such capabilities so that they can carry out what is being called the new field of synthetic biology. In this new field of scientific research, the intention is to test specific hypotheses about how fundamental life processes operate at the micro level. The aim is to be able to develop artificial models of how such processes operate in nature and then to test predictions from the models in real circuits that have been synthesized in living tissues. Such work involves mathematicians and engineers besides life scientists, but surprisingly fast progress is being made in these complex tasks.[15]

Coming at the problem of understanding the mechanisms of life from the other end, systems biologists are asking questions at the macro level about how the parts of whole biological organisms operate together.

Systems biology has been described as "an emerging field that is characterized by the application of quantitative theoretical methods and a tendency to take a global view of problems in biology."[16]

While such thinking is not new in biology, the widespread appreciation of the value of studying dynamic behavior in such complex biochemical networks indicates, surely, the emergence of a mechanistic science and associated technology.

One way to view the future of biology is to envisage it as having the capability to analyze the global network of biochemical interactions, and then to zoom down to specific biochemical pathways, and then down further to the interactions between the proteins of a particular part of a biochemical pathway.[17] Given such powerful possibilities, it is little wonder that Matthew Meselson, professor of molecular biology at Harvard, said in 1999 that

> during the century ahead, as our ability to modify fundamental life processes continues its rapid advance, we will be able not only to devise additional ways to destroy life, but will also be able to manipulate it—including the processes of cognition, development, reproduction and inheritance.[18]

As all previous scientific and technological revolutions have been extensively employed for hostile purposes, as Meselson also pointed out, it will be a difficult task to prevent the new life sciences from being used in exactly the same manner.

Conclusion: What Needs to Be Done

From the foregoing analysis, it is evident that we face a multifaceted problem. We need to close down and prevent the initiation of state-level offensive biological weapons programs, and we increasingly will have to face the prospect of the capacity to cause havoc on the part of substate groups (terrorists) or even deranged individuals. Furthermore, our agriculture is already vulnerable to large-scale attack from such groups. Better intelligence on potential proliferators, and an international determination to react very strongly to any hostile use of chemistry and biology, can help to convince potential proliferators that the costs will far outweigh the benefits of the misuse of the new knowledge for hostile purposes. But such measures will clearly not suffice—in particular, such preventive actions by single or small groups of states are unlikely to be an adequate deterrent.

A sensible additional means of minimizing the risks is for states to exercise effective control of exports of agents and equipment that might be misused. While this in itself cannot prevent all possibilities of misuse, it can certainly make proliferation more difficult. Similarly, while it is possible to go overboard on defensive and emergency response measures, the sensible strengthening of normal public health and emergency planning procedures (including exercise training) can help to both minimize the consequences of any attack and persuade those with hostile intent that they are unlikely to be successful.

What is being described, therefore, is what the International Committee of the Red Cross has called a "web of prevention."[19] The term describes a multilaterally implemented, integrated set of policies that together reduce all aspects of the risk. However, to achieve that end, the web of policies has to be bound together by the internationally accepted norm that modern biology and chemistry will not be misused for hostile purposes.

That norm is embodied in the 1925 Geneva Protocol, which bans the use of biological and chemical agents for hostile purposes, and in the BTWC and the 1997 Chemical Weapons Convention (CWC), which further ban development, production, and so on. The CWC is a modern agreement with strong provisions and organizational backup. There may be concerns about how well it will stand up to technological change and military interests in so-called nonlethal chemical weapons,[20] but such concerns are nothing compared to the fears engendered by the weaknesses of the BTWC.

Biology is an area of extremely rapid scientific and technological change, as we have seen, but the Cold War–era BTWC lacks any organization to properly oversee its adequate development; and following the failure of the decadelong negotiations on a verification protocol in 2001, it still lacks any effective means of confirming that the states parties are living up to their obligations. In such circumstances it is natural that suspicions abound. However, we are not bereft of options for strengthening the BTWC and thus, indirectly, the web of prevention.[21] An inter-review conference process was agreed to in 2002 and has led to productive discussions on national legislation and biosecurity (2003), disease monitoring and investigations (2004), and codes of conduct for scientists (2005). The latter discussions encouragingly evidenced a much greater involvement of life scientists and their professional organizations than had been shown in the past and suggested a growing sense of responsibility among scientists for protecting the results of their civil work from malign misuse. Action on these discussions has been discussed at the Sixth BTWC

Review Conference in 2006, and clearly, joint action on these issues will help to reinforce the web of prevention.

However, much more is at stake in 2006. The acrimony following the failure of the protocol negotiations fatally damaged the 2001 Fifth Review Conference, and no agreement on the operation of the convention was possible. As the convention was not thoroughly reviewed in 1996 because of the ongoing protocol negotiations, it has not been thoroughly assessed since 1991. While it may be necessary to wait some time before the issue of verification can be resurrected, it is essential that the convention be given some permanent organizational support and that further actions—such as a new inter-review conference process—also find agreement to keep the process of strengthening the BTWC in operation. Failing this, we face the prospect that a weakened central element of the web of prevention will remain unaltered when the Seventh Review Conference is scheduled in 2011. Given the pace of scientific and technological change and the irresistible spread of new capabilities because of commercial considerations, it is necessary to ask whether the BTWC will still be functioning in such circumstances. And without it, what other parts of the web of prevention will remain effective as restraints against the proliferation and potential use of biological agents for hostile purposes, and what will be the state of the CWC regime?

Notes

1. M. R. Dando, *Biowar and Bioterror: A Beginner's Guide* (Oxford: Oneworld, 2006).

2. "Convention on the Prohibition of the Development, Production, and Stockpiling of Bacteriological (Biological) and Toxin Weapons and on Their Destruction," Geneva, 1972, http://www.opbw.org/convention/conv.html (accessed 16 November 2005).

3. M. R. Dando, V. Nathanson, and M. Darvel, *Biotechnology, Weapons and Humanity* (London: Harwood Academic, 1999).

4. J. B. Petro, T. R. Plasse, and J. A. McNulty, "Biotechnology: Impact on Biological Warfare and Biodefense," *Biosecurity and Bioterrorism* 1, no. 3 (2003): 161–168.

5. R. J. Jackson et al., "Expression of Mouse Interleukin-4 by a Recombinant Ectromelia Virus Suppresses Cytolytic Lympocyte Responses and Overcomes Genetic Resistance to Mousepox," *Journal of Virology* 75, no. 3 (2001): 1205–1210.

6. J. Cello, A. V. Paul, and E. Wimmer, "Chemical Synthesis of Poliovirus cDNA: Generation of Infectious Virus in the Absence of Natural Template," *Science* 297, no. 5583 (August 2002): 1016–1018.

7. A. M. Rosengard et al., "Variola Virus Immune Evasion Design: Expression of a Highly Efficient Inhibitor of Human Complement," *Proceedings of the National Academy of Sciences of the United States of America (PNAS)* 99 (2002): 8808–8813.

8. M. Madjid et al., "Influenza as a Bioweapon," *Journal of the Royal Society of Medicine* 96 (2003): 345–346.

9. Debora MacKenzie, "US Scientists Resurrect Deadly 1918 Flu," *NewScientist.com News Service,* 5 October 2005, http://www.newscientist.com/article .ns?id=dn8103 (accessed 16 November 2005).

10. George Poste, "Advances in Biotechnology: Promise and Peril?" (speech at the Second National Symposium on Medical and Public Health Response to Bioterrorism," Washington, DC, 28–29 November 2000). Available at http://www.upmc-biosecurity.org/pages/events/bioterror2000/hend/hend .html.

11. J. Tian et al., "Accurate Multiplex Gene Synthesis from Programmable DNA Microchips," *Nature* 432, no. 7020 (December 2004): 1050–1054.

12. P. Carr et al., "Protein-Mediated Error Correction for de Novo DNA Synthesis," *Nucleic Acids Research* 32, no. 20 (2004): e162.

13. K. Pekrun et al., "Evolution of a Human Immunodeficiency Virus Type 1 Variant with Enhanced Replication in Pig-Tailed Macque Cells by DNA Shuffling," *Journal of Virology* 76, no. 66 (2002): 2924–2935.

14. J. Lieberman et al., "Interfering with Disease: Opportunities and Roadblocks in Harnessing RNA Interference," *Trends in Molecular Medicine* 9, no. 9 (2003): 397–403.

15. M. Albert et al., "Computational Design of Receptors for an Organophosphate Surrogate of the Nerve Agent Soman," *Proceedings of the National Academy of Sciences of the United States of America* 101, no. 21 (May 2004): 7907–7912.

16. A. Goldbeter, "Computational Biology: A Propagating Wave of Interest," *Current Biology* 14 (2004): 601–602.

17. P. Aloy and R. B. Russell, "Structure-Based Systems Biology: A Zoom Lens for the Cell," *FEBS Letters* 579, no. 8 (2005): 1854–1858.

18. Matthew Meselson, "The Problem of Biological Weapons" (paper presented at the 1818th Stated Meeting of the American Academy of Arts and Sciences, Cambridge, MA, 13 January 1999), http://www.pugwash.org/reports/ cbw/cbw5.htm.

19. See Appendix 2 in Malcolm R. Dando, *Biotechnology, Weapons and Humanity II* (London: British Medical Association, 2004).

20. Malcolm R. Dando, *The Danger to the Chemical Weapons Convention from Incapacitating Chemicals,* CWC Review Conference Paper, no. 5 (Bradford, UK: University of Bradford, April 2003).

21. See Dando, *Biowar and Bioterror.*

Part 2

Assessing the Threat: Differing Perceptions

5

Knowledge Gaps
and Threat Assessments

PETER R. LAVOY

THE USE OF BIOLOGICAL WEAPONS BY UNSCRUPULOUS STATES OR NONSTATE TER-
rorist groups has become one of the world's most frightening security
threats.[1] Fear spreads because of the international community's rapidly
growing understanding of the lethal characteristics of biological agents,
the size and sophistication of some countries' previous biowarfare programs, and the vulnerability of populations and armed forces to biological attacks. However, biodefense efforts are hampered by a disturbing
lack of knowledge about the actual biological weapons that certain
countries or terrorist groups now possess and about how they could
employ these weapons to achieve their political, military, or psychological goals.

Two significant knowledge gaps create particularly large obstacles
for governments to assess the vulnerability of their populations, environments, and armed forces to biological attacks and to calibrate the
resources required to fashion effective biodefense polices. The first
information problem comes from not knowing which countries, substate
entities, and nonstate groups may be pursuing or already possess
bioweapons programs, and also from not knowing the sophistication of
these programs in terms of weaponization of biological agents, dissemination techniques, and the integration of biological warfare into military or terrorist strategies. Drawing on declassified US government
assessments, I show the great difficulty the United States has experienced in accurately assessing the bioweapons capabilities of the Soviet
Union during the Cold War, Iraq prior to 2003, and Al-Qaida today.

The second knowledge gap lies in establishing when state and nonstate actors actually have employed bioweapons in the past; the objectives
behind the attacks that have occurred; and the tactical and strategic effects

of such use on human, animal, or environmental targets. I examine four cases of suspected bioweapons use during the Cold War and post–Cold War periods to demonstrate how challenging it is for governments to identify and characterize the use of bioweapons and to identify the perpetrator of the alleged attack.

Deficiencies in the preparedness of Western governments and armed forces to deal with modern-day bioweapons threats are at least partially due to the psychological, bureaucratic, and political conditions that ensue from these two knowledge gaps. I describe several policymaking problems that these knowledge gaps have caused. Finally, I outline three corrective approaches that might help policymakers and analysts gain a better appreciation of how biological agents could be used in state and nonstate asymmetric strategies.

My aim in this chapter is to identify constructive ways for the United States and its allies to overcome formidable policy problems and to improve the preparedness of their societies and armed forces to combat these menacing threats.

The First Knowledge Gap: Capability Assessments

Since the mid-1990s, US government spokespeople have asserted that approximately one dozen countries either possess or are actively pursuing offensive biological warfare agents.[2] Concern about the development and possible use of biological weapons by these and other countries has led to a significant amount of intelligence and policy attention being paid to this problem during that period. However, it remains extraordinarily difficult to ascertain which countries and terrorist groups have weaponized biological agents. It is even harder to characterize the scope and sophistication of suspected bioweapons programs.

Because bioweapons can be produced in small-scale facilities and are easily concealed, they are very difficult to detect through overhead surveillance or by other intelligence collection techniques. The fact that virtually all of the technology, materials, and equipment required to produce bioweapons can also be found in legitimate scientific and commercial enterprises makes it difficult to distinguish a bioweapons production facility from a vaccine plant or some other peaceful venture in the life sciences. Most countries can obtain pathogenic microorganisms from supply houses, university or research laboratories, and hospitals. In addition, skilled scientists and engineers are able to isolate indigenous pathogenic microorganisms compatible with bioweapons production and develop them for offensive use.[3] Moreover, the technical skills required to start and operate a bioweapons program are consistent with relatively basic training in microbiology.

Also contributing to the difficulty the US government and its allies have in identifying and characterizing the bioweapons capabilities of various countries and terrorist organizations have been the extensive "denial and deception" techniques that all bioweapons producers and recipients have implemented to conceal their programs from foreign and domestic scrutiny. After conducting a detailed review of the track record of the US intelligence community to correctly characterize modern weapons of mass destruction (WMD) threats, the US WMD Commission recently reported, "Most of the traditional Intelligence Community collection tools are of little or no use in tackling biological weapons."[4] The formidable difficulties involved in ascertaining the existence and level of sophistication of offensive bioweapons programs can be illustrated more clearly by three cases: (1) the Soviet bioweapons program during the Cold War, (2) the Iraqi bioweapons program from 1991 to 2003, and (3) Al-Qaida's efforts to obtain bioweapons in the months leading up to its notorious 11 September 2001 terrorist attacks.

The Soviet Biowarfare Program

One of the biggest intelligence failures of the Cold War was the inability of Western governments to accurately assess the scope, sophistication, and purpose of the Soviet Union's offensive bioweapons program, especially from the late 1940s to the late 1970s. As a result, efforts to understand how Moscow might employ bioweapons against the US and European populations or armed forces were based almost entirely on speculation and inference. From the testimony of Soviet defectors and other information that Western governments managed to acquire after the breakup of the Soviet Union, it gradually became apparent that for at least several decades, Moscow had orchestrated an enormous, diversified, and secretive bioweapons research and development and production enterprise, only a very small portion of which Western governments ever detected or comprehended during the Cold War.

Shortly after the conclusion of World War II, US authorities suspected Moscow of carrying out an extensive offensive bioweapons program, but they had no evidence to support this belief. In the first National Intelligence Estimate (NIE) produced on the subject, at the beginning of 1951, the US intelligence community wrote, "The Soviets are capable of producing a variety of agents in sufficient quantities for sabotage or small-scale employment," and "by 1952 at the latest, the Soviets probably will be capable of mass production of BW agents for large-scale employment."[5] During this very unstable period of the East-West military competition, another world war loomed as a real threat. If a general war were to break out, US officials feared, the Soviet Union would employ chemical and biological weapons in its initial military maneuvers. With this concern looming in the background, the US Central Intelligence Agency (CIA) reported in September 1951 that the Soviets were capable of launching a clandestine bioweapons attack against key individuals and installations, livestock, and possibly crops in the United States.[6] However, no firm evidence was cited to support these contentions. In fact, after an exhaustive review of all US intelligence on Soviet bioweapons capabilities, conducted a decade later, the CIA was forced to acknowledge that there was "insufficient direct evidence on which to base a firm assessment of Soviet BW offensive activities." The United States was not able to identify the specific bioweapons that Moscow was assumed to be developing, the dissemination techniques it was pursuing, or even the production facilities that presumably were involved in this effort.[7]

When US intelligence analysts still had not been able to obtain any reliable evidence about Soviet biological warfare doctrine and capabilities by the mid-1960s, they departed from their earlier assumption of a robust and highly capable Soviet biological warfare menace to what they came to believe was a more realistic view of "limited BW activity and the unsure potential of BW weapons."[8] As a result, the 1964 NIE on the Soviet biological warfare threat reported "no positive indications of any Soviet effort to produce and stockpile BW weapons," no information on any facility devoted to offensive bioweapons research, and no awareness of any bioweapons delivery systems or field testing. Perhaps because of these gaping knowledge voids, that particular NIE went on to say, "The Soviets have no present intention to employ BW in military operations."[9]

In reality, the biological warfare threat had not changed significantly. In fact, the earlier estimate was much closer to the truth. The Soviet Union was expanding its offensive bioweapons production program and devising new plans and techniques to deliver large amounts of pathogens and toxins against Western civilian and military targets, including the preparation from 1960 onward of ballistic missiles for bioweapons delivery roles.[10] However, the dearth of information about actual Soviet plans and capabilities resulted in a radical shift in the biological warfare threat perception in the mid-1960s, which in turn led the

US government to devote a relatively low level of civilian and military resources to counter that threat—and soon to get out of the offensive biological warfare business altogether.

Because the US intelligence community could not gather enough information to confirm the presence of a Soviet offensive bioweapons program, and because Washington was not putting a great deal of effort into its own offensive or defensive bioweapons programs at the time, analysts may have engaged in a form of mirror imaging and down-played the Soviet threat. I suspect this explanation has merit; but it should not be overstated. The United States had been ramping up its own offensive bioweapons program between 1956, when President Dwight D. Eisenhower directed US military forces to "be prepared to use chemical and biological weapons in general war,"[11] and late 1961, when President John F. Kennedy and Secretary of Defense Robert S. McNamara authorized resources for a crash bioweapons production program. While significant progress was made in the production and weaponization of pathogens for assassination missions, however, the US capacity for employing bioweapons against large-scale military targets was still quite limited in the early and mid-1960s. In fact, it was not until the late 1960s that US researchers solved most of the technical problems associated with large-scale fermentation, purification, concentration, stabilization, drying, and weaponization of pathogenic microorganisms for military uses. But even these agents were not actually weaponized. When President Richard M. Nixon decided to terminate the offensive bioweapons program in 1969, the US bioweapons arsenal consisted only of stocks of antipersonnel and anticrop agents (and there were no munitions filled with the latter).[12]

The shortage of firm indications about the Soviet bioweapons program remained a major problem throughout the Cold War, but later US intelligence estimates were less likely to downplay the threat. For example, the next NIE on the subject, which came out in 1969, reported, "In previous years, virtually all available evidence could be related to Soviet work in epidemiology, public health, and sanitation, and defensive aspects of biological warfare, but recent evidence points to the development of BW weapons." The evidence in question pertained mainly to Soviet work on the aerosolization of botulinum toxin.[13]

Confirmation of a large-scale Soviet bioweapons production program finally came after Western intelligence sources determined that an unusual anthrax epidemic, which led to the death of about seventy people in the Soviet city of Sverdlovsk (present-day Yekaterinburg) in April and May 1979, had been caused by the accidental escape of an aerosol of anthrax pathogen from a secret military facility in the city. Although the US government account of this epidemic was disputed for many years by Soviet officials and even by some nongovernmental analysts in the West,[14] the matter was finally put to rest when an independent team of researchers obtained detailed epidemiological and patho-anatomical proof of the location and date of the accidental airborne release of the anthrax pathogen.[15] Largely because of the Sverdlovsk anthrax epidemic, by 1986, the CIA had acquired enough information to assess that "the Soviets maintain the world's most comprehensive chemical and biological warfare program" and that this capability constituted a "serious threat" to the North Atlantic Treaty Organization (NATO) and to several other countries friendly to the West.[16]

Western governmental estimates of Soviet bioweapons capabilities improved later in the Cold War, but important questions remain even today about the full spectrum of Soviet biological warfare activities, and also about the bioweapons inventories that Russia, Ukraine, and other former Soviet republics may now possess. The US State Department reported in August 2005 that despite Russia's claim that it had dismantled its offensive bioweapons capability by 1992, Moscow continues to maintain an offensive bioweapons program in violation of the 1972 Biological and Toxin Weapons Convention:

> The United States continues to assess that Russia maintains a mature offensive BW program and that its nature and status have not changed. Russia's BW capability builds on capabilities and expertise inherited from the far more extensive Soviet BW program that dates back to the 1920s. Since the Soviet era, elements of that former Soviet BW program have been subject to varying degrees of downsizing and restructuring. There have also been severe cuts in funding and personnel at some key BW facilities. However, some key elements of the former Soviet program may remain largely intact and may support a mobilization capability for the production of biological agents and delivery systems. The United States continues to receive unconfirmed reports of some ongoing offensive biological warfare activities, and key officials from the Soviet offensive BW program continue to occupy influential positions.[17]

Iraq's Mysterious Bioweapons Program

The dramatic controversy that surrounded (and to some extent still surrounds) Iraq's post–Gulf War bioweapons program is testimony to the scope of today's bioweapons policymaking problem. Despite years of UN inspections and the failure of the dedication of large portions of US,

British, Australian, and other national intelligence assets to uncover Iraq's WMD programs, most policymakers and intelligence agencies incorrectly believed that Saddam Hussein had maintained a large-scale, operational bioweapons program—chiefly, it now seems, because of the Iraq regime's extensive denial and deception activities and, in particular, its systematic pattern of noncooperation with UN inspection teams.[18]

For example, the controversial October 2002 NIE, *Iraq's Continuing Programs for Weapons of Mass Destruction,* assessed that "all key aspects—R&D, production, and weaponization—of Iraq's offensive BW program are active and . . . most elements are larger and more advanced than they were before the Gulf War." It concluded that Iraq had "some lethal and incapacitating BW agents and [was] capable of quickly producing and weaponizing a variety of such agents, including anthrax, for delivery by bombs, missiles, aerial sprayers, and covert operatives." It specified that smallpox and "genetically engineered BW agents" might be part of Iraq's offensive bioweapons program. Further, it stated, "Baghdad has established a large-scale, redundant, and concentrated BW agent production capability."[19] From this and other intelligence assessments that appeared around the same time, US, British, and Australian policymakers were told with "high confidence" that Iraq presented a growing bioweapons threat to its neighbors and coalition forces in the region.

The Iraq Survey Group (ISG) concluded in September 2004 that the October 2002 intelligence assessment had been wrong:

> With the destruction of the Al Hakam facility [in 1995], Iraq abandoned its ambition to obtain advanced BW weapons quickly. ISG found no direct evidence that Iraq, after 1996, had plans for a new BW program or was conducting BW-specific work for military purposes. Indeed, from the mid-1990s, despite evidence of continuing interest in nuclear and chemical weapons, there appears to be a complete absence of discussion or even interest in BW at the Presidential level.[20]

Yet even after the ISG had pored over thousands of intelligence reports, inspected facilities all over Iraq, and conducted interviews with dozens of officials and workers associated with Iraq's bioweapons program, many important questions remained unresolved, including questions about the fate of Iraq's stocks of bulk bioweapons, missing bulk agent storage tanks, the remains of a significant portion of Iraq's bioweapons seed stocks, and "the nature, purpose and who was involved in the secret biological work in the small IIS [Iraqi Intelligence Service] laboratories discovered by the ISG."[21]

The recent report of the US WMD Commission sheds light on some of these mysteries. It confirmed the finding of the ISG that for all intents and purposes Iraq had abandoned its bioweapons program—though Saddam Hussein had attempted to keep his scientists together and was intent on reconstituting his WMD production programs after international sanctions against his country had been lifted. The commission observed that while the intelligence community had been mistaken about most aspects of Iraq's WMD capabilities, "one of the most painful errors" concerned the bioweapons program.[22] One of the reasons cited for this intelligence failure was the community's overreliance on a single, bad human intelligence source (code-named Curveball).

A deeper problem, which had also impaired analysis of the Soviet bioweapons threat in the 1960s, was the tendency of the intelligence community to deal with the dearth of reliable information by rallying behind one hypothesis to explain the conduct of the adversary. In the Soviet case, because US officials had been unable to gather sufficient evidence to confirm the presence of an offensive bioweapons program, and because the US government had not been putting much effort into its own offensive bioweapons program at the time, analysts engaged in a form of mirror imaging and discounted the Soviet threat.[23] In the Iraq case, intelligence analysts went in the other direction. They regarded Iraq's past use of chemical (and possibly biological) weapons, its successful concealment of its bioweapons program both before and after the Gulf War, and its unwillingness to cooperate with UN inspectors as "proof" of the continued presence of a significant offensive bioweapons capability. When Curveball's fabrications were thrown into the mix, the outcome was a strong—but completely mistaken—belief in a large-scale and growing Iraqi bioweapons threat. As the WMD Commission describes in great detail, the US intelligence community erected sturdy psychological, bureaucratic, and political barriers to prevent serious consideration of alternative hypotheses to this dominant and mistaken view of Saddam's willingness and wherewithal to conduct germ warfare.[24]

Al-Qaida's Bioweapons Capability

Assessing the covert bioweapons capabilities of substate or nonstate terrorist groups is even more challenging than discerning state programs, and thus the intelligence policy problem is potentially even more vexing. The CIA released an unclassified report in May 2003 stating that "al-Qaida and associated extremist groups have a wide variety of potential agents and delivery means to choose from for chemical, biological, radiological, or nuclear (CBRN) attacks." It cited as evidence the observation that "several groups of mujahidin associated with al-Qaida have attempted to carry out 'poison plot' attacks in Europe with easily produced chemicals and toxins best suited to assassination and small-scale scenarios." It further reported that key Al-Qaida members were interested in obtaining spray devices to disseminate bioweapons agents: "Both 11 September attack leader Mohammad Atta and Zacharias Moussaoui expressed interest in crop dusters, raising our concern that al-Qaida has considered using aircraft to disseminate BW agents." Finally, the report indicated that, based on documents recovered in Afghanistan in the summer of 2002, Al-Qaida had mastered crude procedures for making mustard agent (along with the chemical warfare agents sarin and VX).[25]

In March 2005, the US WMD Commission provided a few more details about Al-Qaida's bioweapons capabilities prior to the war in Afghanistan. It observed that Al-Qaida's bioweapons research and development program in Afghanistan was "extensive, well-organized, and operated for two years before 11 September, but intelligence insights into the program were limited."[26] In Afghanistan, Al-Qaida operatives with special training worked at two sites containing commercial equipment that could be used for the production of bioweapons agents.[27] Despite four years of conducting the global war on terrorism, however, little firm information was available in the public domain about the bioweapons capabilities of Al-Qaida—and much less reliable data has come to light about the bioweapons potential of any other current terrorist organization. The WMD Commission concluded that "outstanding questions remain about the extent of biological research and development in pre-war Afghanistan, including about the reliability of the reporting" of the US intelligence community.[28]

Despite the paucity of detailed information, US officials have made several assumptions to help bound the bioterrorism threat. According to the previously cited unclassified May 2003 report prepared by the CIA, Al-Qaida's main interest in bioweapons probably is to inflict mass casualties; however, any actual bioweapons attack by the group—and especially by associated extremists—will probably be small-scale, incorporating relatively crude delivery means and easily produced or obtained toxins.[29] This assessment is based on the presumption that neither Al-Qaida nor any other nonstate actor would be able to assemble the production infrastructure and scientific expertise required to develop advanced bioweapons on a large scale or sophisticated systems to deliver them effectively.

Identifying which biological agents Al-Qaida could employ is very difficult. Terrorists might be inclined to experiment with a greater number of agents than would state actors. Some agents that are not lethal enough to be used on a battlefield are sufficiently hazardous to kill people in more enclosed or heavily populated areas. But the CIA believes that "most scenarios could cause panic and disruption." In its view, as stated in 2003, mass destruction would be an unlikely result of bioterrorism.[30] Because there still is not a firm handle on the bioterrorism threat, however, there is a real possibility that the knowledge gap concerning capability will complicate governmental efforts to sufficiently comprehend and effectively deal with the threat.

The Second Knowledge Gap:
The Use and Effects of Bioweapons

One of the great attractions of biological weapons is the wide variety of effects they are capable of producing on humans (from simply incapacitating the target population to causing mass deaths), livestock, and agriculture without the likelihood of detection. The individual or group behind a bioweapons attack has good reason to be confident that identification can be evaded. Moreover, because the effects of biological attacks are potentially not dissimilar to the effects of naturally occurring diseases (or possibly also to the accidental release of pathogens), there often will not be any certainty that an attack has even occurred.[31] Thus, the history of biological warfare is characterized by uncertainty, controversy, and inference. For example, the most vicious case of biological warfare in the twentieth century, the deliberate infection of Chinese prisoners and citizens with bubonic plague between 1940 and 1942 by the Japanese Imperial Army's notorious Unit 731, was formally confirmed only in August 2002 by a district court in Japan (although the court refused to award damages to the families of the estimated tens of thousands of Chinese victims)—and yet many important details about this case remain controversial.[32] Beyond this episode, many other allegations of the use of bioweapons during large-scale wars have been levied, as the United States knows all too well.

Allegation of US Bioweapons Use

On more than one occasion, the US government has found itself accused of having used bioweapons against its adversaries. The most controversial episode was during the Korean War, when North Korea, China, and the Soviet Union each claimed that the United States had dropped insects and animals infected with smallpox, plague, cholera, anthrax, and other diseases to contaminate military troops and citizens in multiple attacks during 1951 and 1952. The Communists appealed to the World Peace Council to investigate their claim. As a result, a committee of scientists under the direction of eminent British chemist Joseph Needham examined autopsy reports and interviewed supposed eyewitnesses and physicians, as well as four US captives who testified to US bioweapons use. The Needham report concluded that the United States had conducted biological warfare by air-dropping deadly biological agents and various items contaminated with these agents.[33]

Although these claims, and their corroboration by several international peace and science organizations, became front-page news in the West, the US government and its allies dismissed them as Communist propaganda. However, the controversy did not completely die away. As late as 1979, in a review of the publicly available evidence, one US author concluded that the United States had experimented with bioweapons during the Korean War against its Communist foes.[34] More recent research drawing on declassified government records shows that although the United States had attempted to accelerate its offensive bioweapons research and development program during the early 1950s, it failed to achieve any meaningful operational capability before the termination of the Korean War—in part because it did not want to violate its commitment under the 1925 Geneva Protocol.[35] This episode shows just how difficult it is to reach a firm conclusion on actual bioweapons use, even when the alleged perpetrator is a relatively open democratic country.

The long-running controversy surrounding this case finally came to an abrupt halt in January 1998, when a reporter for the Japanese newspaper *Sankei Shimbun* published twelve Soviet documents dating from February 1952 to June 1953 to prove that the Communist charges about US behavior had been contrived and were completely without merit.[36] It turns out that the Chinese government had concocted the bioweapons story to discredit and isolate the United States from the international community so that Washington would be less likely to employ nuclear weapons against the Chinese or the North Koreans, and so that the Communists would come out on top in the eventual cease-fire negotiations. The documents revealed that the Chinese had helped the North Koreans stage two false regions of infection by dispersing cholera bacteria obtained from corpses in China; had prepared medical personnel to compose statements alleging that the United States had spread smallpox; and might even have deliberately infected prisoners sentenced to execution with cholera and plague bacilli.[37] Although the Soviet ambassador to North Korea had initially assisted in this deception, Soviet premier Georgy Malenkov, who succeeded Joseph Stalin, ultimately demanded that the Chinese and North Koreans stop slandering the United States, but the controversy did not die away because the issue continued to be championed by international peace and science organizations.

The elaborate Communist biological warfare ruse during the Korean War demonstrates three important points. First, it is extremely difficult to authoritatively validate that bioweapons have been used at a particular site, and even harder to identify the source, especially when there is a lengthy delay before the inspecting parties have access to the scene where the attack supposedly occurred. The Chinese and North Koreans showed that it is relatively easy to plant enough circumstantial "evidence" to raise significant suspicion that a deliberate attack has occurred. Second, this episode revealed that allegations of bioweapons use can have tremendous propaganda value, and that even a well-meaning nongovernmental organization (NGO)—in this case the World Peace Council—can unwittingly be drawn into an elaborate deception campaign. Because of the inherently ambiguous nature of the evidence, the preconceptions and prejudices of different parties, be they states or NGOs, are likely to influence how they interpret the merits of a particular case. Moreover, the stain of even an allegation of a bioweapons attack is difficult to wipe away, because it is even harder to prove that bioweapons were not used than it is to suggest that a deliberate bioweapons attack might have occurred.

Finally, the uncertainties and controversies that are likely to surround future allegations of bioweapons use will pose enormous challenges for policymakers and military planners, regardless of which side is alleged to have employed biological agents. Either a government and its armed forces will be forced to dedicate significant resources to proving that they did not conduct biological warfare, as the United States had to do in the 1950s, or they will have to devote almost as many resources to proving that the other side actually did engage in this behavior, as the United States did in the early 1980s to show that the Soviets had used chemical and toxin agents against Afghanistan and that the Vietnamese had employed similar agents against Laos, Cambodia, and Thailand.

The Yellow Rain Controversy

In the early 1980s, the US government went from being the accused to the accuser when it claimed that it had accumulated evidence of the use of various toxic agents in war-torn Afghanistan and in Southeast Asia by the Soviet Union and Soviet client states. Beginning in the fall of 1978, US intelligence analysts began collecting reports that aircraft operated by Soviet or Soviet-backed Vietnamese forces had sprayed anti-Communist Hmong resistance fighters from Laos with a mysterious substance that had left horrific burns and lesions on their skin and in some cases had caused severe illness and death. The refugees called the toxic substance "yellow rain." Based on field investigations conducted in October 1979, US State Department and Army analysts speculated that the Vietnamese had conducted a series of attacks against Hmong fighters who had taken refuge in Vietnam with as many as three different toxic agents, including one that caused internal bleeding.[38]

Shortly after Ronald Reagan became US president in January 1981, US authorities received additional reports of similar attacks along the Cambodia-Thailand border. Laboratory tests of plant specimens taken from the infected region indicated the presence of an unusually high level of trichothecene mycotoxins—harsh natural poisons that are produced by various molds that grow on wheat, corn, millet, and other grains. Despite the presence of large gaps in the accumulated evidence on possible toxin warfare and despite significant doubt among many of the intelligence and scientific analysts who had examined this evidence,[39] Secretary of State Alexander Haig announced in September 1981 that the United States had accumulated "physical evidence" that Moscow and its clients in Southeast Asia had conducted warfare using "three potent mycotoxins."[40]

Like many other allegations of bioweapons use, this case has never been settled. A team of scientists led by Harvard biologist Matthew Meselson—who just prior to this episode, as a government consultant, had questioned the US government's claim that the Sverdlovsk disaster had been caused by an accident inside a Soviet anthrax production facility (although he later validated this claim for the public record)—presented a strong, detailed case that the yellowish samples found in Southeast Asia, based on which the US government had made its allegations of toxin warfare, were actually innocuous yellow feces dropped by swarms of honeybees, not the residue of biological attacks. Meselson and his colleagues further pointed out that only a very small number of the samples collected in Southeast Asia and analyzed in US laboratories had been judged to contain mycotoxins and that these few positive identifications had taken place in two US government-contract laboratories that used unreliable scientific methods that could easily yield false positives. Moreover, British, Canadian, French, and Swedish investigations into the yellow rain allegations have yielded no evidence to sustain the US allegations.[41]

The question of whether Soviet and Vietnamese troops employed toxins (or other chemical or biological agents) against anti-Communist insurgents in Southeast Asia remains a matter of great controversy. Regardless of whether the US government's mycotoxin allegations were valid or not, Washington claims to have additional evidence of the use of some kind of biological or toxin weapons (or possibly novel chemical weapons) in Vietnam, Laos, and Cambodia during the late 1960s, 1970s, and into the early 1980s.[42] The fact that US officials have still not been able to fully identify the precise bioweapons that Communist forces may have employed testifies to the extreme difficulty in identifying and characterizing bioweapons use. And by no means have these difficulties been confined to Southeast Asia, as US officials monitoring the Soviet occupation of Afghanistan soon discovered.

Soviet Use of Chemical and Biological Weapons in Afghanistan

Soon after the December 1979 Soviet invasion of Afghanistan, Afghan resistance fighters and civilians began reporting that Soviet military forces had mounted chemical and biological attacks against them with helicopters, fixed-wing aircraft, artillery, and mines. To US government officials, the similarity of these allegations to the claims about toxin warfare in Southeast Asia was striking. Eyewitness reports from journalists operating in Afghanistan provided additional evidence. According to one US report, Dutch journalist Bernd de Bruin filmed two episodes in June 1980 in which Afghan residents of a village near Jelalabad experienced skin lesions and subcutaneous bleeding after being exposed to a sticky yellow powder that had been poured out of canisters dropped by a Soviet Mi-24 helicopter. De Bruin reportedly also developed similar symptoms and severe illness.[43] Although little reliable evidence has been produced in the public domain to confirm allegations of Soviet use of chemical and biological weapons in Afghanistan, Ken Alibek, a scientist who had formerly worked in the Soviet bioweapons program, reported that these allegations were probably true:

> Several months before Soviet forces withdrew from Afghanistan in 1989, I was told by a senior officer in the Fifteenth Directorate that the Soviet Union used biological weapons during its protracted struggle against the mujaheddin. He said that at least one attack with glan-

ders took place between 1982 and 1984, and there may have been others. The attack, he claimed, was launched by Ilyushin-28 planes based in military airfields in southern Russia.[44]

As with the claims about Vietnamese use of toxins against resistance forces in Southeast Asia, controversy still surrounds allegations of Soviet employment of chemical and biological weapons in Afghanistan.

Foot-and-Mouth Disease in Taiwan

The problem is even more challenging when it comes to discerning biological attacks against agricultural or livestock targets. For example, in March 1997, Taiwanese authorities first reported a widespread outbreak of foot-and-mouth disease, a highly contagious viral disease of cloven-hoofed animals. Foot-and-mouth disease, comprising over seventy different strains, is one of the most infectious viruses known, capable of spreading as a wind-driven aerosol over 170 miles from its source.[45] In little over a month, foot-and-mouth disease had spread throughout Taiwan, requiring government authorities to slaughter more than 8 million pigs. This completely shut down the country's valuable pork exports. The source of the viral outbreak was reportedly traced to a single pig from Hong Kong. Immediately, China was suspected of deliberately introducing the disease into Taiwan, but no formal allegations were ever levied. The disease has had a long-term impact on Taiwan's economy. The ultimate costs to that nation are estimated to be at least US$19 billion—US$4 billion to diagnose and eradicate the disease and another US$15 billion in indirect losses from trade embargoes.[46] The lingering question is whether this was an act of biological terrorism or warfare, or simply a natural outbreak. The answer may never be known. This is yet another case that illustrates the difficulty policymakers face in fashioning effective policies to deal with the modern-day threats of biological terrorism and biological warfare.

The Effects of Uncertainty

The paucity of information about many aspects of today's biological weapons threat significantly complicates civilian and military biodefense efforts. As described above, two knowledge gaps lie at the root of the problem. The first pertains to poor knowledge about the scope and sophistication of the bioweapons programs that states and nonstate groups might possess. The other concerns the identification, characterization, and attribution of possible attacks involving bioweapons. Because of these two factors, psychological, organizational, political, and military conditions arise that make it extremely difficult for governments to develop effective strategies and focus adequate resources to manage the risks associated with possible biological outbreaks. Below I discuss five such debilitating effects that knowledge gaps might have on policymaking.

The first effect of knowledge paucity on policymaking is psychological. It can be difficult for the human mind to imagine the horrific consequences of an event when these consequences have never been witnessed—at least conclusively. Nuclear weapons have been employed in warfare, and even though their use occurred sixty years ago, the physical and social consequences of their use are indelibly etched in our minds. This, I think, at least partially explains the tremendous hue and cry over the threat of dirty bombs, or radiological dispersal devices, which do not have nearly the same potential for death and destruction as does the employment of most bioweapons. In contrast, because there have been few biological attacks in recent decades; because relatively few deaths have resulted (except for the horrendous employment of biological agents by Japan in China and against military prisoners during World War II[47]); and because so many biological outbreaks have been shrouded in secrecy and controversy, it is very difficult for policymakers to imagine the physical and social effects of biological outbreaks and to take effective action to mitigate these effects.

A related psychological factor possibly contributing to the policymaking problem stems from mirror imaging. Because all Western governments have abandoned their offensive bioweapons programs (and many never even initiated such programs), Western officials might have a harder time imagining that other countries are actively pursuing these capabilities, or that they would ever use bioweapons. Humans sometimes have a tendency to imprint their own values even on their adversaries. This point should not be overstated, but it might help to explain why some government officials and military officers neglect what could in fact be a very menacing threat.

The second effect is political. In the post–Cold War era, it has been difficult to dedicate significant resources to counter poorly understood defense challenges, especially when there are so many clearly defined social and defense problems that do require large amounts of funding. How do you convince lawmakers to fund programs to counter a threat that appears to be so remote and poorly defined? It is much easier to ignore the problem or simply to make a token effort. This is not to discount the serious attention and resources that actually have been devoted to the problem; but the tendency might account for why more has not been done.

A third effect has to do with organizational and bureaucratic politics. Because of intense staffing demands already operating within the national security bureaucracies and armed forces of Western governments, it is difficult to establish dedicated offices or to appoint senior officials or even policy analysts to focus exclusively on the bioweapons threat and response. At best, biological defense portfolios are combined with chemical warfare issues and more often with both nuclear and chemical weapons responsibilities, despite the important distinctions between these weapons categories.[48] As a result, relatively few civilian officials and military officers have developed the experience and expertise required to deal with bioweapons threats effectively.

A fourth effect takes place in the area of military planning. Defense planners have a very difficult time planning against nebulous bioweapons threats. The military prefers to, and probably must, plan against "validated" threats. That is, evidence of a particular military threat is scrutinized closely by intelligence professionals and must be judged to be both sufficiently grave and probable to make it into the bureaucratic process of determining military priorities, plans, and requirements. Because it costs so much money and drains so many other resources to organize, train, and equip military forces to counter numerous validated threats, there always will be significant bureaucratic opposition to rank possible but unconfirmed military risks ahead of other, known threats in the military planning process. Therefore, the military validation of bioweapons threats is up against difficult odds because of the severe knowledge gaps that exist.

A related military effect is that military organizations, like most other complex organizations, are reluctant to undergo a radical transformation to deal with a very different kind of challenge, such as that posed by possible military or terrorist employment of bioweapons. Truly effective military operations against bioweapons-armed adversaries would probably entail radical changes to the way armed forces organize, train, and equip themselves, and also to what capabilities would need to flow first into a theater of war and to how a war would be planned and conducted. Since the mid-1990s or so, to the extent that Western militaries have tried to rethink their planning, equipment, and force structure requirements for dealing with novel, asymmetric threats, almost all have focused primarily on the chemical warfare threat because it is much better understood and the responses are potentially much less sweeping. The biological defense mission is still generally seen as an add-on to the chemical defense mission.

A fifth negative effect occurs at the international level. Largely because of the knowledge gaps described above, it is very difficult for allies and coalition partners to achieve a political consensus that specific bioweapons threats deserve serious, coordinated attention. Outside the United States (and a handful of other countries, such as Israel), the prospect of bioweapons use by adversary states or terrorist groups is still considered to be a "risk," not an actual military or terrorist threat worthy of urgent attention. A case in point is the relatively lackluster effort that NATO and the European Union have undertaken to deal with the prospect of bioweapons use.[49]

Managing Uncertainty

Unfortunately, there are no surefire solutions for mitigating the deleterious effects caused by the huge knowledge gaps surrounding the acquisition and possible use of bioweapons. The lack of information about the scope and sophistication of the bioweapons capabilities that certain countries and terrorist organizations now possess, as well as about the character and perpetrator of actual or suspected bioweapons attacks, makes it difficult for policymakers, military forces, and their publics to devise effective responses to mitigate contemporary bioweapons challenges. The situation is not entirely bleak, however. Some approaches have the potential to ameliorate the daunting policy problems that frustrate effective biodefense strategies. Following are three sets of measures to improve policymaking on bioweapons issues.

The first step to reduce the consequences of policy problems related to insufficient knowledge is to try to gain more information about the character and scope of existing bioweapons production programs and to learn more about the cases in which bioweapons have been used, have possibly been used, or were claimed to have been used. Regarding the first knowledge gap, the US WMD Commission report identified new collection methods and organizational solutions to improve the integration and effectiveness of the US intelligence community. Aside from these measures, which are being implemented, the commission proposed other steps to upgrade analytical expertise and procedures, including strengthening long-term and strategic analysis and encouraging diverse and independent analysis (through red teaming, alternative hypothesis development, counterfactual analysis, and related techniques). In particular, an emphasis on gaining more knowledge about the identity, goals, and capabilities of potential state and nonstate actors could be a particularly useful improvement, especially if this is done with an eye toward assessing indicators that could serve as warning signs about the existence of bioweapons production programs and possible bioweapons use. The implementation of these recommendations should improve the quality of intelligence about bioweapons programs.[50] A thorough reexamination of past instances of possible or actual bioweapons use could similarly increase the baseline of knowledge about the physical, political, and social effects of biological outbreaks, which, in turn, could enable policymakers to fashion more effective strategies to deter, defeat, defend, and mitigate the consequences of bioweapons use.

A second step would be to accept that even if the recommended transformation of the intelligence community results in more knowledge about bioweapons threats, large information gaps would remain. Many of these gaps are unavoidable, for they are inherent in the nature of bioweapons development, production, storage, and potentially even use. Government policymakers and military planners thus must learn to deal with biological risks more effectively in the absence of unambiguous intelligence. Military acquisition and war planning processes should be based, at least in part, on planning scenarios that feature robust bioweapons employment contingencies. The same bioweapons scenario approach should be pursued to help determine realistic biodefense strategies for protecting the livestock, agriculture, and population of the homeland.

A third measure for improving policymaking on bioweapons issues is to imagine a future threat environment that could be very different from the past. As noted above, robust biowarfare and bioterrorism scenarios must be utilized in high-level planning and acquisition processes so that we come to understand the vulnerability of potential civilian and military targets to biological attack and can develop effective strategies and capabilities for overcoming these vulnerabilities. In the scenario-building process, when defense planners decide upon the assumptions to make for state or terrorist bioweapons capabilities and delivery methods, their concepts of use, their target selection, and their operational effectiveness, they should not base their calculations solely on a reading of the past. For various reasons, the perpetrators of bioweapons attacks during and after the Cold War have underachieved. Although these attacks have produced fatalities, psychological stress, and significant diversions of public funds and other resources, they have not reached their potential for mass death and destruction. Future users of bioweapons may be much more effective and sophisticated than previous perpetrators. They might use larger quantities of more lethal agents. They might select targets more carefully in terms of the intended political or military impact. They might disseminate bioweapons more stealthily and effectively, using novel delivery means. And they might manage to integrate bioweapons attacks with other means of destruction and disruption to create devastating asymmetric strategies. We can hope that bioweapons users will continue to underachieve. But hope is not an effective strategy.

Conclusion

There is little consensus on the nature of the threat now posed by biological terrorism. The US government insists that one of its most important missions is to be prepared for the threat of biological terrorism and spends about US$7 billion a year on biodefense.[51] Many nongovernmental specialists disagree. They claim that the threat is overstated, and that public funds should be redirected, for example, to improve public health capacity in the event of a naturally occurring biological outbreak.[52] The one thing upon which almost everyone agrees is that US biodefense efforts could be improved. However, the counterproliferation and homeland security programs of the United States and many of its allies lack the strategic focus that is required to deter, defend against, and ultimately defeat contemporary and future bioweapons threats because of the existence of certain debilitating psychological, bureaucratic, and political conditions that ensue from the significant paucity of information about today's biological weapons threat.

In this chapter, I analyzed two knowledge gaps that have impaired the performance of governments in assessing the vulnerability of their populations, environments, and armed forces to biological attacks and in allocating appropriate resources for effective biodefense strategies.

First, policymakers and intelligence analysts do not have a good handle on the countries and nonstate organizations that are pursuing or already possess bioweapons programs and also the sophistication of these programs in terms of weaponization, dissemination techniques, and the integration of biological agents into asymmetric strategies. As I documented, the United States has experienced difficulty in accurately assessing the bioweapons capabilities of the Soviet Union during the Cold War, Iraq prior to 2003, and Al-Qaida today.

Second, it has always been hard to know when state and nonstate actors have employed bioweapons in the past; the objectives behind their attacks; and the various effects of these attacks on human, animal, and environmental targets. I presented four cases of suspected bio-weapons use to show how challenging it is for governments to identify and characterize biological agent use and to identify the perpetrator of alleged attacks.

I also described five deleterious effects that ensue from these two knowledge gaps. Psychological effects hinder the ability of policymak-ers to think through the physical and social consequences of biological outbreaks and to take effective action to mitigate them. Politically, it is difficult for government officials to dedicate the substantial resources that probably are required to counter bioterrorism when there remains so much uncertainty about this threat. The same problem takes place in government bureaucracies, where competing demands make it almost impossible to secure many senior officials and experts dedicated to biodefense. Militarily, the difficulties involved in validating a biologi-cal warfare threat assessment, even at the classified level, mean that the military services are not required to devote meaningful resources to this problem, and that military planners are not forced to plan against robust biological threats. Finally, knowledge gaps also complicate the ability of differently positioned and resourced governments to agree on the seriousness of the bioweapons threat and the correct set of measures that are needed to counter it.

Finally, I provided three corrective measures to assist policymak-ers and analysts in gaining a better appreciation of how biological agents could be used in state and terrorist asymmetric strategies. Vari-ous organizational modifications and analytical strategies, some of which were highlighted in the 2005 US WMD Commission report, could go a long way toward minimizing knowledge gaps and reducing the barriers they pose to homeland security and counterproliferation efforts. In particular, greater use of planning scenarios, featuring robust but realistic biological agent attacks, might enable civilian and military officials to devise more effective biodefense strategies and better prior-itize the allocation of precious resources. Through these and other measures to reduce knowledge gaps and improve threat assessments, the United States and its allies should be better able to counter the very real menaces of biowarfare and bioterrorism.

Notes

1. The US government's view of today's bioweapons threat is expressed by Under Secretary for Arms Control and International Security Robert Joseph:

"With today's dual-use capabilities and access to particular pathogens, some of which occur naturally, the bioterror challenge presents a low-cost means of a potentially high-impact attack." Remarks made at the University of Virginia Miller Center, 9 December 2005, http://www.state.gov/t/us/rm/57874.htm (accessed 12 December 2005). A counterperspective holds that bioterrorism is not an acute threat. For examples, see Malcolm Dando, *Bioterrorism: What Is the Real Threat?* Science and Technology Report, no. 3 (Bradford, UK: Department of Peace Studies, University of Bradford, March 2005), available at http://www.carnegieendowment.org/static/npp/ST_Report_No_3.pdf (accessed 12 December 2005); Milton Leitenberg, "Biological Weapons and 'Bioterrorism' in the First Years of the 21st Century" (unpublished paper, 15 May 2002), available at http://www.carnegieendowment.org/pdf/npp/Bioterror21.pdf (accessed 12 December 2005); and Anthony H. Cordesman, "Outside View: Crying Wolf on Bioterror?" *Washington Times,* 14 June 2005, http://washingtontimes.com/upi-breaking/20050610-061616-5870r.htm (accessed 12 December 2005).

2. For example, see US Department of Defense, *Proliferation: Threat and Response* (Washington, DC: US Government Printing Office, January 2001), p. 114. Even after the 2003 Iraq war, administration officials still believe that this is about the right number of bioweapons programs around the world. See Mitchell Reiss (then director of policy planning in the State Department), "Steps to a Brighter Future: The Bush Administration's Non-proliferation Policy" (remarks to the 2004 Carnegie Endowment International Nonproliferation Conference, Washington, DC, 21 June 2004, http://www.state.gov/s/p/rem/34267 .htm (accessed 7 November 2005).

3. For example, *Bacillus anthracis* can be cultured from infected animals or isolated from contaminated soil. *Coxiella burnetii,* the causative agent of Q fever, can be obtained from disease-ridden sheep.

4. Commission on the Intelligence Capabilities of the United States Regarding Weapons of Mass Destruction, *Report to the President of the United States* (Washington, DC: GPO, 31 March 2005), p. 34, http://www.wmd.gov/about .html (accessed 7 November 2005) (hereafter cited as the WMD Commission report).

5. US Central Intelligence Agency (hereafter CIA), *Probability of Soviet Employment of Biological and Chemical Warfare in the Event of Attacks upon the US,* NIE-18 (10 January 1951), p. 1, declassified document available in Declassified Documents Reference System (DDRS), item no. CK3100219039. The CIA based this assessment on information contained in the 1951 "Hirsch Report" on Soviet chemical and biological warfare efforts compiled by a former Nazi intelligence officer from documents found in Germany's wartime intelligence files.

6. CIA, *Soviet Capabilities for a Surprise Attack on the Continental United States Before July 1952,* Special Estimate (SI) 10 (15 September 1951), pp. 11–13.

7. CIA, Office of Scientific Intelligence, *The Soviet BW Program,* Scientific Intelligence Research Aid 61-3 24 April 1961); available at the CIA's Freedom of Information Act (FOIA) website, www.foia.cia.gov (accessed 7 November 2005) (hereafter cited as CIA-FOIA).

8. Wilton E. Lexow and Julian Hoptman, "The Enigma of Soviet BW," *Studies in Intelligence* 9 (Spring 1965), CIA-FOIA, http://www.fas.org/irp/threat/cbw/sibw1965.pdf.

9. CIA, *Soviet Capabilities and Intentions with Respect to Biological Warfare,* NIE 11-6-64 (26 August 1964), pp. 1–3, CIA-FOIA.

10. See Ken Alibek, with Stephen Handelman, *Biohazard* (New York: Random House, 1999), especially pp. 29–43.

11. Eisenhower's directive can be found in NSC 5602/1, 15 March 1956, p. 4, DDRS no. PD00470.

12. Information contained in US National Security Council Interdepartmental Political-Military Group, *Annual Review of United States Chemical Warfare and Biological Research Programs,* 1 November 1970, pp. 20–21; declassified document available in the Digital National Security Archives, item no. TE00135. For background on the US biowarfare program, see David R. Franz, Cheryl D. Parrott, and Ernest T. Takafuji, "The US Biological Warfare and Biological Defense Programs," in *Medical Aspects of Chemical and Biological Warfare,* ed. Frederick R. Sidell, Ernest T. Takafuji, and David R. Franz, 430–431 (Washington, DC: Office of the Surgeon General, Borden Institute, Walter Reed Army Medical Center, 1997); Ed Regis, *The Biology of Doom: The History of America's Secret Germ Warfare Project* (New York: Holt, 1999), especially pp. 182–198.

13. CIA, *Soviet Chemical and Biological Warfare Capabilities,* NIE 11-11-69 (13 February 1969), pp. 9–10, CIA-FOIA.

14. See, for example, Elisa D. Harris, "Sverdlovsk and Yellow Rain: Two Cases of Soviet Noncompliance?" *International Security* 11, no. 4 (Spring 1987): 41–95.

15. Matthew Meselson et al., "The Sverdlovsk Anthrax Outbreak of 1979," *Science* 266 (18 November 1994): 1202–1207. For detailed background on the Sverdlovsk accident and the Soviet attempts to cover it up, see Jeanne Guillemin, *Anthrax: The Investigation of a Deadly Outbreak* (Berkeley: University of California Press, 1999).

16. CIA, *Soviet Chemical and Biological Warfare Program,* NIE 11-17-86/S (August 1986), p. 1, CIA-FOIA.

17. US Department of State, *Adherence to and Compliance with Arms Control, Nonproliferation, and Disarmament Agreements and Commitments* (Washington, DC: Bureau of Verification and Compliance, 30 August 2005), http://www.state.gov/t/vc/rls/rpt/51977.htm (accessed 7 November 2005). For background, see Lester C. Caudle, "The Biological Warfare Threat," in Sidell, Takafuji, and Franz, *Medical Aspects of Chemical and Biological Warfare,* pp. 454–455.

18. For a public summary of Britain's post–Iraq war (2003) intelligence assessment, see the Butler Review of Intelligence on Weapons of Mass Destruction, 14 July 2004, http://www.globalsecurity.org/intell/library/reports/2004/butler-report.pdf (accessed 5 December 2005).

19. US National Intelligence Council, *Iraq's Continuing Programs for Weapons of Mass Destruction,* NIE 2002–16HC (October 2002), pp. 6–7; portions declassified in April 2004, available at the National Security Archives website,

http://www.gwu.edu/~nsarchiv/NSAEBB/NSAEBB129/index.htm (accessed 7 November 2005).

20. CIA, *Comprehensive Report of the Special Advisor to the DCI on Iraq's WMD,* 30 September 2004, http://www.cia.gov/cia/reports/iraq_wmd_2004/chap6.html (accessed 7 November 2005).

21. Ibid.

22. WMD Commission report, p. 48.

23. Ironically, mirror imaging has, more often than not—at least in the US-Soviet experience—led intelligence analysts on both sides to exaggerate the military capabilities and hostile intentions of the adversary. For background, see Robert B. Bathurst, *Intelligence and the Mirror: On Creating an Enemy* (London: Sage, 1993).

24. WMD Commission report, pp. 168–177.

25. CIA, Directorate of Intelligence, *Terrorist CBRN: Materials and Effects,* CTC 2003-40058 (May 2003), http://www.cia.gov/cia/reports/terrorist_cbrn/terrorist_CBRN.htm (accessed 7 November 2005).

26. WMD Commission report, p. 269.

27. Ibid.

28. Ibid., p. 270.

29. CIA, *Terrorist CBRN.*

30. Ibid.

31. These points are illustrated in the Monterey WMD Terrorism Database, which is the largest open-source catalog of worldwide incidents involving the acquisition, possession, threat, and use of WMD by substate actors since 1900. This source contains information on over twelve hundred acts of WMD terrorism, half of which were acts of bioterrorism. Half of these events were hoaxes or pranks, and only half of the groups or individuals behind these attacks have been identified. See http://cnsinfo.miis.edu/db/wmdt/index.htm. (Subscription required.)

32. "Biological Warfare in China Confirmed," *World War II* 17, no. 5 (January 2003): 12. For background, see Sheldon H. Harris, *Factories of Death: Japanese Biological Warfare, 1932–45, and the American Cover-Up* (New York: Routledge, 1994).

33. Jeanne Guillemin, *Biological Weapons: From the Invention of State-Sponsored Programs to Contemporary Bioterrorism* (New York: Columbia University Press, 2005), p. 100.

34. Stephen L. Endicott, "Germ Warfare and 'Plausible Denial': The Korean War, 1952–1953," *Modern China* 5, no. 1 (January 1979): 79–104.

35. Examples include Regis, *Biology of Doom,* pp. 143–151; Conrad C. Crane, "'No Practical Capabilities': American Biological and Chemical Warfare Programs During the Korean War," *Perspectives in Biology and Medicine* 45, no. 2 (Spring 2002): 241–249; Guillemin, *Biological Weapons,* pp. 96–106.

36. Yasuro Naito, "Soviet Documents Reveal PRC, DPRK, Fabrications," *Sankei Shimbun* (Tokyo), 8 January 1998, reprinted in English in the US Foreign Broadcast and Information Service, 8 January 1998, no. FTS19980111000717.

37. A comprehensive treatment of the subject is provided in Milton Leitenberg, "New Russian Evidence on the Korean War Biological Warfare Allegations:

Background and Analysis," *Cold War International History Project Bulletin: Cold War Flashpoints,* no. 11 (1 March 1999), http://www.wilsoncenter.org/index.cfm?topic_id=1409&fuseaction=library.document&id=37 (accessed 7 November 2005).

38. Jonathan B. Tucker, "The 'Yellow Rain' Controversy: Lessons for Arms Control Compliance," *Nonproliferation Review* 8, no. 1 (Spring 2001): 28; Judith Miller, Stephen Engelberg, and William Broad, *Germs: Biological Weapons and America's Secret War* (New York: Simon and Schuster, 2001), p. 78.

39. For details, see Julian Robinson, Jeanne Guillemin, and Matthew Meselson, "Yellow Rain: The Story Collapses," *Foreign Policy,* no. 68 (Autumn 1987): 100–117.

40. Alexander M. Haig Jr., "A Certain Idea of Man: The Democratic Revolution and Its Future," *Current Policy,* no. 311 (Washington, DC: US Department of State, Bureau of Public Affairs, 13 September 1981).

41. Robinson, Guillemin, and Meselson, "Yellow Rain"; Eliot Marshall, "Yellow Rain Evidence Slowly Whittled Away," *Science* 233, no. 4759 (4 July 1986): 18–19; Thomas David Inch, Examination of Witness, Select Committee on Foreign Affairs Minutes of Evidence, UK Parliament, 18 June 2003, www.publications.parliament.uk/pa/cm200203/cmselect/cmfaff/813/30618a02.htm (accessed 7 November 2005).

42. For background, see Tucker, "'Yellow Rain' Controversy," pp. 37–38.

43. Gary B. Crocker, "The 'Yellow Rain' Issue: Evidence of Chemical and Toxin Weapons Use in Laos, Cambodia, and Afghanistan," *Comments on Toxicology* 2 (Special Issue on "Yellow Rain," 1988): 7, cited in Tucker, "'Yellow Rain' Controversy," p. 28.

44. Alibek, *Biohazard,* p. 268.

45. Floyd P. Horn and Roger G. Breeze, "Agriculture and Food Security," in *Food and Agricultural Security: Guarding Against Natural Threats and Terrorist Attacks Affecting Health, National Food Supplies, and Agricultural Economics,* ed. Thomas W. Frazier and Drew C. Richardson, Annals of the New York Academy of Natural Sciences 894 (New York: New York Academy of Sciences, 1999): 9–17.

46. Henry S. Parker, *Agricultural Bioterrorism: A Federal Strategy to Meet the Threat,* McNair Papers 65 (June 2003), http://www.ndu.edu/inss/mcnair/mcnair.html (accessed 7 November 2005).

47. For background information, see Harris, *Factories of Death;* Peter Williams and David Wallace, *Unit 731: The Japanese Army's Secret of Secrets* (Sevenoaks, Kent, UK: Hodder and Stoughton, 1989).

48. James J. Wirtz, "Introduction," in *Planning the Unthinkable: How New Powers Will Use Nuclear, Biological, and Chemical Weapons,* ed. Peter R. Lavoy, Scott D. Sagan, and James J. Wirtz (Ithaca, NY: Cornell University Press, 2000), pp. 3–8.

49. NATO, "The Threat of Weapons of Mass Destruction," *NATO Topics,* 18 February 2005, http://www.nato.int/issues/wmd/index.html (accessed 7 November 2005); European Union, *EU Strategy Against the Proliferation of Weapons of Mass Destruction,* European Union Fact Sheet, 26 June 2004, http://europa.eu.int/comm/external_relations/us/sum06_04/fact/wmd.pdf

(accessed 7 November 2005); Peter R. Lavoy and Gayle D. Meyers, "US Counterproliferation Cooperation with Allies," in *Avoiding the Abyss,* ed. Jim A. Davis and Barry R. Schneider (Montgomery, AL: USAF Counterproliferation Center, Maxwell Air Force Base, March 2005), pp. 321–324.

50. A good discussion of how the transformation of the US intelligence community might improve knowledge of WMD threats is provided in Arnold W. Nash III, "Intelligence Reform and the Implications for North Korea's Weapons of Mass Destruction Program" (master's thesis, Naval Postgraduate School, Monterey, CA, September 2005), http://www.ccc.nps.navy.mil/research/theses/nash05.pdf (accessed 7 November 2005).

51. The White House, Office of the Press Secretary, *Defending Against Biological Terrorism,* Fact Sheet, 5 February 2002, http://www.state.gov/t/np/rls/fs/2002/7884.htm (accessed 12 December 2005).

52. See the three examples cited in note 1.

6

Why Do Conclusions from the Experts Vary?

Marie Isabelle Chevrier

At first glance, assessments of bioterrorism, whether they are billed as "risk" assessments, "threat" assessments, or "vulnerability" assessments, appear to vary widely. At one end of the spectrum are statements such as the one made in 1998 by former US secretary of state George P. Shultz. Referring to the possible use of chemical or biological weapons, Shultz claimed, "Realistically we must face up to the likelihood that it is not a question of 'if' but of 'when.'"[1] In contrast, noted terrorism expert Brian M. Jenkins reasons,

> Contrary to what some assert, it is *not* just a matter of time before we witness an attempt at mass murder using chemical or biological weapons. Such an event may occur, but it cannot confidently be predicted on the basis of what we know today about the motives and interests of terrorists.[2] (emphasis added)

Further, George Smith, a senior fellow at GlobalSecurity.org, asserts that "much of the literature on chemical and biological terrorism published in the United States is replete with errors, exaggeration, and scaremongering."[3]

Bioterrorism assessments involve gathering and analyzing relevant information to predict the likelihood that a nonstate actor will deliberately disseminate a disease-causing pathogen or a biologically derived poison to cause illness or death to a target civilian population.[4] Bioterrorism assessments may also attempt to predict the likely agents of choice, the likely actor(s), the method of dissemination, or the consequences of a bioterrorist act in terms of casualties and fatalities.

Bioterrorism assessments are not new, but their number has increased rapidly following a series of shocking events. The first was the release of the chemical agent sarin in the Tokyo subway in 1995. The second was the bombing of the federal building in Oklahoma City the same year. The third was the 11 September 2001 attacks on the World Trade Center and the Pentagon, followed shortly after by the fourth event, the mailing of letters containing anthrax spores to members of the US Congress and others. While the first three of these events were not bioterrorist attacks, apprehension about mass casualty terrorism and the use of a nonconventional weapon in Tokyo led many researchers to reconsider the prospects of bioterrorism.

Prior to the 1995 attack in the Tokyo subway, some assessments had been devoted to the terrorist threat of biological or toxin weapons.[5] Since the 1995 attack and the extensive media coverage that followed, however, the bioterrorism threat has been the subject of numerous scholarly books and articles—not to mention the mind-boggling number of reports, studies, articles, and published testimonies emanating from institutions, governments, and the popular media. The threat of bioterrorism has also captured the imagination of novelists, screenwriters, and film and television producers.

This chapter analyzes the ways in which a number of scholars have attempted to come to terms with bioterrorism and more specifically with the prospect of a deliberate dissemination of a biological agent or toxin with the intention to cause mass casualties. Most of the assessments also discuss potential bioterrorist acts that would result in far fewer casualties, either because the perpetrators do not intend to cause mass casualties or because their intended acts do not produce the desired results. Problems with assessments of bioterrorism are manifold, including difficulties in defining what constitutes terrorism and terrorist groups; the paucity of historical data; the dangers associated with predicting the future based only on historical data; the difficulty of establishing the veracity of information; the problem of establishing the expertise needed to objectively assess bioterrorism; the difficulty of understanding the intentions and motivations of terrorist groups; the problems in identifying the difference between a threat and a risk; and so on. This chapter focuses on the following question: Do respected, credentialed scholars come to different conclusions in their bioterrorism assessments? If they do, why? If not, why do perceptions of the threat differ from experts' judgments?

This chapter examines a number of aspects of the assessments in question. First, how do different researchers frame the question or problem in their assessment? Second, what data do the researchers consider relevant to their analyses? Third, what methods do the researchers use to analyze the data? Fourth, what conclusions do the authors draw from their analyses of the data and their methodologies? Most assessments include policy prescriptions along with their estimates of the future likelihood of bioterrorist attacks. Thus, a final question the chapter seeks to answer is, what do the authors emphasize in their analyses or conclusions? The bulk of the assessments examined in this chapter do not vary greatly in their estimates of the probability of future bioterrorism, rather they place emphasis on different facets of the problem and disagree about what should be done to minimize that probability, and how to deal with it.

This chapter is not a comprehensive catalog of bioterrorism assessments. Instead, I have chosen the assessments according to the following criteria: First, the assessments are limited to those undertaken after Aum Shinrikyo released sarin in the Tokyo subway in 1995. Second, I focus principally on assessments that are relatively long or part of a lengthy process. I have done this in order to concentrate on those assessments that look at the issue in greater depth and on those that are anthologies that cover a number of diverse views. All assessments are from nongovernmental sources, and newspaper articles have been excluded. Finally, I concentrate primarily, but not exclusively, on assessments of bioterrorism threats written by people or organizations that have a record of publishing on biological weapons or biological warfare. The events mentioned above have drawn a large number of people to the "sexy" new topic of biological terrorism, but a familiarity with the field of biological weapons and biological warfare adds to the credibility of the assessments. At the same time, including only established authorities would discount newcomers who can add greater creativity or new ways of thinking about the issue to this discussion. Hence, a number of the anthologies include new thinkers, especially those with expertise in terrorism rather than in biological weapons. A marriage of these two areas of expertise is desirable when tackling this problem.[6]

In the following, I first examine the different ways in which assessments frame the question or questions that they are attempting to answer. Second, I address the data that different assessments examine and consider relevant. Third, I look at assessments undertaken between 1995 and 2001. I next summarize assessments that have been published since 2001. Finally, I offer observations and comments based on a comparison of the assessments. Table 6.1 compares the assessments in an easily accessible and concise format.

Table 6.1 Bioterrorism Assessment

Author	Question	Data and Methodology	Principal Conclusions	Emphasis
Tucker 1996	Is another terrorist attack like that of Aum Shinrikyo using chemical or biological weapons likely?	Major chemical and biological incidents; terrorism trends; technical aspects	Large-scale chemical or biological attacks are unlikely. Terrorists motivated by religious or racist fanaticism are particularly dangerous.	Counterterrorism policies are needed to reduce likelihood and impact. Religious fanaticism is particularly worrisome.
Tucker et al. 2000	What are the motivations of terrorists who have used, acquired, or shown an interest in chemical or biological weapons?	Historical case studies of chemical or biological weapons acquisition or use and allegations without proof	The use of chemical or biological weapons is strikingly infrequent. The process by which terrorists select their weapons is poorly understood. Terrorists who use chemical and biological weapons manifest traits of paranoia and grandiosity; are innovative in their use of violence; and tend to escalate over time. They may use chemical or biological weapons for tactical rather than strategic use.	Governments cannot be complacent, particularly about terrorist groups that receive state sponsorship.
Roberts et al. 1997	Do the Tokyo and Oklahoma City incidents signal a new, more destructive terrorism era and with chemical, biological, or nuclear weapons?	Technical and political barriers; proliferation from state programs; terrorists' motivations and methods; reasons for historical nonuse	Events cannot be taken as a harbinger of a new era of destructive terrorism using unconventional means. The likelihood of bioterrorism is possible but not probable, and mass casualties are unlikely; the problem is growing; the United States is vulnerable; government policies should decrease ease of acquisition and mitigate consequences.	US vulnerabilities must be minimized.

(continues)

Table 6.1 continued

Author	Question	Data and Methodology	Principal Conclusions	Emphasis
Roberts et al. 2000	How do terrorist mindsets interact with circumstances, capabilities, and opportunities that may lead to nuclear, biological, or chemical weapons use?	Motivations of right-wing groups and lone operators; implications of collapsing states, organized crime, and asymmetric conflict; changing technology; and political violence	Whether terrorists will use chemical, biological, or nuclear weapons to carry out catastrophic attacks is unknown. The assumption that catastrophic (>1,000 fatalities) terrorist attacks involving WMD are imminent or inevitable is not supported by research. New terrorism has not supplanted the old. Interest in nuclear, biological, and chemical weapons remains low.	Something new is afoot. Terrorism is changing in many ways. There is plenty of evidence of rising interest in chemical and biological weapons. How best to prepare for contingencies?
Wilkening 1998	Is the proposition valid that chemical and biological weapons threats are growing?	Historical chemical and biological incidents; proliferation; state and terrorist motivations; and US vulnerability	Future biological and chemical weapons episodes will be small, unsophisticated attacks. Expected outcome, (probability times consequences) may be comparable. The logic that the threat is growing appears valid. This does not necessarily imply that threats are likely. Hurdles to chemical and biological weapons acquisition remain. A vast majority of terrorist groups are not interested; religious and nihilist groups are a disturbing trend. Those inclined toward using WMD are likely to have a distinctive signature, increasing detection.	Prudence demands that steps be taken to cope with the potential for biological and chemical weapons threats across the entire spectrum.

Pre-9/11

(continues)

Table 6.1 continued

Author	Question	Data and Methodology	Principal Conclusions	Emphasis
Smithson and Levy 2000	Why would terrorists want to follow Aum Shinrikyo's path? Who would be the most likely copycats, and why hasn't Aum Shinrikyo been copied?	Terrorism history; feasibility debate; analysis of federal programs	Small attacks are likely where a few, not thousands, would be harmed. Using chemical and biological weapons to cause mass casualties is not easy. The weapons of choice for terrorists remain truck bombs and other conventional tools that are less technically demanding, less resource-intensive, and less dangerous to the perpetrators.	Expertise from the former Soviet Union should be hired; greater emphasis should be placed on first responders.
Stern 1999	What if terrorists went nuclear?	Terrorism trends; proliferation of nuclear, biological, and chemical weapons; new terrorists; changing motivations; breakup of the Soviet Union; chemical and biological weapons are proliferating to states; advances in technology	There is an increased risk that terrorists will use nuclear, biological, or chemical weapons against civilian targets. Most terrorists will probably continue to avoid WMD.	The risk is growing. There is devastating potential loss.

Pre-9/11

(continues)

Table 6.1 continued

Author	Question	Data and Methodology	Principal Conclusions	Emphasis
Zilinskas 1999	What are the effects of recent and anticipated advances in biotechnology and the effects of this on perfecting biological weapons?	The effect of biotechnology to enhance biological agent utility and to enhance the ability of agents to withstand stress	It is highly probable that a terrorist or criminal will use food-borne or waterborne biological agents or toxic chemicals in the next five years. The probability that a terrorist or criminal will carry out an airborne attack is low. Emerging infectious diseases are the greatest biological threat to the United States.	A meaningful or adequate risk assessment is not possible. Fundamental information about the intentions and capabilities of terrorists is lacking and unobtainable.
Zanders 1999	What is the potential for terrorists to acquire chemical and biological weapons?	Use of assimilation model to analyze Aum Shinrikyo and Rajneesh cases, applying this to analyze the terrorist threat	The acquisition of chemical and biological weapons by terrorists is feasible. Terrorist organizations face enormous obstacles. If terrorists acquire a chemical or biological weapons capability, it is highly probable that the quality of the agents will be well below that of similar agents in military arsenals.	The norms against acquisition of chemical and biological weapons have been greatly strengthened. Major impediments to widespread use of chemical and biological weapons by terrorists remain.
Tucker 2003	What should be done?	Anthrax letters; Al-Qaida's interest in biological weapons	The threat of bioterrorism is real and growing.	National and international policies are needed to restrict access to pathogens.

Pre-9/11

(continues)

Table 6.1 continued

Author	Question	Data and Methodology	Principal Conclusions	Emphasis
Roberts 2003	Are we facing an imminent major bioterrorism attack?	11 September 2001; Al-Qaida; distinguishes "risk" from "threat"	There is a huge difference between using these weapons and exploiting their full lethal potential. The threat is not easily knowable, and much is a mystery. Al-Qaida, Iraq, home-grown US terrorists, and copycats are risks. Personal risk is very low. Societal risk is higher.	There is disagreement on what to do. The United States remains vulnerable. Breathtaking gambles are being undertaken, but we do not and cannot know that Bush's strategy of preventive war and regime change is wrong.
Zilinskas et al. 2004	What can be done to improve threat assessments and develop risk assessment methods for bioterrorism?	Discussion of applicability of different assessment methodologies, including quantitative risk assessment models	Quantitative risk assessment depends on reliable data. Data regarding targets and agents are available; data on bioterrorist intent and on the frequency of types of attack are nearly nonexistent. Large uncertainties remain. Assumptions and judgments, rather than statistical data, must provide the basis for predictions. Neither the targets nor the person or group responsible for the anthrax letters could have been predetermined.	Prescriptions: threat assessment with information on a specific threat; vulnerability analysis for preparedness and response plans; comparative ranking of plausible and credible attack scenarios
Dando 2005	What is the real bioterrorism threat?	Open scientific literature	There are real threats from terrorists with biological agents, but they do not include WMD attacks on people. Agriculture bioterrorism is worrisome. An aerosolized WMD bioattack is only possible under a state program.	Very little has changed, except the renewed perception of threat. We must prevent the militarization of biology in order to prevent terrorist capabilities.

Pre-9/11

(continues)

Table 6.1 continued

Author	Question	Data and Methodology	Principal Conclusions	Emphasis
Danzig 2003	How best can we counter the threat of biological attacks on our civilian population?	Organize responses around representative, most significant risks; case-capabilities approach	Terrorists may inflict great trauma by using biological agents. Most significant near-term risks are large-scale outdoor aerosol anthrax and smallpox attacks; dissemination of botulinum toxin in cold drinks; and an attack that spreads foot-and-mouth disease to livestock. In the immediate future, most attacks are likely to be versions, often lesser versions, of these cases.	Places emphasis on vulnerability. Bioterrorists could reload and attack again easily; therefore, exceptional preparation is needed.
Salerno et al. 2004	What is the risk of bioterrorism?	Historical cases and technological requirements	Significant financial resources and technical sophistication are required to develop and deploy a biological weapon causing a high-consequence event. Bioterrorists, who generally lack the technical skills and financial resources of states, are currently considered capable of perpetrating low to moderate attacks with biological weapons.	Advances in and increased availability of biotechnology will enhance the capabilities of both states and nonstate actors over time.
Leitenberg 2004	Was the US postal attack an indication of what may be experienced with increasing frequency, or was the attack the latest in a series of essentially anomalous events?	Historical cases	The most serious threat in the long term remains the proliferation of state-sponsored programs.	Public health effects were small and adequately dealt with. Consequences outside public health were enormous. Determining the likelihood of similar attacks depends crucially on the identification of the perpetrator.

Framing the Question

Nearly all of the analysis undertaken prior to 1995, and much of it since, has combined chemical and biological weapons (CBW) threats. A significant portion of the analysis has combined biological threats with nuclear and radiological weapons threats. To further complicate the picture, some assessments examine threats from both states and nonstate actors. Thus, determining how the conclusions drawn from these assessments apply specifically to bioterrorism can be prone to errors of interpretation.

A researcher who poses the question "How likely is it that there will be a terrorist attack using anthrax or smallpox that produces more than a thousand casualties in the next five years?" is necessarily going to predict a much smaller probability than a researcher who asks, "How likely is it that a terrorist group or rogue state will use chemical or biological agents in the future?" The latter way of framing the question will almost certainly lead to a conclusion that such an event is inevitable, that indeed it is a question of when, not if. One group of researchers, for example, has focused on covert attacks by states or nonstate actors using nuclear, chemical, or biological weapons.[7] Thus, readers should carefully take note of the way in which a question is framed when they interpret the conclusions and apply them to other situations.

Data and Methodologies

Researchers typically take into account empirical data on terrorist use of biological agents in their assessments.[8] Others add empirical data on terrorism in general, including data on the propensity of terrorist groups to intentionally cause or accept greater numbers of casualties and fatalities. Most researchers examine the evidence for and implications of the changing motives and aspirations of terrorist groups. Many look at the differences between the "old terrorists"—commonly left-wing, nonreligious groups with exclusively political motives and frequently with aspirations to govern—and "new terrorists"—often right-wing, religiously fervent groups that combine political and religious or apocalyptic motives.[9]

In addition, some researchers examine limited empirical data and theoretical data about the motivations of actors or about decisionmaking processes, or they create hypothetical, what-if scenarios about the future. They might take as a given, for instance, that a nonstate actor wants to cause mass casualties and is attracted to biological agents, and they might ask, "How difficult would it be to acquire, produce, and disseminate biological weapons?" Still others might examine advancements in the science underlying biological weapons and the spread of that scientific knowledge. Indeed, some inferences are drawn by applying existing technical and scientific knowledge to the assessment of hypothetical attack scenarios. Researchers justify the use of theoretical or hypothetical methods by recognizing that the past is not a perfect predictor of the future, particularly when predicting the likelihood of low probability events with few or no precedents.

Many bioterrorism assessments include descriptions of state biological weapons programs, particularly the programs in the former Soviet Union, Iraq, and South Africa. The existence and extent of these programs is used to support different arguments. Some researchers argue that state biological weapons programs are a more serious threat than possible acts by nonstate actors. Others draw attention to the theoretical possibility that nonstate actors could acquire biological weapons from state programs or former state programs and use such weapons, thereby bypassing technical barriers to agent production.

The most germane empirical data for predicting a bioterrorist event with "mass" fatalities would arise from such an event having already happened.[10] However, there are no actual occurrences that fall into this category. There are two known cases of a successful, deliberate dissemination of biological agents by a nonstate actor that produced some casualties, and nearly all researchers acknowledge the influence of these events on their thinking.[11] In 1984, members of the Rajneesh religious sect in Oregon introduced salmonella bacteria in salad bars to cause sickness. There were no deaths and no indication that the group's intention had been to cause death. The group had intended to incapacitate a large part of the local population, preventing it from voting in a local election.

In September and October 2001, five letters containing anthrax spores were sent through the mail in the United States to different recipients. Twenty-two persons contracted the disease, and five died. No person or group has, to date, been convicted, confessed, or claimed responsibility for mailing the letters. Four of the five letters—the fifth was never recovered—warned that the envelopes contained anthrax or that the recipients should take antibiotics. Without such an indication, many more people are likely to have contracted the disease, and it is likely that many more would have died. A reasonable inference is that the sender had not intended to cause widespread disease or death.

In addition to these two cases, on four separate occasions Aum Shinrikyo, the infamous Japanese group, intentionally sprayed a slurry containing a strain of *Bacillus anthracis* that at least some members of the group thought would cause disease. No cases of anthrax were reported. The biological agent that the group obtained was a vaccine strain of the bacterium that could not have caused disease. Moreover, the method of dispersal may not have produced a mist that could have been inhaled deep into the lungs. There were reports that the equipment had not produced the appropriate particle size and that the nozzles had become clogged.[12] The group had intended to cause fatalities but did not succeed in producing a disease-causing biological agent and did not successfully disseminate the relatively innocuous biological agent that it had obtained and produced. This failure is considered reassuring by some researchers; even with significant financial assets and scientific expertise, the group was not successful in carrying out its intentions. Others regard it as a lucky miss and conclude that copycat actors could avoid Aum Shinrikyo's mistakes.

Another incident involved the acquisition of a biological toxin with no attempted use. In 1991, some members of the Minnesota Patriots Council, an antigovernment group, obtained a kit through the mail containing about a dozen castor beans and photocopied pages of instructions on how to extract the deadly toxin ricin from the beans. One member of the group successfully extracted less than a gram of ricin from the beans. Other members transported and stored the powder for a year before the wife of one of the members contacted the police and turned the powder over to them. The powder was stored in a baby food jar within a coffee can. The amount of ricin recovered in the jar could theoretically have poisoned and killed between one hundred and one hundred fifty people if successfully disseminated.[13]

Additional empirical evidence deemed relevant by some researchers is the increase in terrorist acts employing explosives that have caused hundreds or more fatalities and casualties. In the 1980s, the conventional wisdom on terrorism was that terrorist groups were not interested in causing many deaths. That perception of terrorist groups has changed because of a series of acts that were intended to, and did, cause hundreds of deaths and injuries. Recent terrorist events are well known and include (but are not limited to) the shooting down of a Pan Am airliner over Lockerbie, Scotland, in 1988, which killed 270 people; the bombing of the Murrah Federal Building in Oklahoma City in 1995, which caused 163 deaths and more than 750 injuries; the 2004 Madrid subway bombings, which killed 190 and wounded over 600; the 2004 bombings in Bali, Indonesia, which killed 186 people and wounded 300; and the attacks of 11 September 2001 in New York and Washington, DC, which killed just under 3,000 people and injured over 6,000.

Analyzing the Assessments from 1996 to 2001

In a seminal article a year after the Aum Shinrikyo sarin attacks, Jonathan Tucker posed the question "How likely is another incident similar to that in the Tokyo subway?"[14] Tucker concluded that "another large-scale chemical/biological terrorist attack remains unlikely."[15] He argued that political restraints operated on politically motivated terrorists but not necessarily on those with other motives. According to Tucker,

> terrorists motivated by religious or racist fanaticism are particularly dangerous because unlike politically motivated groups, they are not subject to rational constraints on the scope of their violent acts, nor are they easily deterrable by credible threats.

While Tucker enumerates disadvantages of chemical and biological weapons, he maintains that

> terrorist groups motivated by religious fanaticism or supremacist ideology might be drawn to C/B weapons if they
> 1. possess the necessary technical know-how;
> 2. are intent on inflicting mass casualties rather than attracting attention to a political cause;
> 3. have no clearly defined base of popular support; and
> 4. are willing to accept substantial physical risks.[16]

Numerous commentaries followed the article, praising, criticizing, or pointing out gaps in the logic or conclusions of the author.

In 2000, Tucker followed up the article with an edited book, an in-depth study of all of the historical cases described above (with the obvious exception of the 2001 anthrax letter attacks).[17] The anthology also includes cases of agent acquisition but not use and cases that turned out to be hoaxes or false allegations. The case studies are carefully constructed using primary source material. The specific questions that the study attempted to answer were these: "What types of terrorist groups or individuals are most likely to acquire and use such weapons, and for what purpose? Further, what types of CBW agents are most likely to be produced, and how would they be delivered?"[18] Tucker sums up the analysis saying that "only a tiny minority of terrorists will seek to inflict indiscriminate fatalities, and few if any of them will succeed."[19] Terrorist organizations that might be attracted to chemical and biological weapons are "individuals or groups motivated by religious fanaticism, supremacist ideology, or apocalyptic prophecy."[20] Tucker recognizes the limitations of the case study approach. He addresses the criticism of "some analysts [who] contend that historical case studies are of limited value for predicting the future threat of CBW terrorism because the nature of terrorism is changing, making it more difficult to extrapolate from past events" by arguing that the supposedly "new terrorism" is "well represented in the historical record." He also acknowledges the small number of cases, and he cautions that any conclusions are "preliminary."[21]

Taking the Tokyo subway attack and the Oklahoma City bombing as a starting point, Brad Roberts led another extensive study published in 1997.[22] Roberts's study attempted to understand the disparity—already existing in 1997—between "dire predictions about the imminence of massively destructive terrorist attacks [that are] at stunning odds with the historical record." The process the study participants used was "to probe beyond conventional wisdoms and to lead a process of inquiry and debate among interested scholars and policymakers."[23] They were asked to evaluate the validity of the proposition that "the attacks in Tokyo and Oklahoma City signal a new era in terrorism, one marked by more massively destructive and indiscriminate attacks with heretofore taboo weaponry." Various researchers examined the technical and political barriers to nuclear, biological, and chemical terrorism;[24] the prospect of the proliferation of weapons from state biological weapons programs;[25] the connection between the motives of terrorist groups and their choice of methods;[26] the technical constraints on bioterrorism;[27] the past relative nonuse of chemical and biological weapons;[28] and policy prescriptions.[29]

Each author who contributed to the anthology examines the question from a different perspective and emphasizes different factors. Nevertheless, nearly all of them reach the same general conclusions. First, the likelihood of biological terrorism is possible but not probable. Second, "there is a wide gap between the possible and the probable."[30] Third, it is unlikely that any biological terrorism that might occur will produce massive casualties. Fourth, over time the probability is growing. Fifth, the United States is vulnerable to bioterrorism. And sixth, government policies can and should be put in place to decrease the ease with which terrorists might produce or acquire biological agents for weapons use and to mitigate the consequences should a bioterrorist attack occur. It is unclear whether James Adams, who looked at proliferation concerns, agrees with the above conclusions. He emphasizes in his conclusion that "the further spread of CBW is inevitable. It is inevitable, too, that CBW will reach the hands of a terrorist or a rogue nation that will consider the use of CBW to be a legitimate act of war." Adams bases this assessment on the view that there is no real price to pay "for acquiring CBW and for passing them along."[31] In the concluding chapter of the anthology, Roberts cautions that

> we should be reticent about embracing unquestioningly the notion that 1995 was a watershed year and that the noted terrorist events are the harbinger of a new wave of terrorism employing weapons of mass destruction . . . The events do reveal American vulnerabilities that must be minimized.[32]

In 2000, Roberts edited a second anthology that assesses terrorist use of nuclear, chemical, and biological weapons.[33] The essays therein consider the goals and motivations of terrorists, their "perspective on the utility of violence," and their sources of support. The authors' task was to struggle with the "circumstances, capabilities and opportunities to take a potential terrorist" down the path leading to the use of nuclear, biological, and chemical weapons.[34] The book's scope is very broad, including the evaluation of right-wing terrorists and lone operators as well as the effects of collapsing states, organized crime, and asymmetrical conflict. The book projects technological change and trends in political violence in the future.

In the opening essay, Ehud Sprinzak describes why "terrorism specialists and top U.S. government officials [have] become so obsessed with the prospect that terrorists, foreign or home-grown, will soon attempt to bring about an unprecedented disaster in the United States."[35] Sprinzak argues that sloppy thinking, vested interests, and morbid fascination have led to what he describes as the "Great Superterrorism Scare."[36] Sloppy thinking occurs when people do not distinguish between mass casualty terrorism, in general, state-sponsored chemical or biological terrorism, small-scale chemical or biological terrorism, and superterrorism. Some people have vested interests in hyping the threat: "The threat of superterrorism is likely to make a few defense contractors very rich, and a larger number of specialists famous and moderately rich." Further, "people love to be horrified."[37] Sprinzak concludes that "there is neither empirical evidence nor logical support to the growing belief that a new 'postmodern' age of terrorism is about to dawn, an era afflicted by a large number of anonymous chemical and biological mass murderers."[38] However, terrorists have a growing interest, Sprinzak says, in small-scale, tactical chemical or biological attacks.

James K. Campbell is specifically concerned about Osama bin Laden's Al-Qaida attempting to use weapons of mass destruction. In a prescient statement, he warns that "low-tech should not be taken as synonymous with amateurism: if the attack results in tens or hundreds of casualties and a tremendous amount of collateral disruption, does it really matter how 'technically' competent the terrorist was?"[39] Campbell observes that

> the motivations, intentions, and capabilities of terrorists are difficult to investigate and analyze . . . [because] they are strategic criminals who operate outside the rule of law . . . [and] conduct their activities in a highly covert fashion in order to evade the authorities.[40]

The uncertainty surrounding any estimate of the likelihood of future terrorist use of nuclear, biological, and chemical weapons is echoed by other authors in Roberts's *Hype or Reality?* and emerges as a theme in other assessments as well. According to Joseph F. Pilat, "The prospects for widespread NBC [nuclear, biological, and chemical] terrorism are then uncertain, in large part because there remain political, technical, and operational obstacles to emerging terrorist threats."[41]

In 2000, Brian Michael Jenkins described points of consensus among experts at a conference on mass casualty terrorism, publishing his findings in Roberts's *Hype or Reality?* First, Jenkins says, there is no support for the "assumption that catastrophic terrorist attacks involving weapons of mass destruction are imminent or inevitable. Historical analysis provides no basis for forecasting catastrophic terrorism involving chemical, biological or nuclear weapons."[42] Terrorism attacks, in general, appear to be increasing, both in absolute numbers and in terms of greater numbers of casualties, but Jenkins attaches caveats to the observation of that trend. He notes that there have been no imitations of the Tokyo chemical attack, in spite of the propensity of terrorist groups to copycat other methods, such as hijackings. He warned at the time that Osama bin Laden was a serious threat. Yet the conference participants agreed that there was ample cause for concern. Jenkins recommended policies of "continued scrutiny, a refocusing of intelligence, and some preparations."[43]

In 2000, a report by the Chemical and Biological Arms Control Institute criticized vulnerability assessments and focused instead on reducing the uncertainty surrounding the threat of terrorist use of biological agents.[44] The report constructed a matrix involving the motivation and capabilities of potential bioterrorists, as well as possible agents, methods of dissemination, and targets. The authors of the report then used this matrix to think through the most likely pathways for bioterrorist attacks ranging from the catastrophic—fifty thousand casualties—to the less worrisome—fifty casualties. In applying the pathways matrix to historical as well as theoretical cases, they found that

> the degree of risk declines as the level of desired casualties increases, *insofar as it becomes less likely . . . As a terrorist seeks higher casualties, fewer pathways are available to achieve that objective, and those that remain are more difficult.*[45] (emphasis in original)

The authors emphasize, however, that "despite the low probability of catastrophic bioterrorism, there is still ample cause for concern."[46] They also stress that the "environment of uncertainty surrounding bioterrorism will remain." Interestingly, the authors point out that change, especially as it relates to technology and potential actors, may not necessarily "make the threat more severe."[47]

In 1998, the respected conservative Hoover Institution at Stanford University inaugurated its national security forum with a two-day conference on the biological and chemical weapons threat. In the proceedings of the conference, published in an anthology, Dean A. Wilkening posits that

> the argument that BCW [biological and chemical weapons] threats are growing rests on three propositions: (1) the capability to make BCW is increasingly available to states, if not terrorist groups; (2) the intention to use these weapons is growing; and (3) civilian populations, and to a lesser extent military forces, are quite vulnerable to BCW attacks.[48]

Wilkening examines each of these propositions and concludes that they are valid, yet the evidence that the threat of chemical and biological weapons attacks is growing "is less compelling than is commonly believed,"[49] and "considerable uncertainty surrounds the degree to which the incentives to threaten or to use BCW are increasing."[50] He argues that "the supply of BCW material, technology, and expertise probably has already spread beyond any state's ability to control it,"[51] but the technological conservatism of most terrorist groups "implies that BCW may not be favored methods of attack."[52] US urban populations, Wilkening notes, are particularly vulnerable. Yet in the book's preface, former secretary of state George P. Shultz ignores these reasoned and nuanced conclusions and asserts that "realistically we must face up to the likelihood that it is not a question of 'if' but of 'when.'"[53] The conference dealt with all chemical and biological weapons threats from states and nonstate actors alike. Thus the "it" that Shultz refers to means any use of chemical or biological weapons, yet the proverbial "it's not a question of 'if' but 'when'" phrase is repeated frequently and applied only to a bioterrorist event.

Writing in 2000, Amy E. Smithson and Leslie-Anne Levy sought to answer "*why* terrorists would want to follow Aum Shinrikyo's path . . . *who* along the spectrum of terrorists groups would be the most likely copycats . . . [and] *why* Aum Shinrikyo's attack has not been duplicated."[54] Their purpose was to "inject an appreciable dose of pragmatism into the what-if frenzy over the chemical and biological terrorism threat and the attendant federal programs."[55] After articulating technical requirements for chemical and biological weapons and an analysis of the Aum Shinrikyo subway attack and the lessons being drawn from it, the authors describe how the common reasoning—that "a rise in terrorist incidents causing mass casualties plus a claimed increase in the availability of unconventional weapons ingredients equals a greater likelihood that terrorists would use mass destruction weapons to kill large numbers of people"—is an amplification of the threat that "can be deflated." As Smithson emphasizes,

> Scientific techniques have indeed advanced, but . . . the obstacles to the successful dissemination of biological agents are such that governments have found it necessary to employ hundreds, even thousands of top-flight scientists, to obtain a mass casualty biological weapons capability . . . All of the publicity about unconventional terrorism fueled the impression that terrorist capabilities and plots involving chemical and biological agents somehow became more substantive and plausible in the late 1990's . . . Unconventional terrorism was tailor made for hyperbole . . . Using chemical and biological weapons in a manner that causes mass casualties is not shake-n-bake easy. The weapons of choice for terrorists remain truck bombs and other conventional tools that are less technically demanding, resource-intensive and dangerous for the perpetrators.[56]

In 1999, Jessica Stern articulated an increasing risk of terrorist use of nuclear, biological, and chemical weapons.[57] She joined other experts concerned about the increasing numbers of "terrorists seeking to conjure a sense of divine retribution, to display scientific prowess, to kill large numbers of people, to invoke dread or to retaliate against states that have used these weapons in the past."[58] Despite her conclusion that "most terrorists will probably continue to avoid WMD [weapons of mass destruction],"[59] her book has a more alarmist tone than others written in this period. The jacket blurb, for example, reads, "As bad as they are, why aren't terrorists worse? With biological, chemical, and nuclear weapons at hand, they easily could be. And, as this chilling book suggests, they soon may well be." Stern understands and describes the disproportionate dread associated with poisons and disease and emphasizes throughout the possibility that such attacks could be successful, seemingly in order to sound a wake-up call and garner support for her policy prescriptions.

In 1999, Jean Pascal Zanders applied the assimilation model to analyze the acquisition of chemical or biological weapons by terrorists. Assimilation is a complex dynamic whereby the weapons acquisition process is examined through both military and political lenses. The model, Zanders argues, is useful "for studying CB weapon armament programs in countries for which limited information is available on decisionmaking processes and the structure of armament programs."[60] Zanders applies the model to the Aum Shinrikyo and Rajneesh cases. He concludes that there "are and will remain major impediments to the widespread use of CB weapons for terrorist purposes." Those impediments include "the norms against . . . acquisition and use of CB weapons [that] have been greatly strengthened" and "the greater awareness of the security risks involved in proliferation," leading to fewer willing partners in the acquisition process.[61] Zanders uses stronger language as well, saying that terrorist organizations "face enormous obstacles on the path to a CB weapon capability."[62]

Looking at chemical or biological attacks only, and at a simple food-borne or waterborne delivery system, Raymond Zilinskas made in 1999 what he described as a "near certain prediction" that such attacks would occur in the next five years and would be "likely to cause casualties ranging in number from a few to hundreds." He based this prediction on the prevalence of "unprotected, unmonitored salad bars and food displays" and the increasing number of "persons with at least a modicum of training in microbiology."[63] Zilinskas came to a different conclusion for airborne attacks, saying that the probability of terrorists or criminals carrying out such attacks is low. The difference, according to Zilinskas, "is that it is technically difficult to formulate pathogens and toxins for airborne dispersal and to operate dispersal mechanisms successfully." Yet Zilinskas is critical of the reliability of risk assessment. He states that

> it is not possible to perform a meaningful or adequate risk assessment
> . . . because the information to do so is not available. If solid infor-
> mation is lacking, the tendency might be to substitute assumptions for
> information. The more assumptions that are made while performing a
> risk assessment, the less rigorous will be the analysis.[64]

He further declares that

> fundamental information about capabilities and intent of domestic ter-
> rorist groups is lacking and probably cannot be obtained . . . The ana-
> lyst would have to make a series of assumptions if he or she wished to
> perform a threat or risk assessment of any one group. The product of
> such a threat or risk assessment would, to my mind, be worthless.[65]

What do these assessments, taken as a whole, tell us? First, there is insufficient historical data to predict future bioterrorist events. A precise quantitative assessment is out of the question. Second, in framing the question, most of the researchers felt that terrorist incidents involving chemical agents were appropriate cases from which to draw inferences about biological terrorism, while acknowledging that the technology for the production and dissemination of a biological agent was usually quite different. Such analysis would overstate the estimated probability of a bioterrorism attack, but few acknowledge or adjust for that. Third, the vast majority of the researchers describe the future likelihood of mass casualty bioterrorism as "low," "unlikely," "possible, but not probable," or some variation thereof, yet none of them ventures a more precise estimation. Does "unlikely" mean one in a hundred, one in a thousand, one in a million, or one in a billion? Especially with regard to small probabilities, the order of magnitude is important. As I remind my children, if someone describes you as one in a million, it means there are a thousand just like you in India. It may well be worth asking researchers to infer ranges, if not point estimates, of probability, even if the results are speculative. If we had several instances of researchers' estimating probabilities as between one in a hundred to one in a thousand over a five-year future period, or one in a million to one in two million over the same period, we could get a better estimation of the acknowledged uncertainty surrounding the predictions. Several researchers distinguish between bioterrorist incidents with few casualties and mass casualty events, describing the former as more likely, but neither the low base probability nor the increase in magnitude is discussed with any precision. Moreover, most of the researchers do not attempt to associate a precise time period with their qualitative predictions.

Researchers agree that the likelihood of mass casualty bioterrorism is low, but they may disagree on how low. They agree that any estimate is surrounded by a great deal of uncertainty but disagree about the magnitude of the uncertainty surrounding their estimates. They generally agree that terrorism trends, especially the trend toward a greater number of events with fatalities in the hundreds, are relevant, but they disagree about what this trend means. Does it mean that terrorists will continue to use explosives to generate large numbers of casualties? Or that they do not need to innovate to other means, like biological agents, to produce desired effects? Or does it mean that terrorists will innovate to biological agents because the public and the media will begin to see explosions as commonplace?

Striking disagreements in these assessments come, however, not in the conclusions about the likelihood of bioterrorism or society's vulnerability, but in the authors' emphasis following their probability estimates. Authors typically discuss their estimates and then add "but . . ." Their emphasis could be described as what the authors say after that "but." Tucker and Wilkening emphasize religious, particularly fanatical, isolated, or millenarian groups. Smithson and Tucker highlight the danger of leaks from state biological weapons programs. Roberts emphasizes the changing nature of terrorism, and Stern focuses on the devastating potential of bioterrorism. Zanders's emphasis is on the many policies that have already been put into place to strengthen the norm against the use of biological weapons. Zilinskas stresses what is unknown and unknowable about terrorists' intentions and capabilities (see Table 6.1).

Analyzing the Assessments from 2001 to 2005

While the United States and the world were still reeling from the effects of 9/11—the most destructive terrorist operation in history—a death from anthrax in Florida and the arrival of letters in US Senate offices and at news organizations containing powdered anthrax spores and warnings to take antibiotics sent analysts back to the drawing board to reconsider assessments of bioterrorism.[66] How did analysts revise their thinking following Amerithrax, and what new risk or threat analysis emerged?

Despite his stated misgivings regarding risk assessment quoted above (or perhaps because of it), Zilinskas convened a workshop with risk assessment professionals and "security and intelligence threat analysts" to improve bioterrorism risk assessment.[67] Publishing their conclusions in 2004, the authors agreed that

> a quantitative bioterrorism risk assessment would need data or *well-informed judgments* on the intent of terrorist groups or individuals, their technical capabilities, the attributes of pathogens or toxins that might be used in a biological attack, target characteristics, and the occurrence (frequency) of various attack scenarios.[68] (emphasis added)

They recognized that "information on intent and capabilities of terrorist groups or individuals who aim to mount biological attacks is extremely difficult to obtain." Further, they found that

> there does not appear to be a consistent pattern that could be used to predict the frequency of other bioterrorist or biocriminal events . . . Large uncertainties will remain. *Assumptions and judgments, rather than statistical data, must provide the basis for predictions.*[69] (emphasis added)

Regarding the potential of quantitative risk assessment, Zilinskas et al. remain skeptical. They write:

> In the future more bioterrorist attacks are likely to occur. If so, each would generate information that is applicable to the performing of subsequent, ever improving, risk assessments. If, however, bioterrorist attacks remain very rare occurrences, and their characteristics differ significantly, then our ability to perform quantitative risk assessments will continue to be hampered by a lack of empirical data.[70]

In 2003, Tucker declared that bioterrorism had changed from "a hypothetical threat . . . [to] a harsh reality" and that the threat was "real and growing." He published a lengthy report that focused overwhelmingly on prescriptions of what should be done nationally and internationally to control access to deadly pathogens, rather than on a reassessment of the risk or threat.[71] In February 2003, Brad Roberts, in a series of lectures, argued that Al-Qaida, Saddam Hussein, home-grown militias, or lone operators and copycats constituted the greatest risks but were not specific threats. He stressed how much is unknown and distinguished between very low personal risk and a higher but not explicit societal risk. There is, he states, a "huge difference between using these weapons and exploiting their full lethal potential."[72]

Prior to 2001, Milton Leitenberg had written about exaggeration, misinformation, and repeated errors in information regarding the possibility of bioterrorism.[73] In 2004, Leitenberg addressed the very specific question of whether the 2001 anthrax letters should alter the widespread, though not universal, agreement that it was theoretically possible but very unlikely, given historical and technical evidence, that a nonstate actor would deliberately and successfully cause mass casualties using biological agents. Leitenberg's answer hinges on who was responsible for the letters: "Should it be the work of a state, or of one or more highly skilled US professionals using professional government facilities, the expectation of a repetition drops drastically."[74]

Richard Danzig introduced a new concept into the discourse in 2003. Historical evidence, he said, supports the fact that attackers who use biological weapons can avoid prompt detection.[75] Moreover, biological terrorists could launch a series of attacks—in Danzig's terminology, they could easily "reload." As a consequence of these two phenomena, the potential outcome of bioterrorist attacks might be catastrophic. Thus, the potential scenarios demand extraordinary preparation.[76]

Malcolm Dando wrote in 2005 that

> a terrorist group . . . could carry out some small to medium scale biological weapons attacks [but] all the technical literature and opinion maintain the view that . . . it is presently still unlikely that a substate group would have the necessary capabilities and resources.

He concludes that "very little has changed except the renewed perception of threat."[77]

Reynolds M. Salerno et al. in 2004 asserted that "the risk of BW use or bioterrorism is not well understood, and the rapid advances of and accessibility to biotechnology have only served to increase confusion." They apply a familiar methodology by combining a historical examination of bioweapons activities with an analysis of the technology needed to acquire and deploy them. They conclude that

> significant financial resources and technical sophistication are required to develop and deploy a biological weapon that could cause a high-consequence event . . . Bioterrorists, who generally lack the technical skills and financial resources of states, are currently considered capable of perpetrating low to moderate consequences with biological weapons.[78]

Nonetheless, the authors agree with Dando that "advances in and increased availability of biotechnology will enhance the capabilities of both states and nonstate actors over time." Unfortunately, but in keeping with such statements found in other threat assessments, their analysis of this critical question is thin. The risk of a nonstate actor's use of a biological weapon is currently considered to be low to moderate (low-to-moderate consequences and low-to-moderate probability). However, "the recent trend in terrorism—highly organized, well financed, and intent on mass casualties—as well as projected rapid advances in biotechnology suggest that the risk of nonstate use of biological weapons is increasing."[79]

In a new twist, the US government has recently turned to so-called science-based threat assessment. Tucker raised a warning in a 2004 article in *Arms Control Today* that assessments that involve "the laboratory development and study of offensive biological weapons agents in order to guide the development of countermeasures" are likely to create more problems than they might solve. The Bush administration is wrong in pursuing such an approach, Tucker argues, for several reasons:

> First, the administration's biodefense research agenda credits terrorists with having cutting-edge technological capabilities that they do not currently possess nor are likely to acquire anytime soon . . . Second, prospective threat-assessment studies involving the creation of hypothetical pathogens are of limited value because of the difficulty of correctly predicting technological innovations by states or terrorist organizations. Distortions such as mirror-imaging—the belief that an adversary would approach a technical problem in the same way as the person doing the analysis—make such efforts a deeply flawed basis for the development of effective countermeasures. Third, by blurring the already hazy line between offensive and defensive biological R&D, science-based threat assessment raises suspicions about U.S. compliance with the Biological and Toxin Weapons Convention (BWC) and fosters a "biological security dilemma" that could lead to a new biological arms race. At the same time, the novel pathogens and related know-how generated by threat-assessment work could be stolen or diverted for malicious purposes, exacerbating the threat of bioterrorism.[80]

In summary, the anthrax letters of 2001 changed assessments of bioterrorism from the 1996–2001 period somewhat, but not substantially. In part, those who assessed bioterrorism were not sure what to make of the letters. The responsible person or group remains unknown. The attacks caused disease in twenty-two people, five of whom died—not hundreds or thousands. The economic consequences and the disruption to the US federal government, including to the postal service and all its employees, were significant and out of proportion to the numbers of casualties, however. The event has been accurately described as "mass disruption" rather than as destruction. The written information in the letters contradicts an assumption that the perpetrator(s) intended any casualties. The attacker demonstrated the capacity to reload, but nearly five years later there have been no repeated instances following the five letters, nor any copycat incidents. The quality of the agent could support a number of different hypotheses about its origin. Researchers seem to recognize that what is known about these attacks and what remains unknown do not substantially alter previous assessments or the uncertainty of their predictions.

The authors surveyed who wrote following the 2001 attacks introduced a number of new concepts into the bioterrorism assessment debate, but most assessments were unconvinced that the risk of bioterrorism had undergone a sea change. Roberts distinguished personal from societal risk, Danzig introduced the concept of reload, and Zilinskas recommended the ranking of plausible and credible attack scenarios. In terms of focus, Tucker's policy recommendations concentrated squarely on the need to restrict access to pathogens. Dando and Leitenberg warned of the dangers of state and state-sponsored activities. Danzig and Roberts emphasized US vulnerability. Salerno et al. worried about the increasing threat over time from the spread of technology. (See Table 6.1 for more details.)

Observations and Comments

Terminology matters, and researchers have done a poor job of being precise about what they mean by the terms that they use. To make cross-comparisons of assessments valid, we need to know that two authors mean the same thing when they use the same words. "Probability" and "likelihood" are estimates of whether a future event will happen in a specific time period.[81] Most authors of bioterrorist assessments mean the same thing when they use these terms. "Risk" is sometimes used as a synonym for "probability." But some use the term "risk" to describe the product of the probability of an event and its likely consequences in terms of the number of casualties. "Threat" is sometimes used interchangeably with "risk," while at other times it is used to describe identified plots or groups for which enough information is available to lead researchers to suspect that future events might be caused by such groups. Several researchers have concluded that the bioterrorism threat is "real" or "real and growing." Another has asked, "What is the real threat?" With the exception of Dando, however, it is unclear whether the authors use the term "real" to mean "nonimaginary," "nonzero," "no longer hypothetical," "not only nonzero but big enough to worry about," "major," or "substantial."[82]

Above I asked: What do qualitative measurements of probability mean? How should we interpret conclusions that contain language such as "not likely," "very unlikely," "extremely unlikely," "possible but not probable," "a small but growing probability," and "virtual certainty"? Moreover, it is important to consider the form of a prediction. Any probability estimates that link parameters with "or" are by definition larger than those linking parameters with "and." If questions are phrased thus: "How likely are terrorist groups *or* lone actors to use *or* threaten to use biological *or* chemical *or* nuclear weapons against the United States *or* its allies?" the probabilities, because they are additive, grow and grow. If, on the other hand, the predictions are more precise, as in the question "How likely is it that a terrorist group will be able to acquire *and* produce *and* successfully disseminate a biological agent to cause mass casualties?" the estimated probability, because it is the product of the separate probabilities, diminishes.

The time frame associated with an assessment is also relevant to the estimated probability. Predictions over longer periods of time, because they are cumulative probabilities, are again by definition larger probabilities than those made over a shorter period of time. Assessments have ranged from "in the next five years" to "in the next century." Short time frames, such as "the next five years" or "the next ten years," also narrow the uncertainty of the prediction. So from a policy and planning perspective, what is the most appropriate time frame to consider? Some threat assessments have begun to tackle the problem by ranking possible events using relative probabilities.

The authors surveyed in this chapter and others conducting bioterrorism assessments typically follow their statements of findings or conclusions with a qualifying "but" or "nevertheless" or a similar phrase, limiting, interpreting, or expanding their stated conclusions. What the author says following the "but" or the "nevertheless" is what I refer to as the "emphasis" and is frequently what distinguishes the assessments from one another. Wilkening, for example, states that future chemical and biological weapons attacks would likely be small and unsophisticated attacks, yet he follows that finding by saying that "prudence demands that steps be taken to cope with the potential for BCW threats across the entire spectrum."[83] Wilkening's emphasis is echoed by other authors who agree that, however small the probability, it is not zero, bioterrorism is possible, and they devote significant work to developing policy prescriptions. Table 6.1 includes a summary of the questions, data and methodology, conclusions, and emphases of works discussed in this chapter.

Conclusion

Assessments of the threat of nonstate actors' using biological agents against the United States or its allies are abundant. An examination of the literature reveals similar arguments, based on similar data, using similar reasoning to reach similar conclusions. Nevertheless, new threat assessments should primarily and explicitly take into account new information or events that would change earlier assessments. If new events using biological weapons occur, researchers should be able to improve the accuracy of their threat assessments. Bayesian analysis would include a reevaluation of earlier probabilities as events unfold. New scientific and technical advances would affect prior probabilities, as would the occurrence or indeed absence of events. If no new successful bioterrorist events occur as time goes on, the probabilities deduced in earlier assessments should logically be revised downward. For example, several assessments prior to 2000 were concerned about millenarian sects' possibly using biological weapons. Now that we are well into the twenty-first century without millenarian bioterrorism, how does that change the previous assessments? Were the assessments wrong? Were we just lucky? Did our preparations prevent such attacks? Designers of threat assessments should ask what would have to occur to change their minds about their conclusions.

Nevertheless, assessments are likely to continue to be hampered by uncertainties. Researchers tackling these questions should make their assumptions explicit and, where appropriate, conduct sensitivity analyses in order for policymakers to draw reasonable conclusions from assessments. Estimates of the likelihood of future bioterrorist events may still be overwhelmed by uncertainty, but proper, multidisciplinary, objective assessments would tend to mitigate any particular agenda of individual authors or groups. Policymakers who must make decisions about how to allocate resources in the presence of such uncertainties would do well to consider the full spectrum of biological risks, from naturally occurring disease outbreaks to deliberate misuse of biology. Doing so would likely increase the efficient allocation of increasingly scarce funds.

Given the glut of commentary about the likelihood of bioterrorism, evaluations of threat assessments should be undertaken with a critical eye. Anyone who says there is a consensus on anything but the simplest truisms is exaggerating or dismissing those who disagree as somehow irrelevant. Commentators should be aware of the credentials of people making the threat assessments. Who is in the best position to make the most unbiased assessments? What expertise ought to be included in a team making an assessment? How do the professional biases and organizational cultures of such teams affect their analysis? How are the assessments funded, and how does the funding source affect the analysis?

Finally, following the attacks of 11 September 2001, much was made of the heuristic "connecting the dots." The information warning of such an attack was available, so the claim went, but nobody "connected the dots." Connecting the dots is not nearly as simple as the analogy of the child's puzzle would suggest. Any five-year-old knows that the dots must be connected in the right order for the intended picture to emerge. Without a preconceived design, linking data points is unlikely to yield a coherent image. A preconceived mental picture, on the other hand, can lead investigators to take any data and fit it to conform to their predetermined figure.

Writing in 2000, Hoffman recognized

> how wide the intellectual chasm separating the academic and policy-making communities over this issue has grown. The position of most academic terrorism analysts has been far more restrained and skeptical than many of their counterparts in government, the military, and law enforcement. Yet, their cautionary appraisals are either dismissed or have long ago been superseded by a policy process that is already plowing full steam ahead.[84]

That gap has continued to grow. The gap has been driven, at least in part, by highly publicized exercises such as Dark Winter and Atlantic Storm, which are not assessments as much as demonstrations of the theoretical power of biological agents through simulations of catastrophic scenarios, regardless of the likelihood of their occurrence or of the decisions made by the participants. Although varying widely in their ultimate policy prescriptions, nearly all of the actual assessments conclude that a successful bioterrorism event causing mass casualties is not likely to be a common, much less an inevitable, event. A critical question for future research, then, is why different policy prescriptions have been based on similar assessments.

In 2000, Jenkins emphasized that the intolerance of policymakers to those who believed there was no cause for panic suggested "that something more fervent than strong convictions is at work here—it is symptomatic of official dogma."[85] Those he described as the "apocalypticians" believed, according to Jenkins, that the notion that "if something bad can happen, someone bad inevitably will do it . . . had become the new orthodoxy." Jenkins continues,

> And as with any orthodoxy it is unforgiving of doubt: Whether terror-ist employment of weapons of mass destruction can be shown to be a clear and present danger is beside the point; the time for discussion is over, the skeptics are told, they can sign on or stand aside.[86]

Jenkins's reflections appear increasingly apt today.

An important theme that emanates from a number of the authors is that the threat of bioterrorism is a component of a larger threat of the use of biological weapons that could come from states or individuals as well as terrorist groups. Labeling the biological weapons threat as ter-rorism attracts attention and resources. Similarly, the bioterrorism threat is a component of the larger terrorism threat. Recognizing the nexus of these two threats—terrorism and biological weapons—is critical as the international community goes beyond assessment to preventive action. Developing policies to minimize the likelihood of deliberate disease, however, requires seeing the bioterrorism threat in this larger context.

Notes

1. George P. Shultz, "Preface," in *The New Terror: Facing the Threat of Biological and Chemical Weapons,* ed. Sidney D. Drell, Abraham D. Sofaer, and George D. Wilson (Stanford, CA: Hoover Institution, 1999), p. xiv.

2. Brian M. Jenkins, "Understanding the Link Between Motives and Meth-ods," in *Terrorism with Chemical and Biological Weapons: Calibrating Risks and Responses,* ed. Brad Roberts (Alexandria, VA: Chemical and Biological Arms Control Institute, 1997), pp. 43–51, 49.

3. George Smith, "Comments on the CRS Report 'Small-Scale Terrorist Attacks Using Chemical and Biological Agents,'" GlobalSecurity.org, http://www.fas.org/irp/crs/RL32391-smith.html (accessed 27 August 2005).

4. Biologically derived poisons are typically referred to as toxins. Ricin is an example. Although toxins are chemical substances that do not reproduce and do not cause contagious disease, they are included in most discussions of bioterrorism because of their biological origins. This is true even if they are chemically synthesized.

5. See, for example, Robert S. Root-Bernstein, "Infectious Terrorism," *Atlantic* 267, no. 44 (May 1991): 48–50; Jeffrey D. Simon, *Terrorists and the Potential Use of Biological Weapons: A Discussion of Possibilities,* Rand Paper R-3771-AFMIC, prepared for the US Armed Forces Medical Intelligence Center (Santa Monica, CA: Rand Corporation, 1989); Joseph D. Douglass Jr. and Neil C. Livingstone, *America the Vulnerable: The Threat of Chemical/Biological*

Warfare (Lanham, MD: Lexington Books, 1987). My doctoral dissertation devotes part of a chapter the terrorist threat; see Marie Isabelle Chevrier, "The International Regime to Control Biological and Toxin Weapons: Is It the Best Way to Minimize the Threat?" (Ph.D. diss., Harvard University, 1991), pp. 45–52.

6. This chapter quotes extensively from the conclusions of the assessments. I have presumed that the authors chose their wording with great care, and I did not wish to distort their conclusions by paraphrasing. In the interest of brevity and the attempt to distill the most important conclusions from the studies, I have summarized and omitted a large amount of information. If I have distorted conclusions by omission, I apologize to the authors and welcome their clarification.

7. See, for example, Richard A. Falkenrath, Robert D. Newman, and Bradley A. Thayer, *America's Achilles' Heel: Nuclear, Biological, and Chemical Terrorism and Covert Attack,* BCSIA Studies in International Security (Cambridge, MA: MIT Press, 1998).

8. While a number of important databases focus on chemical and biological terrorism, only Seth Carus limits the data to biological agents, which he defines as including toxins. See W. Seth Carus, "Bioterrorism and Biocrimes: The Illicit Use of Biological Agents Since 1900" (working paper, Center for Counterproliferation Research, National Defense University, Washington, DC, 1998, rev. February 2001).

9. The dividing line between the two is, of course, not so simple or neat. There is an array of characteristics that distinguish terrorist groups from one another, and religious terrorists are not a new phenomenon. Moreover, terrorist groups may have mixed religious and political motives.

10. Researchers differ about what constitutes mass fatalities—and mass casualties—or they fail to articulate a definition. Most researchers, however, would include an event with more than a thousand fatalities in this category. Events that result in hundreds of fatalities may or may not be considered mass casualty events, depending, in part, on the number of nonfatal casualties and on whether or not the number of fatalities is closer to one hundred or one thousand.

11. Other cases of deliberately disseminated biological agents more accurately fall into a category of crimes using biological agents—those directed at specific individuals or at groups but that have no political intentions and are not meant to cause widespread fear. For more information on those cases, see Carus, "Bioterrorism and Biocrimes."

12. Milton Leitenberg, "The Experience of the Japanese Aum Shinrikyo Group and Biological Agents," in *Hype or Reality? The "New Terrorism" and Mass Casualty Attacks,* ed. Brad Roberts (Alexandria, VA: Chemical and Biological Arms Control Institute, 2000), pp. 159–170.

13. For a fuller description of this event, see Jonathan B. Tucker and Jason Pate, "The Minnesota Patriots Council, 1991," in *Toxic Terror: Assessing Terrorist Use of Chemical and Biological Weapons,* ed. Jonathan B. Tucker, 159–183 (Cambridge, MA: MIT Press, 2000).

14. Jonathan B. Tucker, "Chemical/Biological Terrorism: Coping with a New Threat," *Politics and the Life Sciences* 15, no. 2 (September 1996): 167–183, 168.

15. Ibid., p. 181.

16. Ibid., pp. 168–169.

17. Tucker, *Toxic Terror.*

18. Ibid., p. 13.

19. Ibid., p. 267.

20. Ibid., p. 266.

21. Ibid., p. 14.

22. Roberts, *Terrorism with Chemical and Biological Weapons.*

23. Ibid., pp. xi–xii.

24. Joseph Pilat, "Prospects for NBC Terrorism After Tokyo," in Roberts, *Terrorism with Chemical and Biological Weapons,* pp. 1–21.

25. James Adams, "The Dangerous New World of Chemical and Biological Weapons," in Roberts, *Terrorism with Chemical and Biological Weapons,* pp. 23–42.

26. Jenkins, "Understanding the Link Between Motives and Methods," pp. 43–51.

27. Karl Lowe, "Analyzing Technical Constraints on Bio-Terrorism: Are They Still Important?" in Roberts, *Terrorism with Chemical and Biological Weapons,* pp. 53–64.

28. Ron Purver, "Understanding the Past Non-Use of CBW," in Roberts, *Terrorism with Chemical and Biological Weapons,* pp. 65–73.

29. Anthony Fainberg, "Debating Policy Priorities and Implications," in Roberts, *Terrorism with Chemical and Biological Weapons,* pp. 75–93; Jonathan B. Tucker, "Policy Approaches to Chemical and Biological Terrorism," in Roberts, *Terrorism with Chemical and Biological Weapons,* pp. 95–111; Frank Young, "The Essential Tasks of Emergency Preparedness," in Roberts, *Terrorism with Chemical and Biological Weapons,* pp. 113–120.

30. Lowe, "Analyzing Technical Constraints on Bio-Terrorism," pp. 63–64.

31. Adams, "Dangerous New World of Chemical and Biological Weapons," p. 41.

32. Brad Roberts, "Has the Taboo Been Broken?" in Roberts, *Terrorism with Chemical and Biological Weapons,* pp. 121–140, 123–124.

33. Roberts, *Hype or Reality.*

34. Michael Moodie, "Introduction," in Roberts, *Hype or Reality,* p. xvii.

35. Ehud Sprinzak, "On Not Overstating the Problem," in Roberts, *Hype or Reality,* pp. 3–16, 5.

36. Superterrorism is defined as "the strategic use by a nonstate organization of chemical or biological agents to bring about a major disaster, with death tolls ranging in the tens or hundreds of thousands." Ibid., p. 9.

37. Ibid., pp. 9–11.

38. Ibid., p. 15.

39. James K. Campbell, "On Not Understanding the Problem," in Roberts, *Hype or Reality,* pp. 17–45, 40.

40. Ibid., p. 19.

41. Joseph F. Pilat, "The New Terrorism and NBC Weapons," in Roberts, *Hype or Reality,* pp. 225–237, 237.

42. Brian Michael Jenkins, "The WMD Terrorist Threat: Is There a Consensus View?" in Roberts, *Hype or Reality,* pp. 241–242.

43. Ibid., p. 250.

44. Chemical and Biological Arms Control Institute, *Biological Terrorism in the United States: Threat, Preparedness, and Response* (Alexandria, VA: Chemical and Biological Arms Control Institute, November 2000).

45. Ibid., p. 20.

46. Ibid., p. 70.

47. Ibid., p. 73.

48. Dean A. Wilkening, "BCW Attack Scenarios," in Drell, Sofaer, and Wilson, *New Terror.*

49. Ibid., p. 109.

50. Ibid., p. 112.

51. Ibid., p. 95.

52. Ibid., p. 107.

53. Shultz, "Preface," p. xiv.

54. Amy E. Smithson and Leslie-Anne Levy, "Ataxia: The Chemical and Biological Terrorism Threat and the US Response," *Stimson Center Report 35* (Washington, DC: Henry L. Stimson Center, October 2000), p. 20.

55. Ibid., p. 7.

56. Ibid., pp. 279–282.

57. Jessica Stern, *The Ultimate Terrorists* (Cambridge, MA: Harvard University Press, 1999), pp. 8–10.

58. Ibid., p. 8.

59. Ibid., p. 70.

60. Jean Pascal Zanders, "Assessing the Risk of Chemical and Biological Weapons Proliferation to Terrorists," *Nonproliferation Review* 6, no. 4 (Fall 1999): 17–34, 24.

61. Ibid., p. 33.

62. Ibid., p. 18.

63. Raymond Zilinskas, "Assessing the Threat of Bioterrorism," testimony before the Subcommittee on National Security, Veterans Affairs, and International Relations, US House of Representatives, 20 October 1999, p. 5. Available at http://cns.miis.edu/pubs/reports/zilin.htm (accessed 1 August 2005).

64. Ibid., p. 11.

65. Ibid., p. 12.

66. For detailed descriptions of the mailing of anthrax letters, see Milton Leitenberg, *The Problem of Biological Weapons* (Stockholm: Swedish National Defence College, 2004), pp. 137–155; Leonard A. Cole, *The Anthrax Letters: A Medical Detective Story* (Washington, DC: National Academy of Sciences, 2003).

67. Raymond A. Zilinskas, Bruce Hope, and D. Warner North, "A Discussion of Findings and Their Possible Implications from a Workshop on Bioterrorism Threat Assessment and Risk Management," *Risk Analysis* 24, no. 4 (2004): 901–908, 901.

68. Ibid., pp. 901–902.

69. Ibid., p. 902.

70. Ibid., p. 907.

71. Jonathan B. Tucker, *Biosecurity: Limiting Terrorist Access to Deadly Pathogens,* Peaceworks, no. 52 (Washington, DC: United States Institute of Peace, 2003), p. 11.

72. Brad Roberts, "Bioterrorism: Calibrating Threats and Responses," informal remarks delivered to the German–US roundtable on countering WMD terrorism, 3 February 2003; George Washington University symposium on bioterrorism, Washington, DC, 14 February 2003; and Fletcher School of Law and Diplomacy public lecture, Tufts University, Medford, MA, 25 February 2003. Copy of the remarks obtained from the author August 2005.

73. Milton Leitenberg, "The Widespread Distortion of Information on the Efforts to Produce Biological Warfare Agents by the Japanese Aum Shinrikyo Group: A Case Study in the Serial Propagation of Misinformation," *Terrorism and Political Violence* 11, no. 4 (Winter 1999).

74. Leitenberg, *Problem of Biological Weapons,* p. 155.

75. Neither the Rajneeshees in Oregon nor the sender of the 2001 anthrax letters were promptly detected or apprehended. The perpetrator of the anthrax attacks in 2001 is still at large.

76. Richard Danzig, *Catastrophic Bioterrorism: What Is to Be Done?* (Washington, DC: Center for Technology and National Security Policy, National Defense University, August 2003).

77. Malcolm Dando, *Bioterrorism: What Is the Real Threat?* Science and Technology Report, no. 3 (Bradford, UK: Department of Peace Studies, University of Bradford, March 2005), http://www.brad.ac.uk/acad/sbtwc/ST_Reports/ST_Reports.htm (accessed 7 August 2005).

78. Reynolds M. Salerno, Jennifer Gaudioso, Rebecca L. Frerichs, and Daniel Estes, "A BW Risk Assessment: Historical and Technical Perspectives," *Nonproliferation Review* 11, no. 3 (Fall/Winter 2004): 25–55, 46–47.

79. Ibid., p. 49.

80. Jonathan B. Tucker, "Biological Threat Assessment: Is the Cure Worse Than the Disease?" *Arms Control Today* 34, no. 8 (October 2004), http://www.armscontrol.org/act/2004_10/Tucker.asp (accessed 10 August 2005).

81. Common and numeric definitions of probability are circular, and the most reliable estimates of probability are based on easily repeatable events such as coin tosses. Experts could argue with this definition, but it is unlikely to raise controversy in this context.

82. Dando is reasonably clear that he means "more likely" or "more worrisome." Dando, *Bioterrorism.*

83. Wilkening, "BCW Attack Scenarios," p. 113.

84. Bruce Hoffman, "The Debate Over Future Terrorist Use of Chemical, Biological, Radiological and Nuclear Weapons," in Roberts, *Hype or Reality,* p. 220.

85. Jenkins, "WMD Terrorist Threat," p. 250.

86. Ibid., p. 251.

Part 3

Managing the Threat: Policy Options

7

When to Cry Wolf, What to Cry, and How to Cry It

Anthony H. Cordesman

THE THREAT OF BIOLOGICAL TERRORISM IS ALL TOO REAL. THERE HAVE ALREADY been a series of low-level and attempted attacks using biological weapons and toxins, and some have had marginal success. The politics and ideology of terrorism continue to remove the past limits to the levels of violence that terrorists are prepared to use and have increased terrorists' willingness to attack populations and innocent targets.

The United States faced actual anthrax attacks during the period September–November 2001 in New York, Washington, DC, and Lantana, Florida. Anthrax-tainted letters and parcels were sent to US senators and media figures like Tom Brokaw, killing five US citizens and infecting a total of twenty-two people.[1] As of 2006, the United States still had not been able to identify the attackers. As a 2005 presidential commission has noted, the United States was fundamentally unprepared for these attacks.[2]

The potential threat is clearly global. While the full details are classified, captured Al-Qaida records show that Islamic extremists and terrorists have an interest in acquiring biological as well as chemical and nuclear weapons. Britain has found elements for preparing ricin attacks, and a number of other European and Asian countries have found evidence of terrorist interest in such weapons.

Moreover, the ease with which bioterrorism can be put into practice is growing. The Internet provides a growing list of sites claiming to provide literature on the manufacture of biological agents and toxins in a wide variety of languages. The dissemination of biotechnology and of dual-use food processing and pharmaceutical equipment is steadily expanding the range of options for producing and weaponizing biological agents.

At the same time, biotechnology is advancing the range of different agents that can be used. Genetic engineering is moving from cutting-edge science to commercial practice; immune and semi-immune strains of major diseases are becoming more common; and new approaches to bioweapons, like attacking human immune systems, are becoming practically applicable. The worst cases in biological warfare are becoming more possible, and the results could be truly grim.

The fact remains, however, that anyone approaching the subject of bioterrorism still has to be extremely careful about "crying wolf." That a threat exists does not predetermine the kind of response that is needed, the priority it should be given, and the level of investment in time, expertise, and money that is required. It is all too easy to cry wolf in a post-9/11 world, but the risk of biological terrorism is only one more of thousands of risks that affect human society.

Triage is just as essential an element of counterterrorism as it is of medicine and public health policy. In a world where car and truck bombs can kill over one hundred people on a crowded street without warning, and where there are so many other competing priorities for government action, one has to be extremely careful about giving any particular threat a priority over others, and even more careful about what to call for in terms of public policy. The years since 9/11 have shown that it is far easier to throw money at a problem than it is to solve that problem, and it is far easier to focus noisily on the worst case than it is to produce credible risk assessments.

What to Cry: The Problem of Intelligence

It has long been clear that tracking any form of biological warfare activity is extremely difficult and that the challenges are growing steadily as nations and terrorist movements have more—and better access to—technology and dual-use facilities and equipment. It has also become clear that this is an area where international cooperation could have great potential value but also presents massive risks, because intelligence collection is heavily oriented toward human intelligence and sensitive sources and methods, and also because intelligence can be so useful to any state or group that can and desires to use it as a "cookbook" for proliferation.

Critical Problems in Superpower Intelligence

Until recently, there was little unclassified analysis of just how serious the problems relating to intelligence on biological weapons and bioterrorism are, even for a power with all of the resources of the United States. This situation has changed. The above-mentioned report (see n. 2), issued on 31 March 2005, shows the extent of the difficulties presented by a bioterrorist target like Al-Qaida. At the same time, the report provides equally important insights into many other types of problems and failings in the US effort to trace biological weapons developments in Iraq, Libya, and elsewhere.

Key Challenges for Action: Improving Intelligence

At the risk of oversimplifying what are very detailed conclusions and recommendations, I summarize below the recommendations made by the commission, each of which can be adapted to the systems used by other nations and to the problem of international cooperation at the global and regional levels:

- The United States should create a new kind of counterproliferation center.
- It should strengthen HUMINT (human intelligence) and MASINT (measurement and signals intelligence).
- It should work with biological science (and delivery-weaponization) experts.
- The Director of National Intelligence (DNI) should use the Joint Intelligence Community Council to form a biological weapons working group.
- The intelligence community needs a targeted, managed, and directed strategy for biological weapons intelligence.
- The National Security Council should form a joint interagency task force to develop a counterbiological weapons plan that draws on all elements of national power.
- The United States should aggressively support foreign criminalization of biological weapons development and the establishment of biosafety and biosecurity regulations under the framework of United Nations Security Council Resolution 1540.
- The development of close relationships with foreign governments on the biological weapons issue is imperative to US efforts to better achieve its goals of monitoring and containing biological threats.
- The United States should remain actively engaged in designing and implementing both international and regulatory inspection regimes.

Important as these recommendations are, there is an equally great need to examine the kinds of attacks that might take place and their real-world lethality, and to provide net technical assessments of the impact of the trends in the technology available to bioterrorists, to defenders, and to responders.

What to Cry: The Problem of Low-Level Attack

Capability analysis has long shown that biological terrorism *can be* one of the four types of terrorism whose lethality justifies its classification as a weapon of mass destruction (WMD). US studies and simulations conducted in the 1960s and during and before the period of the Biological and Toxin Weapons Convention (BTWC) found that covert biological attacks could have the lethality of nuclear weapons. These simulations included large-scale field tests using dry particulates similar to weaponized anthrax.

It should be noted, however, that the attacks analyzed by the Office of Technology Assessment (OTA) assumed the use of highly advanced, weaponized, dry storable, and coated anthrax powder of precisely the right particle size, and like many studies of the day, the OTA ignored many of the major uncertainties that affect the real-world lethality of biological weapons.

There is no way of knowing when, if at all, bioterrorists might acquire weapons this lethal—if, in fact, these weapons are truly capable of such lethality in an operational mode. Limited experiments using trained microbiologists who are not familiar with weapons production have raised serious doubts about the capability of individuals or small teams to create such weapons without making seemingly minor errors that severely weaken or eliminate the lethality and life of the weapons, the ability to disseminate them (particularly in the case of coated weapons), and the capability to scale up laboratory samples to the amounts needed for weapons use.

In mid-March 2005, however, a study of possible attack scenarios, developed for defense and response planning by the US Department of Homeland Security (DHS), was inadvertently published on the Internet. Among many other cases, the following examples of bioterrorism as real-world, near-term possibilities were given, and the study stated that these examples were based on current options that terrorists might actually be able to use:[3]

- Spread pneumonic plague in the bathrooms of an airport, sports arena, or train station, killing 2,500 and making 8,000 ill worldwide.

- Infect cattle with foot-and-mouth disease in several places, re-sulting in hundreds of millions of dollars in losses.
- Expose an estimated 350,000 people to an anthrax attack through terrorists' spraying the biological weapon from a truck driven through 5 cities in 2 weeks; an estimated 13,200 people could die.

These examples are only one set of possible high-level cases in a long list of cases and scenarios that have been examined by governments and research organizations in recent years. While serious uncertainties continue to affect estimates of lethality and of how easily certain bio-weapons can be produced and disseminated, every government that has seriously examined bioterrorism in terms of technical capability has con-cluded that it could result in large casualty numbers, high levels of lethal-ity, massive damage to food supplies, and great economic costs.[4]

Is the Most Likely Attack a "Low" Attack?

Like chemical and radiological terrorism, however, most real-world bio-logical terrorism, such as the events in the list above, might take the form of attacks where there is little real damage in terms of lethality, and where the main impact might be a mix of panic and expensive over-reaction. The probability of some variation of a worst-case biological attack may well be very limited in the near term. It is far from clear that real-world biological terrorism will go beyond the limited spread of toxin or agents that cause casualties in double or triple figures at most.

The history of bioterrorism consists so far largely of a series of small incidents, failed plans, and ineffective strikes. The anthrax attacks by the Aum Shinrikyo group in Tokyo in 1995 are the clearest example of attempted acts of biological terrorism that involved serious financial resources mixed with some credible scientific talent. Nevertheless, the end result was a total nonevent that was detected only after the group had succeeded in using chemical weapons.[5]

Similarly, studies of the anthrax attacks in the United States in Sep-tember 2001 initially indicated that the terrorists may have succeeded in creating the kind of dry, storable anthrax powder milled and coated in ways that could produce high lethality. Further examination indicated, however, that the particles were not coated in such a way or milled to the kind of size necessary for the large-scale dissemination that would lead to high concentrations of inhalational anthrax.

This does not mean that even a low-level bioterrorism incident with minimal casualties could not have a massive impact in terms of panic and its political and economic effects; and a series of well-distributed low-level attacks might well be a substitute for one massive attack, or at least they might produce far more serious effects than a single incident. The anthrax attacks in the United States in the fall of 2001 killed only five and sickened only twenty-two people, but they still led to widespread panic, closing US government and postal facilities; to massive public expenditures; and to preventive actions, like the treatment of some twenty thousand people for possible exposure to anthrax. They also led to tens of thousands of hoax attacks all over the world, many of which forced governments to react.

Lethality is only one measure of the impact of bioterrorism, and in most real-world attacks, lethality may be far less important than the other impacts of such attacks. At the same time, we should take great care not to assume that biological attacks necessarily become weapons of mass media, weapons of mass panic, or weapons of mass expenditure. Initial attacks might produce such effects, but governments, the media, and the public may well have a more rapid learning curve than some analysts expect. The following points need to be implemented as preventive measures:

- Warning, intelligence, detection, defense, and response must be capable of dealing with low-level attempts and attacks, including a series of attacks that may not use the same agent.
- The modeling and analysis of bioterrorism and bioweapons must be parametric and must explicitly model uncertainty.
- Governments must have clear plans for dealing with public information and warning to counter panic, to inform the media, and to minimize economic impacts.
- National and international efforts are needed to establish suitable controls on equipment and supply sales and access to key facilities.
- Suitable national and international legislation and law enforcement procedures must be created to deal with low- and high-level threats.
- The possibility of establishing an international system for tracking individuals with special expertise should, at the very least, be examined, as should procedures for vetting and clearing workers and researchers.
- There must be education on the real-world capabilities and limits of bioterrorism.
- Specialized elements to track and analyze the risk and effects of low-level attacks must be created.

- The risk of agricultural and food attacks must be reexamined.
- Local decontamination capabilities must be reexamined.

What to Cry: Uncertainties in High-Level Attack

The problems in characterizing and analyzing bioterrorism are different in the case of high-level attacks. The key problems for public policy are how to distinguish the worst case from the real case and how to make sure that defenders and responders are fully aware of the uncertainties that they may face.

Unfortunately, it has almost become fashionable to hold war games or simulations based on worst cases to dramatize the risks of covert, terrorist, or proxy attacks and to model attacks at the scare level. In far too many cases, the assumed lethality of a given form of bioattack is based on uncertain criteria, and the modeling is weak; there is inadequate parametric analysis; and the analysis or simulation is based on dubious mathematics and assumptions.[6]

There may have been a time when dramatizing worst cases was necessary to win the attention of policymakers. Most governments and international organizations, however, now recognize the risk of high-level attack. What they need are valid attack models on which they can base public policy. They need real-world capability studies—and not horror shows—and explicit models of uncertainty to prepare them for attacks that may be extremely difficult to characterize.

At the broadest level, far more peer review and red teaming is needed with regard to virtually every aspect of the analysis of high-level attacks and to the ways such analysis is translated into guidance for planning. There are, however, a number of areas that need special attention.

Lethality

The tendency to game worst-case attacks often arises from the assumed lethality of such attacks. In many cases, historical data are adapted with little real analysis, and no effort is made toward parametric modeling. Microbiologists note that the real-world lethality of many agents can vary by four to six times, depending on the exact agent used, the nature of its dissemination, and the precise conditions under which it is disseminated. Potential worst cases may look very different if they involve actual attacks perpetrated by relatively unskilled or inexperienced terrorists.

As mentioned above, limited experiments using trained microbiologists who are not familiar with weapons production leave serious doubts about the capability of individuals or small teams to create such weapons without their making seemingly minor errors that severely weaken or eliminate the lethality and life of the weapon, reduce their ability to disseminate the weapon (particularly in the case of coated weapons), and limit their ability to scale up laboratory samples to the amounts needed for weapons use.

There is no expert agreement on the probable level of capability that current and future terrorists and extremists have of producing and using specific biological agents; on how soon advanced or highly lethal weapons can be deployed, if at all; and on the most likely method of dissemination and attack. Neither terrorists' interests nor their activities imply competence, but there is no way to deny that competence is possible—particularly if a state actor should furnish assistance.[7]

There is no meaningful data based on actual war or on human testing of biological weapons, but the former Soviet Union and other nations have learned that actual virulence is always an uncertainty, and lethality can also vary or decay sharply if the agent is not stable or is not the product of very experienced, well-financed, and well-equipped experts. Even highly advanced weapons developed by states can present major effectiveness problems. People are not evenly distributed or constantly and evenly distributed and exposed, and military forces may be protected, warned, or sheltered. Meteorological factors like wind speed, temperature and inversion, moisture and rain, and sunlight can have a significant impact. In terms of terrain conditions, there are few open, smooth plains, and most people live in built-up areas. Aerosols can quickly agglomerate or become sediments. Explosive dissemination can destroy a large amount of an agent, and even pneumatic dispersal can be inefficient. Delivery to a target can be affected by navigation, targeting, mechanical problems, equipment malfunction, and a host of other factors.

As pointed out above, the level of uncertainty in the operational use of a bioagent would probably exceed two orders of magnitude for even the most advanced military effort by a state and could easily reach four to six orders of magnitude. At the bottom end of the range, a bioterrorist attack might mirror the Aum Shinrikyo model and produce zero casualties and effect. At the top end of the range, even classified models and estimates contain so much uncertainty that only a series of actual attacks could begin to establish the probable area coverage and casualty impact, although the Centers for Disease Control and Prevention (CDC) and the Defense Threat Reduction Agency have made efforts to develop far more reliable parametric estimates.[8]

However, there are several factors that could increase the impact of an attack. One is the panic factor and the political, economic, and disruptive impacts of a limited success, or even public knowledge that an attack was under way or had been carried out.

Lethality and other impacts of bioweapons use can vary considerably when a mix of agents is involved. Most US and former Soviet Union planning for biological warfare called for a mix of biological agents to be used—so-called biological cocktails. At least some research has been done on mixes that are likely to cause responders to focus on the first source of lethality, leading them to the wrong response.

Other simulated attacks have modeled the use of one biological agent as a means of greatly increasing the lethality of another. The modeling of simultaneous and sequential attacks with one agent is uncertain enough, but there are no rules that say a sophisticated terrorist group, or one aided by a state actor, could not use similar cocktails.

Sequential or disperse attacks could cover very wide areas rather than the single area assumed in many lethality calculations. Multiple attacks on urban areas, sequential attacks on such areas, and the use of a mix of agents could greatly increase the lethality and other effects of such weapons and could greatly complicate the treatment of both infectious and noninfectious agents. Terrorists and extremists may or may not face physical and financial limitations in carrying out such complex attack patterns, but there are scarcely any rules, and even one attack on a major transportation hub like an airport could have the effect of multiple attacks as infected passengers subsequently move and disperse.

Manufacture, Weaponization, and Dissemination

The lethality of a disease or toxin cannot be separated from the way in which it is manufactured, processed, weaponized, and disseminated. It is clear from past US, Russian, and European research and development in biological weapons that every step in this chain can radically alter the real-world lethality and effect of such weapons.

An examination of the unclassified literature on bioterrorism raises serious questions about just how much empirical research has actually been done on what terrorists can or cannot do in these areas, and also on possible actions by those states that might carry out covert or proxy attacks. Some literature assumes that highly lethal bioterrorism is well within the grasp of well-organized terrorist groups, and other literature draws virtually the opposite conclusion.

In the past, conventional wisdom indicated that the manufacture, weaponization, and dissemination of bioweapons were technically difficult and required major resources. However, given the recent proliferation of dual-use technologies and know-how, the technical difficulties are diminishing with time.

The dissemination of the necessary equipment and technology. While terrorists and extremists have not demonstrated advanced skills to date, the equipment and technology to make bioweapons are becoming far more widely disseminated—and at a very high rate. Developing countries are moving into the field very quickly, although little concrete data are available on just how quickly this trend is moving ahead.

However, studies of the 2001 anthrax attacks in the United States have revealed a far broader spread of relevant biological, food processing, and pharmaceutical facilities than the authorities previously believed, and the spread is even broader if we consider those who might manufacture an agent and who are willing to take serious risks with their own lives or the lives of those around them. The cost and availability of many items of relevant dual-use equipment were found to present significantly fewer problems than expected, and security measures and controls were sometimes limited, token, or nonexistent.

The extent of the proliferation of bioweapons may be uncertain, but the extent of the proliferation of biotechnology is not. A now dated 1999 survey of fourteen hundred US academic institutions found that 16 percent of the institutions possessed human, animal, or plant pathogens that appear in the draft BTWC's list of biological agents. Another 11 percent had high-level containment facilities; 7 percent were conducting research on vaccines; 5 percent were performing research for the military or the US Department of Energy to develop defenses against biological weapons; and 3 percent had high-volume bioreactors.[9]

In the twenty-five years that followed the development of recombinant DNA technologies, over two thousand biotech firms were founded in the United States alone. By the year 2000, there were roughly thirteen hundred US companies actively commercializing biotechnology. They employed between one hundred eight thousand and one hundred sixteen thousand people, and the market for such products was estimated to have grown from US$7.6 billion in 1996 to US$24 billion in 2006. These figures do not include the growth of agricultural biotechnology, which may be as significant a source of threats as the technology tailored to deal with humans, and for which spending was projected to grow from US$295 million in 1996 to US$1.74 billion in 2006. Unlike most companies, biotech firms also train a large number of individuals in research and development. They spent US$69,000 per employee on research and development in 1995, compared to a US corporate average of US$7,651.[10] While there are no precise figures, much of this activity involved foreign scientists and technical personnel. Japan's and Europe's pharmaceutical and biotechnological markets have also experienced similar significant growth.

Technology transfer from the former Soviet Union is also a potential problem, although there is little evidence of such a risk to date. The Cold War biological effort involved some sixty thousand to seventy thousand people.[11] There is no meaningful current account of their whereabouts. It is clear, however, that at least seventy-five thousand Russian scientific workers emigrated between 1989 and 1992, and many have left the former Soviet Union since. There are also repeated unconfirmed reports that some of these scientists are working in Iran and North Korea.

It seems possible that a comprehensive net technical assessment might show that the difficulties relating to the manufacture, weaponization, and dissemination of bioweapons are being steadily reduced by the spread of biological facilities, dual-use equipment, and technical skills. Unlike chemical weapons and most nuclear weapons, biological agents are generally compact and low in weight. They can be disseminated in a wide variety of ways—by insects, through water and food supplies, through contact, in powders and liquids, and by aerosol.

However, terrorists' ability to produce aerosols is another key issue. The US Department of Defense reports that the dissemination of infectious agents through aerosols, either as droplets from liquid suspensions or as small particles from dry powders, is by far the most efficient method.[12] Tests conducted during the 1950s and 1960s showed that an aerosol cloud of fine particles (2–5 microns) behaves more like a gas than a suspension and penetrates interior as well as exterior spaces. The United States found that release from ships, aircraft, and tall buildings could achieve some lethality over distances of fifty to a hundred miles, although without approaching anything like a uniform density.[13]

The problems of integrating the hardware for line-source delivery,[14] the agent, the munitions, and suitable vehicles need to be reexamined, as do possible solutions related to the fact that the effectiveness of biological warfare munitions is dependent on meteorological conditions and exposure to daylight. Covert attacks could now involve a wide range of different methods of delivery. Since only relatively small quantities of a relatively impure agent are required for terrorist use, the range of possible agents is almost unlimited.

US Department of Defense estimates indicate that the quantity of an agent used could be small (a single gram, possibly less). The production and purification methods and the dissemination means could range from simple to complex. All elements of such a program might go undetected until an agent has been used. Broad areas or individual buildings are potential targets. In the case of buildings, off-the-shelf aerosol generators could be used to disperse a biowarfare agent into the air intake ducts of the target structure, especially in the case of toxins, where far fewer toxic agents could be employed. The necessary quantity of the agent would be much less than for other targets.

Technological Change and the "Twelve Monkey" Problem

Another area of uncertainty that merits close examination is the combined impact of the progress taking place in the biological sciences and the dissemination (or proliferation) of the facilities and equipment that can be used to produce biological agents for terrorism.

While bioterrorism is an immediate risk, no assessment of the technical and practical issues surrounding the use of biological weapons by terrorists or states in covert and proxy operations can focus merely on the present. Biological weapons belong to an area where the rapid pace of technical change means a constantly increasing ability to make far more effective weapons. Biotechnology can offer many benefits.[15] At the same time, genetic engineering and other new technologies can now be employed to overcome product deficiencies in the classic agents and toxins normally investigated in such assessments. Moreover, toxins that exist in nature in small amounts were once considered insignificant potential threat agents because of their limited availability. However, the US Department of Defense estimates that a number of natural toxins could now be produced through genetic engineering techniques in sufficient quantities for an adversary to consider producing them as an offensive weapon. There are many microorganisms, or their metabolic by-products (toxins), that can now meet all the criteria of effective biowarfare agents.[16] Studies like those of the Jason Summer Study also indicate that this situation will become much more serious in the future.

Furthermore, advances in technology need to be carefully examined to determine the extent to which they will allow small terrorist groups or individuals to carry out more successful attacks using both existing biological weapons and new forms of weapons. Just as the emphasis on terrorist groups like Al-Qaida sometimes leads analysts to ignore the threat from state actors, it can also lead analysts to ignore the threats posed by disturbed individuals or small, ad hoc groups of individuals who may have considerable expertise and act for motives that are too extreme to be predictable. The "twelve monkey" problem (named after the erratic and unpredictable actions of such a group in the motion picture *Twelve Monkeys*) does not seem real now, but this is no guarantee for the future, and the technical options should be continually monitored.

Key Challenges for Action: Improving the Response to High-Level Attacks

The time for bringing the risk of biological terrorism to the public's attention by focusing on worst cases is long past. There is a need to develop scientifically rigorous data on what kinds of large-scale attacks can and cannot be carried out, and there is also a need for a net technical assessment of the trends in the biological sciences and in the methods of manufacture, weaponization, and dissemination of biological agents. Such a rigorous approach already exists in many laboratories and research centers, but it is often lacking at the broader public policy level, and many research and study projects focus more on the "drama" of potential attacks than on probable scenarios.

Many of the options discussed above for characterizing attacks and for dealing with low-level attacks apply also to high-level attacks. Further action should include the following factors:

- Reliable parametric models of lethality tied to different methods of manufacture, weaponization, dissemination, and attack should be created.
- National and international efforts are needed to create standardized and rigorous large-scale attack models for public policy and planning purposes.
- Transparency is needed at the national level, and a comparative analysis of programs is needed at the international level to determine the areas where cooperation and synergies are possible, and where national programs may be similar enough to exchange training methods, technology, and other program information.
- Net technical assessment is needed of the trends in the biological sciences and in the dissemination of equipment and usable facilities.
- Better indicators and analysis are needed to aid national intelligence, warning, characterization tracking, and response systems.
- Options for international cooperation at the "fusion level" need serious examination.

Modeling, simulation, and gaming of high-level attacks, as well as defense and response, need to be extended to the international level.

How to Cry It:
The Problem of Resources and Levels of Effort

Many countries have started responding to the threat of biological terrorism, as have international organizations like the UN, the World Health Organization (WHO), and Interpol. Each country has taken a somewhat different approach, depending in part on its own approach to government, its perceptions of the threat, and its resources and capabilities.

The practical problems arise from the very different levels of available resources among countries, a lack in many of national expertise, and very different perceptions of the threat. The developed world is just beginning to establish national defense and response capabilities. In many countries in the developing world, surplus resources and expertise are negligible, although such countries can and are being used by potential bioterrorists.

The Practical Minimum

There is only a limited amount of literature on the detailed programs of those countries that have started to create biodefense capabilities, and in many cases budget and program data are very limited, and they discuss the goals and intentions in much more depth than the ongoing efforts. Most of the national plans of such countries do, however, seem to include many of the elements of the near-term strategy that were recommended by the CDC Strategic Planning Workgroup before 9/11 triggered most of today's activity and that are described in somewhat similar forms in various UN, WHO, and Interpol studies.[17]

However, bioterrorism is a field where there is little transparency on the scale of national efforts and on the details of the efforts a country has under way that could shape an informed public policy debate or foster detailed international cooperation at the working level. It is difficult, in most cases, to know how much research and at what level the various countries and international organizations are really engaged in; how they are using the money they spend; and the extent to which their efforts reinforce other efforts or needlessly duplicate them.

"Prudent Minimalism" or "Inglorious Excess":
The United States as a Case Study

One thing is clear: no other country is spending more than the United States. The 2006 US budget request for homeland defense—including

US$9.5 billion in spending by the Department of Defense but excluding state and locally funded expenditures—is US$49.9 billion.[18] This is a US$3.9 billion increase over the 2005 budget and is higher than the total defense expenditures of Britain, France, and Germany. The request for the DHS alone is US$26.7 billion, and the total homeland security spending request is US$32 billion without the Department of Defense, and US$47.5 billion with it.[19]

There is no precise way to distinguish US spending on the response to and defense against bioterrorism from spending on many other aspects of homeland defense, and this illustrates the general need for more transparency if any realistic assessment is to be made of the adequacy of national plans or of the opportunities for international cooperation. The DHS does not provide a breakdown of its spending, nor do recent studies by the US Office of Management and the Budget, the Congressional Budget Office, and the General Accounting Office.[20] If one looks at the data in the president's 2006 federal budget request, there are no data on biological programs per se, but the data do provide a total for all activity directly related to all forms of catastrophic or chemical, biological, radiological, or nuclear threats. These data show that such spending has risen to a total of close to US$4 billion.

Another way of looking at US spending is to look at the president's request in areas that affect health and emergency services. If one exempts all spending in the US Department of Defense—which has a substantial role in dealing with bioterrorism—planned US spending would total some US$5.6 billion in 2006 and would rise to US$7.2 billion in 2010. These figures, however, do not include substantial spending relating to bioterrorism, but they do include areas of health and medical spending on other threats. It is striking that total US spending for all forms of homeland defense will rise from US$47.5 billion in 2006 to US$52.8 billion in 2010.

The highest estimate of spending relating to bioterrorism that seems to be available is in an analysis by the Chemical and Biological Arms Control Institute (CBACI) of all federal programs relating to defense and response that have some impact on biodefense. The CBACI states that spending in this area rose from US$1.52 billion in 2001 to US$6.4 billion in 2002, US$11 billion in 2003, and US$11.9 billion in 2004.[21] A review of the 2005 and 2006 US budgets, including the annual impact of the US$5.6 billion that Congress appropriated for Project BioShield, gives a rough estimate of a current total—using the same methodology as the CBACI—of some US$14 billion, although it must be stressed that at most only about one-third of these funds can be directly attributed to biological defense and response.

The seriousness of the anthrax attacks in the United States, and the broader impact of 9/11, help to explain why the United States has made such massive increases in its efforts to deal with bioterrorism and with the risk of covert and proxy biological attacks since early 2002.

The United States is scarcely alone in developing measures to improve its defense against and response to bioterrorism or in its attempts to detect bioterrorist threats. Several nations, including Britain, have created their own homeland defense programs; the WHO is seeking to create a global vaccine storage program; and Russia has adapted some of its former biological warfare programs to defense measures.

The fact remains, however, that no other country in the world comes close to the United States in its efforts relating to bioterrorism. This inevitably has led to a debate in which some US citizens question how usefully much of the money allocated to the US effort is being spent, while others feel that spending is still inadequate.

Finding the Golden Mean: Key Challenges for Action

At this writing bioterrorism policy is very much a moving target. At least some countries and organizations are moving more quickly than their open literature suggests, and the sheer scale of the global effort that has emerged since 9/11 makes any attempt at undertaking a comparative analysis difficult and uncertain.

For all of the above reasons, there is also no reliable way to establish what level of effort is needed or how valid the US program is as a model for other countries. The DHS is, in fact, now in the process of reexamining its current biological warfare programs as part of a general review of its efforts, and significant changes may come in the very near future.

But countries should be able to learn a great deal from each other: there is no need for duplicating efforts in many areas, and there are many opportunities for cooperation and synergy. To take full advantage of their own efforts, individual countries should

- move toward international cooperation in the areas listed above;
- provide maximum transparency regarding their national programs, including research and development, defense, and response efforts, and regarding their budgets;
- create international and regional centers to coordinate key activities;
- create international and regional centers to exchange data on methods of defense and response;
- exchange data on methods of program management and measures of effectiveness;

- focus on common efforts to develop high-cost defense and response systems, such as detection and warning systems and networks, and produce and stockpile vaccines;
- create transparency in their progress regarding international cooperation;
- develop independent sources for the comparative analysis of national and international programs, levels of effort, and strategies.

How to Cry It:
The Threat from Man Versus the Threat from Nature

Virtually all public policy is forced to suboptimize in given areas. In most cases, it is difficult or impossible to make valid trade-offs between the very different areas of government activity. Such trade-offs can also be very difficult to validate in given areas. For example, there is no clear way to establish trade-offs among efforts for dealing with bioterrorism, other forms of terrorism involving WMD, and all forms of terrorism. Ultimately, one must fall back on politics and judgment.

However, there does seem to be a clear need for a great deal more exploration in order to determine the proper mix of trade-offs between preparing for biological terrorism and improving our ability to deal with natural diseases. The worst case that the DHS developed for emergency defense and response planning purposes in July 2005 did not involve a biological or nuclear weapon but a natural outbreak of flu.[22] This scenario produced some eighty-seven thousand fatalities and three hundred thousand hospitalizations and had an economic impact cost of some US$70 billion to US$160 billion.

There is also considerable disagreement among experts as to whether the current emphasis on bioterrorism is diverting resources and talent from other areas in such a way that the actual risk of mass casualties is being increased, because the state's ability to cope with natural outbreaks has been reduced. A total of 758 scientists wrote an open letter, published in *Science* magazine on 4 March 2005, to Elias Zerhouni, head of the National Institutes of Health. They described the allocation of some US$14 billion in US funding to biological terrorism as an expensive diversion from higher priority medical and research needs. The letter might seriously understate some of the potential risks posed by bioterrorism, but it cannot be ignored in a world with so many other medical and public health needs.[23]

It is worth noting that both the US National Intelligence Council (NIC) and the WHO have made it clear that there is no better way to estimate the probability of a major outbreak of a new strain of a lethal infectious disease, or the rate at which treatment-resistant diseases become more lethal, than to identify the precise level of risk from bioterrorism.

Like a truly lethal biological attack, natural diseases remain a possibility that cannot be translated into any kind of real probability. At the same time, the NIC study noted that the cost impacts of even one existing form of a new disease could be staggering compared to most scenarios for biological attack: "By 2000, the cumulative direct and indirect costs of AIDS alone are likely to have topped $500 billion."[24]

Key Challenges for Action: Integrating Biodefense and Public Health Activity

The practical problem for both national policy and global cooperation is determining the extent to which investments in defense against and response to biological terrorism are competing with those in natural disease research, and in defining possible synergies. At present, public policy tends to separate such efforts, both at the national and global levels. This encourages waste, duplication, the failure to share progress, and the failure to develop inclusive information, defense, and response systems. A more valid approach might be to

- directly integrate planning for bioterrorism and natural disease (outbreak) warning; research, development, test, and evaluation; defense; and response;
- create similar programs for dealing with threats to agriculture and livestock;
- provide as much transparency on national efforts as possible;
- task the WHO with seeking international cooperation and with creating a coordinated plan;
- task the Food and Agriculture Organization of the United Nations (FAO) with a similar role in dealing with threats to agriculture and livestock;
- create international stockpiles of vaccines and medicines designed to deal with both bioterrorism and natural outbreaks and medical needs.

The Challenge of International Cooperation

It is obvious from the above analysis that the world is beginning to react to the threat of bioterrorism. It is equally clear, however, that nations and international organizations still face a wide range of challenges in understanding this threat, prioritizing it, and choosing a course of action for public policy. There are also many areas where difficult choices need to be made about the resources required and the resources that can be made available.

The Real-World Problem

There are serious real-world limits to the level of transparency that nations and international organizations can and should provide. The wrong kind of details can provide both a warning and an aid to terrorists.

Broad international cooperation can also be a dangerous goal if it is pushed to unrealistic limits. Security could become more difficult, and some nations are part of the problem, not the solution. This includes nations that proliferate, sponsor, or tolerate terrorist activity and that are shifting from a past focus on conventional warfare to a focus on asymmetric conflict. Bioterrorism is not simply the province of nonstate actors; it cannot be divorced from the risk of covert action by states, false flag operations, and the use of terrorist organizations as proxies.

The states most suspected of having clandestine biological warfare programs are Iran, North Korea, and Syria. These states are not reckless and would almost certainly be very careful about transferring weapons to any extremist or terrorist group they did not totally control. The problem with "rational actor" arguments, however, is that they do not necessarily apply in a crisis or in a period of acute tension, and one side's definition of rational bargaining may differ strongly from another's—particularly if the opponent has massive conventional and nuclear forces.

Nevertheless, transparency and cooperation are key to any effort to prevent bioterrorism, to deal with its potential impact, and to create cost-effective programs. No nation other than the United States can afford a national program on anything like the scale required; and the United States cannot simply isolate itself from the needs of its allies or its own needs from them. As shown above, natural biological threats cannot be ignored simply because the focus is on terrorism.

Key Challenges for Action: Strengthening International Cooperation

There are still many areas where collaborative international planning and analysis, and international cooperation, could be of great value. Many areas are already being explored by the UN, by other global international organizations like Interpol, and by regional organizations like the North Atlantic Treaty Organization, the European Union (EU), and the Association of Southeast Asian Nations. Such cooperation sometimes leads to more rhetoric than action and to the creation of more dialogue and study groups than actors, but it is clear that these efforts are vital.

It is striking that even in the EU—which seems to be the regional body best suited to effective regional cooperation in dealing with bioterrorism and other major threats—little progress has been made in the several years since 9/11 and since the Madrid bombing, as noted by EU antiterrorism coordinator Gijs de Vries: "The main thrust of Europe's defense against terrorism remains firmly at the level of national governments . . . In several of our countries we must do more to speed up the implementation of our legislation."[25]

International cooperation might make a difference in the following areas:

- It could end the compartmentalization of national analysis, planning, and programs that artificially distinguish between domestic and international terrorism, and between attempted and successful incidents. The focus should be on high-risk forms of terrorism and on combining warning and analytic functions.
- It could create hierarchies of intelligence to allow the maximum sharing of data at the national and international levels in a standardized and near real-time form.
- It could establish an international center or centers for tracking, characterizing, and analyzing terrorist incidents, terrorists, and terrorist activities.
- It could create secure regional centers that could operate at high levels of classification and security for tracking, characterizing, and analyzing terrorist incidents, terrorists, and terrorist activities.
- It could create a specialized element in such a center or centers for tracking and analyzing covert and proxy biological attacks and other forms of WMD attacks.
- It could set international standards for incident reporting for both attempted and actual attacks.
- It could establish suitable controls on the sale of equipment and supplies and on access to key facilities.
- It could create suitable international legislation and law enforcement procedures to deal with low- and high-level threats.
- It should include at least the initial examination of the possibility of creating an international system for tracking individuals with special forms of expertise, as well as procedures for vetting and clearing workers and researchers.

- It should create standardized and rigorous large-scale attack models for public policy and planning purposes.
- It should aid the serious examination of options for cooperation at the fusion level.
- It should lead to international and regional centers to coordinate key activities, and other centers to exchange data on methods of defense and response.
- It should task the WHO with the coordination of a plan for dealing with bioterrorism, natural outbreaks, and immunity problems.
- It should task the FAO with a similar role in dealing with threats to agriculture and livestock.
- It should help to produce international stockpiles of vaccines and medicines designed to deal with both bioterrorism and natural outbreaks and with medical needs.
- It should encourage the exchange of data on methods of program management and on measures of effectiveness.
- It should lead to the development of independent sources of comparative analysis of national and international programs, levels of effort, and strategies.

In addition, there may be more challenging opportunities that also deserve consideration in the long run. These include the following:

- The creation of an authority equivalent to the International Atomic Energy Agency within the framework of the BTWC
- The strengthening of the WHO and the FAO to deal with both bioterrorism and outbreaks
- The creation of international and regional centers for cooperation; and a possible expansion of Interpol or the creation of a new Interpol-type body

It is far easier to invent new tasks for the UN and other international organizations than it is to give them the resources and cooperation they need to implement such tasks. It is far easier to talk about the "international community" than it is to face the many reasons why it does not exist and why nations oppose each other rather than cooperate with each other. In the real world, progress is likely to be grindingly slow, and a significant number of governments will be part of the threat and not of the solution. The fact remains, however, that the long-term incentives for cooperation are high, and the long-term risks and costs of noncooperation could be serious. Moreover, if bioterrorism does become a reality, the need for large-scale cooperation may become real virtually overnight—and planning and preparation can greatly ease the strain of crisis-driven action.

Notes

1. Daniel B. Jernigan et al., "Investigation of Bioterrorism-Related Anthrax, United States, 2001: Epidemiologic Findings," *Emerging Infectious Diseases* 8, no. 10 (October 2002), http://www.cdc.gov/ncidod/EID/vol8no10/02-0353.htm (accessed 9 January 2006).

2. Commission on the Intelligence Capabilities, *The Commission on the Intelligence Capabilities of the United States Regarding Weapons of Mass Destruction: Report to the President of the United States* (Washington, DC: US Government Printing Office, 31 March 2005), pp. 502–503.

3. US Department of Homeland Security, *Planning Scenarios,* Homeland Security Council, July 2004, http://www.globalsecurity.org/security/library/report/2004/hsc-planning-scenarios-jul04.htm; Lara Jakes Jordan, "Federal Officials Catalogue Possible Terror Attacks," Associated Press, 16 March 2005.

4. These risks are also scarcely a twenty-first-century or post–Cold War concern of governments. See Erhard Geissler and John Ellis van Courtland Moon, *Biological and Toxin Weapons: Research, Development, and Use from the Middle Ages to 1945* (New York: Oxford University Press, 1999).

5. See the work by Kyle B. Olson of Research Planning, Inc., cited on the Centers for Disease Control website.

6. For unclassified technical background, see the Center for Counterproliferation Research, *The Effects of Chemical and Biological Weapons on Operations: What We Know and Don't Know* (Washington, DC: National Defense University, February 1997); P2NBC2 Report no. 90-1, Physiological and Psychological Effects of NBC Environment and Sustained Operations on Systems in Combat, *P2NBC2 Test Reports,* "Technical Papers and Bibliographies," CB-013725.0 (Ft. McClellan, AL: US Army Chemical School, 4 January 1990); P2NBC2 Report no. 90-2, Physiological and Psychological Effects of NBC Environment and Sustained Operations on Systems in Combat, *P2NBC2 Test Reports,* "Program Overview," CB-013726 (Ft. McClellan, AL: US Army Chemical School, 4 January 1990); P2NBC2, Physiological and Psychological Effects of NBC Environment and Sustained Operations on Systems in Combat, *P2NBC2 Test Reports,* "Program Wrap-Up, Annotated List of Findings," EAI Report 69-2/95/002F (Ft. McClellan, AL: US Army Chemical School, January 1995); John A Mojecki, "Combined Arms in a Nuclear/Chemical Environment (CANE), Phase IIA; Summary Evaluation," ORI, Inc. for Commandant (Ft. McClellan, AL: US Army Chemical School, 31 May 1987); Ali S. Khan, Alexandra M. Levitt, Michael J. Sage, et al., Centers for Disease Control, *Biological and Chemical Terrorism: Strategic Plan for Preparedness and Response Recommendations of the CDC Strategic Planning Workgroup,* 49 (RR04) (21 April 2000), pp. 1–14, available at http://www.cdc.gov/epo/mmwr/preview/mmwrhtml/rr4904a1.htm; Jeffery D. Simon, *Terrorists and the Potential Use of Biological*

Weapons: A Discussion of Possibilities, Rand Report R-3771-AFMIC (Santa Monica, CA: Rand Corporation, December 1989), http://www.rand.org/pubs/reports/2005/R3771.pdf; Brad Roberts, ed., *Terrorism with Chemical and Biological Weapons: Calibrating Risks and Responses* (Washington, DC: Chemical and Biological Arms Control Institute, 1997); Ron Purver, *Chemical and Biological Terrorism: The Threat According to the Open Literature* (Ottawa, ON: Canadian Security Intelligence Service, June 1995); George W. Christopher et al., "Biological Warfare: A Historical Perspective," *JAMA* 278, no. 5 (6 August 1997).

7. For insights into these issues, see Peter R. Lavoy, "Biological Weapons in Adversary Asymmetric Strategies: Overcoming the Knowledge–Policy Problem"; Milton Leitenberg, "Assessing the Biological Weapons and Bioterrorism Threat"; John A. Gilbert, "Calibrating the Threat of Biological Attack"; and Marie Isabelle Chevrier, "Assessing Bioterrorism: Risk, Threat, and Vulnerability; Why Do the Conclusions of the Experts Vary?" (papers presented at the conference "Meeting the Challenges of Bioterrorism: Assessing the Threat and Designing Biodefense Strategies," Center for Security Studies, Swiss Federal Institute of Technology, Fürigen, Switzerland, 22–23 April 2005).

8. For additional papers on this issue, although dated, see "Briefing on the Jason 1997 Summer Study"; Steven M. Block, "Biological Warfare Threats Enabled by Molecular Biology"; and Malcolm R. Dando, "The Impact of Biotechnology," all in *Hype or Reality? The "New Terrorism" and Mass Casualty Attacks,* ed. Brad Roberts, 193–206 (Alexandria, VA: Chemical and Biological Arms Control Institute, 2000). Also see *Combating Terrorism: Need for Comprehensive Threat and Risk Assessments of Chemical and Biological Attacks,* GAO/NSIAD-99-163 (Washington, DC: US GAO), p. 12.

9. Ronald M. Atlas and Richard E. Weller, "Academe and the Threat of Biological Terrorism," *The Chronicle of Higher Education,* 45, no. 49 (13 August 1999).

10. Office of Technology Policy, *Meeting the Challenge US Industry Faces in the 21st Century: The US Biotechnology Industry* (Washington, DC: Department of Commerce, 2000), pp. 9–10.

11. Roberts, *Hype or Reality,* p. 87.

12. For more information, see http://www.defenselink.mil/pubs/prolif/access_tech.html.

13. Chris Bullock, "Biological Terrorism," transcript of a program on biological warfare chaired by Professor D. A. Henderson, director of the Johns Hopkins Center for Biodefense Studies, 29 August 1999, http://abc.net.au/rn/backgroundbriefing/stories/1999/48674.htm.

14. Line-source delivery means a delivery system in which the biological agent is dispersed from a moving ground or air vehicle in a line perpendicular to the direction of the prevailing wind. Point-source is another delivery system.

15. See the forecast in National Intelligence Council, *Global Trends 2015: A Dialogue About the Future with Nongovernment Experts* (Washington, DC: CIA, December 2000), http://www.infowar.net/cia/publications/globaltrends2015/.

16. For a good technical summary of the issues involved in making such weapons, see Office of Technology Assessment, *Background Paper: Technologies*

Underlying Weapons of Mass Destruction, OT A-BP-ISC-115 (Washington, DC: US Government Printing Office, December 1993).

17. Khan, Levitt, Sage, et al., Centers for Disease Control, *Biological and Chemical Terrorism.*

18. The department plays a major role in defense, response, and research. For example, it is actively involved in efforts like an international program to develop a new plague vaccine. See David McGlinchey, "Pentagon to Participate in International Plague Vaccine Effort," GovExec.com, 18 April 2005, http://www.govexec.com/dailyfed/0405/041805d1.htm.

19. For a detailed analysis of some aspects of US homeland defense efforts, see Jennifer E. Lake and Blas Nuñez-Neto, *Homeland Security Department: FY2006 Appropriations,* RL32863 (Washington, DC: Congressional Research Service, 14 April 2005).

20. The best current analysis of the US Department of Homeland Security budget is in the US Office of Management and Budget analytic section of the FY2006 US federal budget, chap. 3, "Homeland Security Funding Analysis." This seems to be the only reliable detailed estimate of costs extending to FY2006.

21. Chemical and Biological Arms Control Institute, *Fighting Bioterrorism: Tracking and Assessing US Government Programs* (Washington, DC: Chemical and Biological Arms Control Institute, 2004).

22. Department of Homeland Security, *Planning Scenarios* (Washington, DC: Homeland Security Council, July 2004), Associated Press, 16 March 2005.

23. "An Open Letter to Elias Zerhouni," *Science* 307 (4 March 2005), http://www.sciencemag.org/feature/misc/microbio/ (accessed 23 March 2005).

24. See http://www.dni.gov/nic/special_globalinfectious.html.

25. Gijs de Vries, Associated Press, 3 June 2005, http://www.homeland security.org/bulletin/060305.htm.

8

More Transparency for a Secure Biodefense

Iris Hunger

The rapid developments in the biosciences, together with the increasing application of biotechnologies and a lack of effective national and international control measures, have resulted in a growing threat from bioweapons, both in the hands of states and in the hands of terrorists. Many of the research, development, production, and testing activities in the biological field are dual-use activities. The differentiation between activities for peaceful—and therefore permitted—purposes and activities for hostile—and therefore prohibited—purposes can be very difficult to ascertain. Therefore, transparency about the activities performed and the willingness of actors to explain them are of the utmost importance in order to allow observers to verify the peaceful nature of such activities.

However, posing as a means to fight bioterrorism, two recent developments have led to a decreasing level of transparency. While transparency—that is, the free exchange of information, samples, and experts, and an open publication policy—has been a value and a goal of the international scientific community for decades, transparent behavior has been restricted since 9/11 by governments, and there are even efforts at self-restriction by the scientific community itself. Conversely, many states have created new or enlarged their existing biodefense programs since the mid-1990s. These often military programs are usually less transparent than civilian activities. This is particularly true where activities are involved that—in the name of biodefense—create offensive capabilities.

In the following, I argue that in order to prevent an erosion of existing international norms against the use of biological agents as weapons, it is essential to reverse the two trends toward more secrecy in the biological field. I analyze in detail the dual-use character of activities in the biological field, noting that not every activity is, in fact, dual use. Further, I explain why transparency is necessary and in which areas of biological activities it is particularly important. I also describe and illustrate two trends toward less transparency. Last, I argue that only if dangerous biological activities are limited to a minimum and carried out in a transparent manner can we prevent the development and use of biological weapons from becoming frequent and widespread.

The Dual-Use Character of Work in the Biological Field

In discussions of biological weapons and the technologies necessary for their development, the term "dual use" appears frequently. Indeed, it is one of the key concepts that anyone dealing with bioweapons control has to memorize and understand. What does dual use mean? It means that the equipment and agents that technicians use, the technologies they apply, and the knowledge they use and generate to produce a biotech product, such as medicines or food, are the same as those used in the production of bioweapons. Dual use is not a characteristic exclusive to biotechnology. To varying degrees, all technologies can be used to good or bad ends. But the degree of dual use is particularly high in the biological sciences: a wide range of activities can be misused for hostile purposes.

Dual-use equipment in the biological field includes such things as fermenters, containment equipment, centrifuges, spray and freeze-drying equipment, aerosol chambers, and DNA synthesizers and sequencers. Biological agents—bacteria, viruses, and fungi—are also dual use. They can be cultured to produce vaccines or to create the fillings for biobombs. Examples of dual-use technologies are genomics, proteomics, micro-array technology, high-throughput screening techniques, fermentation technology, site-specific mutagenesis, and knockout mice. Dual-use knowledge comprises, for instance, laboratory protocols for growing certain agents, designs of buildings for biocontainment facilities, and experimental data on animal aerosol studies. Even the results of biological research can be of dual use. Scientists do not always know whether their planned research activities will yield results that are wide open to misuse for hostile purposes. It is important to note also that knowledge, technology, and equipment are needed together. A fermenter is of no use if one does not know how to operate it. Mastering fermentation technology is of no use if one does not know the specific parameters for producing a particular agent. Dual-use items are found in academic and industrial research laboratories, teaching facilities and hospitals, and industrial production facilities such as antibiotic production facilities and breweries. In general, such items are widespread, and there is a large commercial trade in them. In addition to their civilian use, dual-use items are also used legitimately in biodefense activities.

But not everything in the biological field is suitable for dual use. The dual-use argument has been put forward to justify questionable activities, such as the secret building and testing of a bioweapon bomblet.[1] The argument goes as follows: as long as scientists do this for threat assessment purposes—that is, defensive and therefore peaceful purposes—there is nothing problematic about it. But while it is true that many activities in the biological field have a strong dual-use character, a number of qualifications have to be made. There are certain areas where activities have very limited use for peaceful applications, and there are even areas that cannot be justified with peaceful intentions at all. In general, on a spectrum of activities that ranges from basic research through applied research to production, the further activities move away from basic research, the better their either peaceful or hostile nature can be judged.[2]

Clearly offensive activities are work on bioweapons munitions and on delivery systems for such munitions. Such work can never be justified as peaceful. It is prohibited without qualification by Article I of the Biological and Toxin Weapons Convention (BTWC)—in contrast to agents and toxins that are prohibited only if there is no peaceful justification for their types and quantities:

> Each State Party to this Convention undertakes never in any circumstances to develop, produce, stockpile or otherwise acquire or retain . . . weapons, equipment or means of delivery *designed* to use . . . agents or toxins for hostile purposes or in armed conflict.[3] (emphasis added)

Of extremely limited nonoffensive use is work aimed at enhancing the characteristics of agents that make them more suitable as weapons. For agents to work effectively as bioweapons, they must fulfill certain criteria. States intending to use bioweapons against (the troops of) other states need to have agents that (1) consistently produce a given effect; (2) are manufacturable on a large scale; (3) are stable during production, storage, and transportation; (4) are capable of efficient dissemination; and (5) are stable after dissemination. In addition, the state using the agent needs to be able to protect itself against that agent, and the state against which the agent is used needs to have difficulty detecting and protecting itself against it. Other "desirable" characteristics of bio-weapon agents are (1) a short and predictable incubation period; (2) a short and predictable persistency, if the contaminated area is to be occupied by the attacker; (3) the capability to infect more than one kind of target through more than one entry portal; (4) the capability to be disseminated by various means; and (5) the capability to produce negative psychological effects in the targeted state.[4]

Not all of these characteristics are relevant to terrorist organizations intending to use bioweapons against a civilian population. A list of the "desirable" characteristics of agents for a bioterrorism scenario includes (1) high morbidity and mortality; (2) the potential for person-to-person transmission, either directly or by vector; (3) a low infective dose and high infectivity by aerosol, with a commensurate ability to cause large outbreaks; (4) the ability to contaminate food and water supplies; (5) the lack of a specific diagnostic test and/or effective treatment; (6) the lack of a safe and effective vaccine; (7) the potential to cause anxiety in the public and in health-care workers; and (8) the potential to be weaponized.[5]

Given these "ideal" characteristics of bioweapon agents, in order to enhance the weapons characteristics of agents, scientists would have to (1) enhance the infectivity and pathogenicity of agents; (2) improve transmissibility; (3) alter agents to evade current detection methods; (4) enhance the resistance of agents to current therapeutics, such as antibiotics, or the resistance to host immunological defenses; (5) improve the ability of an agent to remain viable and virulent during production, weaponization, storage, transport, and during and after its release into the environment; (6) facilitate the dissemination of agents as fine particle aerosols, or through the contamination of food or water sources; and (7) assemble oligonucleotides to synthesize the genome of agents.[6] These activities are therefore of extremely limited nonoffensive use.

Besides these two areas of work—weaponization work with no nonoffensive use and work to enhance weapons characteristics with extremely limited nonoffensive use—the following activities are also very close to the offensive side of the spectrum: the mass production of agents that have no commercial application, and the open-air field testing of live biological agents.

The Need for Transparency

Because differentiating between peaceful and hostile activities can be difficult (it has been said frequently that the differentiation often hinges on intentions, which are notoriously difficult to judge), transparency about activities performed and the willingness to explain them is of the utmost importance in order to allow observers to verify the peaceful (or otherwise) nature of biological activities. The level of transparency depends on the availability of relevant information and—in a broader sense—on the openness of a system (a government or a company, for instance) to external observers. The virtues of transparency as a means of improving the effectiveness of control regimes have been touted repeatedly and consistently. In order to regulate states' or nonstate actors' behavior and to assess the effectiveness of such regimes, observers must have information about the activities they want to regulate. Yet most security regimes fail to produce accurate and timely information, making it difficult to assess actors' compliance and the effectiveness of regimes, and to decide on the evolution of a regime and on the sanctioning of violators.[7]

Transparency serves three different purposes. It deters violations of agreed-upon norms. It also reassures states and societies that others are not misusing technologies and goods for prohibited purposes. And it may also reveal problems in a security regime that actors have not recognized before.[8] In addition, transparency has other positive effects. In a 2004 report on transparency and secrecy as regards nuclear weapons, a number of additional positive effects were listed.[9] Transparency has positive effects on foreign relations, arms control and disarmament, and verification. It promotes the peaceful application of technology, and this includes the promotion of trade for peaceful purposes. Transparency allows peer review and free scientific exchange and thereby improves the quality of science. It further allows an informed public debate. If transparency is the norm, then trust in the classification that is applied increases. Transparency makes work in relevant facilities more attractive, thereby ensuring that good people can be recruited. And it decreases costs.

There are several ways to promote transparency. Transparency is fostered first and foremost by the collection, processing, analysis, and dissemination of relevant information. The timely, accurate, and comprehensive reporting by leading states is another important factor that promotes transparency. If reporting is rewarded and disincentives to reporting—for example, requests for excessive amounts of information—are removed, then transparency is encouraged. And a last factor in encouraging transparency is the removal of obstacles to reporting, such as complicated reporting forms.[10]

Judging whether a certain activity in the biological field is peaceful requires information about the context in which the activity is being carried out, and the context can only be understood if relevant information is available. Is the activity done in a military or a civilian facility? What security arrangements are present? Do the scientists involved publish regularly and participate in international conferences? Does the activity fit the stated peaceful aim?[11]

Transparency is particularly important when activities toward the offensive end of the spectrum, as described above, are carried out for peaceful purposes, because such activities are especially prone to misperception. Biodefense programs often fall into this category of work that requires a maximum of transparency. The necessity of transparency for verifying compliance with the prohibition of bioweapons in such cases has been expressed repeatedly. Ken Alibek, who spent much of his life working in the hidden bioweapons program of the former Soviet Union, has said that work on biodefense has to be done openly if at all.[12] Recently, Malcolm Dando explained the need for transparency as follows:

> Great care will be needed to ensure that the research into [the terrorist] chemical and biological threat is seen to be clearly and purely defensive and has no potential for being misperceived as being offensive and thereby fostering the initiation of offensive biological and chemical weapons programmes in other states. Only by maximising transparency in the UK's research into the biological and chemical terrorism threat, demonstrating clearly its purely defensive nature, can this counter-productive result, which will actually increase the threat not diminish it, be avoided.[13]

An important additional reason why transparency is essential, in particular for biodefense programs, is given by Roger Roffey:

> Under certain circumstances, research laboratories can drift from purely defensive research to offensive work for defensive reasons and then, through a gradual process, to purely offensive R&D work. This process can take place over a long period of time, and it can be difficult for individual scientists to recognize that it is happening—especially in large "compartmental" programmes where only those working at the highest levels have the complete picture.[14]

Given the necessity of transparency in the biological field, two developments are essential. Existing transparency in the life sciences must not be decreased; it must be protected. Transparency in biodefense programs must be increased. As illustrated in the following two parts of this chapter, the current developments are, however, completely the opposite of what is needed. The biosciences are becoming less open, and biodefense programs are being enlarged without becoming more transparent.

Toward Less Openness in the Biosciences

Transparency—that is, the free exchange of information, samples, and experts—has been a value and a goal of the scientific community for decades. Four values in particular have guided academic research: (1) a commitment to openness; (2) a resistance to classified research; (3) the maintenance of open relationships between universities and industry, including foreign industry; and (4) the encouragement of relations with foreign students.[15] All of these values are currently under pressure. Since the terrorist events of 2001, governments have restricted openness in the biosciences, and there are even efforts at self-restriction by the scientific community. These developments are by far the most pronounced in the United States. Following the attacks on 11 September 2001 and the anthrax letter attacks shortly after, scientists and politicians began to wonder whether the open exchange of scientific information might not lead to terrorists' more easily acquiring bioweapons.

The move toward less openness is reflected in the reemergence of the category of "sensitive but unclassified" information in the United States in 2002. This categorization allows government agencies to place restrictions on unclassified scientific research and communication while saving themselves the trouble of designating projects as "classified." In January 2002, as part of the effort to safeguard such sensitive but unclassified information, the Bush administration began withdrawing from public access more than sixty-five hundred declassified documents that related to sensitive chemical and biological warfare information.[16] Some have questioned whether the information should have been declassified in the first place, noting that it frequently consists not of basic science but of technical production and process information.[17]

The new regulatory efforts are most actively pursued in the United States. The United States has the largest biotechnology sector, ranking first by a wide margin in terms of number of publications, number of biotech companies, and number of biotech patents. The regulation of this large part of the worldwide biotechnology sector is particularly important in order to avoid the misuse of biotechnology for biowarfare or bioterrorist use. The United States is also by far the most active in research on particularly dangerous agents, thereby creating most of the knowledge that could be misused by terrorists. The biosciences used to be less regulated in the United States than, for instance, in Europe, where discussions about genetically engineered food and reproductive cloning have resulted in a much more guarded attitude toward the life sciences. All relevant laws and regulations that Germany presented during the 2003 Expert Meeting on Security and Oversight of Pathogenic Microorganisms and Toxins in Geneva, for instance, with one exception, date (in their latest amended version) from before the anthrax letter attacks in the United States.[18]

Publication Restrictions

Traditionally in Western states, the results of basic research have been openly published. Control over such research was possible only if selected projects were classified. Increasingly, there are two additional ways in which the exchange of information on research is being limited. One is through the export controlling of information, that is, through the control of the transfer of knowledge to foreign nationals. The export of intangibles has received heightened attention in technology-exporting states. The second way is by attaching prepublication review clauses to grants and contracts.

Experts are also discussing whether certain parts of publications—especially the methods sections of scientific papers—should under certain circumstances be deleted to avoid aiding terrorism. In February 2003, the editors of more than twenty scientific journals announced that they would review and then edit or reject articles that could endanger national security. This voluntary self-censorship is seen by some as a response to the threat of government censorship in the United States.[19] A security review is likely to increase editors' awareness of the security aspects of publications. While it might be burdensome, the little evidence available suggests that it has not significantly influenced publications. It is unclear whether this is due to the fact that publications are not security sensitive, or because contentious publications are withheld.[20]

The scientific community has been protesting against restrictions on the publication of research. Ronald Atlas, president of the American Society for Microbiology, has argued that placing major barriers in the path of the flow of information ultimately may contribute to terrorism by interfering with our ability to prepare and respond to the threat of the misuse of science by bioterrorists . . . If scientists cannot assess and replicate the work of their colleagues, the very foundation of science is eroded . . . Indeed the risk to public health and safety may be greater from restricting research than from allowing the publication of research that could be read by a wrongdoer. Restricting research findings may in fact have no effect on deterring terrorists.[21]

Restrictions on scientists' ability to publish their results, to have them peer reviewed, and thus to improve the quality of science go directly against the traditional value of transparency in the sciences and against the need for transparency in order to allow the verification of the peaceful nature of activities in the biological field.

The Regulation of Work with Dangerous Pathogens

Regulations on work with dangerous pathogens used to focus on avoiding harm to the researchers and the environment. The United States began to tighten regulations after a microbiologist in Ohio ordered plague bacteria through the mail from the American Type Culture Collection in 1995, presumably for terrorist purposes. Since that incident, researchers have had to notify the authorities of the shipping and receipt of selected agents and toxins and justify their procurement. Since the anthrax letter attacks in 2001, the rules on work with pathogens have been further tightened. Now all facilities and persons possessing, using, or transferring selected live pathogens have to register with the US government. Registered facilities must make inventories of their pathogens, keep track of who is working with them and where they are working with them, and implement safeguards to prevent unauthorized access. Registered persons have to get approval from the US Federal Bureau of Investigation before they are allowed to work with pathogens under regulation. It seems that the new regulations have had a chilling effect on US academic research. The burden of the resulting paperwork has created disincentives to work with selected agents. And there are even indications that laboratories have destroyed rare archival stocks of agents that could be useful for forensic investigations and biodefense work.[22]

Tracking Foreign Scientists and Students

Since 2001, certain categories of persons in the United States have been prohibited from working with selected pathogens. Among those are people—excluding permanent residents—from countries on the US list of states that sponsor terrorism.[23] Those countries are currently Cuba, Iran, Libya, North Korea, Sudan, and Syria.

In addition, US entry procedures and the enforcement of such procedures have been tightened. This has resulted in declining numbers of foreign students enrolling in US colleges and universities. The countries most affected by these measures are China and India. Graduate-level applications from students from these two countries have declined by 76 percent and 58 percent, respectively, between the fall of 2003 and the fall of 2004.[24] The data for fall 2006 indicates that this downward trend has been stopped, although the current number of international graduate-level applications is still much lower than it was in 2003.[25] Increased security has also discouraged students and scholars from attending scientific conferences in the United States.

The Increase in Secret Biodefense and Bioweapons Activities

Many states have created new or enlarged their existing biodefense programs since the early 1990s. Since 1992, Australia, Belarus, Belgium, Italy, Japan, Poland, South Africa, Spain, and Switzerland have declared that they have initiated a biodefense program.[26] In general, these often military programs are less transparent than civilian activities. This is particularly true where activities are involved that—in the name of biodefense, for example threat assessment—create offensive capabilities. Under the BTWC's confidence-building measures, states have to declare the existence of their biodefense activities, general information about them, and the facilities involved in such activities. Biodefense funding has risen substantially in many countries that have provided information on such programs, although not to the same extent as in the United States. Australia spent A$250,000 in 1994 and A$1.65 million in 2002. France spent F14 million in 1991 and F8 million in 1999. Russia declared that it had spent 50 million rubles in 1998 and 165 million rubles in 2002. Britain declared that it had spent £10 million in 1991, compared to £24 million in 2002. Spending in Canada and Germany stayed roughly the same between 1991 and 2002.[27]

The increase in biodefense activities is again particularly pronounced in the United States. The US biodefense program was essentially unclassified after the unilateral renunciation of the offensive biowarfare program in 1969. Only one small classified component remained within the

Department of Defense that dealt with analytical threat assessment. Sometime in the 1990s this changed; when exactly and why remains unclear.[28] Now, not only is the Department of Defense running a biodefense program, but the Central Intelligence Agency (CIA), the Department of Energy, the Environmental Protection Agency, the Department of Health and Human Services, the Department of Agriculture, and the newly established Department of Homeland Security all have such programs. Whole projects have obviously been carried out in secrecy, although some have been revealed over the last few years.

Three secret programs were uncovered in the fall of 2001 by the *New York Times*. In order to assess whether it was possible to detect the secret setting up of a bioweapon agent production facility, the Defense Threat Reduction Agency of the Department of Defense initiated Project Bacus. Microbiologists and engineers purchased components on the open market, built a fully functional facility, and in two test runs in 1999 and 2000 produced simulated bioweapons agents.[29] In 1997, the CIA initiated Project Clear Vision, under which it secretly built and tested a model of a Soviet bioweapon bomblet.[30] The US Defense Intelligence Agency of the Department of Defense carried out Project Jefferson, aimed at producing genetically engineered anthrax, replicating earlier work by Russian scientists after failing to obtain a sample of the manipulated strain from Russia.[31]

None of these three projects was reported to member states of the BTWC, as was required by the confidence-building measures under that treaty. There is no security requirement to keep secret the fact that these projects were or are being carried out for threat assessment purposes. Transparency would have supported the claim that these activities were defensive in character. Or, as James Leonard, head of the US delegation that negotiated the BTWC, said, public disclosure is important evidence that the United States is proceeding with a "clean heart."[32] Of course, the details of the three projects need to be kept secret, as detailed information could aid proliferators.

The investigation of the anthrax letter attacks in 2001 revealed the previously unknown fact that the United States has continued to produce dried, weaponized anthrax spores for testing purposes since 1969. Why this was necessary and how much was produced remain unclear. In addition, the United States began in the early 1990s to study explosive and nonexplosive means of delivering dangerous microorganisms as aerosols. For that purpose, three existing large aerosol test chambers were adapted for use with biological agents. This work had not been classified but was known about by only a small technical community.

Both activities have not been reported under the confidence-building measures of the BTWC.[33]

Something that the United States did report in its confidence-building measures submission of 2000 is its design and fabrication of simulated bioweapon warheads. The activities conducted in one of the biodefense programs were described as follows:

> Analysis of earlier known or suspected warhead designs, intelligence estimates and engineering judgment were the basis for postulating the ABO [agents of biological origin] threat warheads. Simulated threat warhead mechanicals were designed and fabricated . . . The simulated threat warhead mechanicals employed in this program were not operational and no aspect of the program makes them either operational or flight worthy designs.[34]

In 2002, the National Biodefense Analysis and Countermeasures Center in Fort Detrick, Maryland, was established. One of the four planned centers—the Biothreat Characterization Center—will carry out a range of studies, including those on genetic engineering, the susceptibility to current therapeutics, aerosol dynamics, and the duplication of threat scenarios, which together "may constitute development in the guise of threat assessment . . . Development is prohibited by the Biological Weapons Convention."[35] The document from which this information was gleaned was briefly placed on a US Department of Defense website. It was quickly removed after it came to the attention of arms control organizations, and it can now be accessed only at a nongovernmental website.[36]

Problematic also are US efforts aimed at exploring biological antimaterial and nonlethal weapons. Antimaterial bioweapons are weapons that degrade or destroy military materials or infrastructure, such as plastics, rubber, or petroleum products. Generally, they are microorganisms genetically modified to enhance the digestion of targeted materials.[37] In 2001, the US Army filed a patent application for a "rifle-launched nonlethal cargo dispenser" that could be used to disperse aerosols, including "biological agents." This, of course, constitutes a weapon that is a delivery system for biological agents, which is clearly prohibited under the BTWC.[38] The US government has in the past refused to provide certain documents on its nonlethal chemical and biological weapons activities to civil society organizations and has ordered the removal of certain such documents from independent websites.

Besides these specific cases of problematic biodefense and bioweapons activities, the overall work with bioweapons-relevant pathogens has increased dramatically since 9/11. For 2005, US$7.6 billion has been requested for civilian biodefense work in the United States, compared to US$414 million in 2001.[39] Work on agents of bioweapon concern has received an enormous increase in funding, while funding for other diseases has been cut considerably. Funding for bacterial agents of bioweapon concern—anthrax, glanders, melioidosis, brucella, and plague—has increased from about US$7.5 million in the period 1999–2001 to about US$185.5 million in the period 2002–2004, in other words an almost twenty-five-fold increase. Funding for viral agents of bioweapon concern—Ebola, Lassa, Marburg, and smallpox—has increased from about US$6 million in the period 1999–2001 to about US$120 million in the period 2002–2004, a twentyfold increase. Funding for work on HIV (human immunodeficiency virus) and tuberculosis dropped by 20 percent during those years. But not only is work on those dangerous pathogens increasing dramatically; the number of people gaining knowledge on how to deal with these agents is also growing drastically. On average, more than 96 percent of the principal investigators in projects on bioweapon agents funded by the US National Institute of Allergy and Infectious Diseases (NIAID)—which is the main institute of the National Institutes of Health that supports biodefense research—have never before received funds for work on those agents.[40] The NIAID developed more than fifty biodefense initiatives in 2002 and 2003, 75 percent of which were new.[41]

Examples of particularly dangerous paths of research on bioweapons-relevant agents are the ongoing work on smallpox and other pox viruses, and the reconstruction of the 1918 influenza virus. Both threaten to bring natural killers that (fortunately) no longer roam the world back to life. While naturally occurring smallpox was eradicated in 1977, stocks of the virus remained in two laboratories, one in the United States and one in Russia. The destruction of the last stocks had been planned for 1999, but with the growing fear that smallpox could be used as a weapon, there was disagreement over whether to destroy the last stocks or allow further research. Final destruction was first delayed until 2002, and then indefinitely. The smallpox research agenda has been enlarged dramatically since the mid-1990s. Research guidelines on work with smallpox—which preclude, among other things, genetic engineering of the virus—are currently under pressure.[42] Recommendations to relax those guidelines—to allow certain forms of genetic engineering of smallpox—were discussed at the World Health Assembly in May 2005 but have not yet been approved. Instead, the Advisory Committee on Variola Virus Research was asked to revisit and review its recommendations.[43] Hopefully, future work with smallpox will not include the distribution of substantive portions of smallpox virus DNA to numerous new laboratories or create genetic constructs that include both smallpox virus DNA and the DNA of other orthopoxviruses.

In the mid-1990s, scientists in the United States started work on reconstructing the 1918 influenza virus. The 1918 influenza virus was particularly aggressive. It killed an estimated 20 million to 40 million people worldwide. Scientists with the US Armed Forces Institute of Pathology were the first to isolate and sequence genetic material from the 1918 influenza virus.[44] They then teamed up with other scientists and succeeded in creating a live virus that contained two genes of the 1918 influenza virus that proved to be very lethal in animal experiments.[45] The researchers then pressed ahead with their work by making a complete reconstruction of the virus, which turned out to kill mice faster than any other influenza virus ever tested before.[46] The scientists argued that such work was necessary in order to see whether existing drugs were effective against such aggressive types of influenza. However, the very threat that they are trying to protect us from is one that they created in the first place.

The exponentially growing research on dangerous pathogens comes at a time when many federal grants and contracts in the United States require tighter prepublication reviews and background checks on any participating foreign researchers. Many awards contain publication restrictions or a variety of clauses restricting the sharing of research results, primarily with foreign nationals.[47] This has introduced an increasing level of secrecy into scientific biodefense work.

Reversing the Trend:
Moving Away from Increased Secrecy

Because of the difficulties in differentiating between peaceful and hostile activities in the biological field, transparency is vital. Transparency is particularly important when work toward the offensive end of the spectrum of biological activities is carried out for peaceful purposes, because such work is especially prone to misperception. Biodefense programs often fall into this category of work, and this necessitates a maximum of transparency. Current developments, however, run counter to the need for more transparency. Transparency—that is, the free exchange of information, samples, and experts, and an open publication policy—has been a value and a goal of the international scientific community for decades; however, it has been limited significantly since

9/11 by governments and to some extent by the scientific community itself. Further, many states have created new or expanded their existing biodefense programs since the mid-1990s, increasing activities carried out in secrecy. These two trends have to be reversed. Transparency in the biosciences has to be protected. Transparency of particularly dangerous dual-use activities has to be increased.

Western states and their allies face new opportunities and also bear a significant amount of the responsibility. Most of the sensitive research projects are still being done in these states, even though biotechnologies are rapidly expanding across the globe. Western states therefore still have a chance to influence how biological research is conducted worldwide in the future and whether or not the hostile use of biotechnology will become a reality on a large scale.

A number of points for action can be identified: (1) projects on weaponization must be stopped; (2) a common understanding has to be developed as to which biodefense projects are so dangerously close to the line between offensive and defensive activities that they cannot be carried out without strict international oversight; international legally binding standards for the review and continuous oversight of such programs have to be developed; (3) transparency needs to be the rule in biological research and development; this does not mean, however, that proliferation-relevant information has to be disclosed; (4) Western states and, in particular, the United States, must lead by example with a special focus on how they design and carry out their biodefense programs; and (5) civil society must push for transparency in biodefense programs, judging the conduct of such projects against the principle of "maximum disclosure."

The dual-use activities that characterize most of the biosciences require transparency so that a nation's citizens and the international community can determine whether or not these activities are peaceful in nature. Transparency is the basis on which bioweapons control—that is, the regulation of access to and the use of biotechnologies—must rest in the long run. It is therefore critically important that we work toward a reversal of the two trends toward more secrecy described above. Only then can we prevent the erosion of the existing international norms against the use of biological agents as weapons.

Notes

1. Milton Leitenberg, *The Problem of Biological Weapons* (Stockholm: Swedish National Defence College, 2004), pp. 180–181.

2. For a comprehensive overview on the distinction of offensive from defensive biological weapons research, see Milton Leitenberg, "Distinguishing Offensive from Defensive Biological Weapons Research," *Critical Reviews in Microbiology* 29, no. 3 (July–September 2003): 223–257.

3. The text of the 1972 Biological and Toxin Weapons Convention can be found at http://www.opbw.org.

4. Stockholm International Peace Research Institute, *The Problem of Chemical and Biological Warfare: A Study of the Historical, Technical, Military, Legal and Political Aspects of CBW, and Possible Disarmament Measures,* vol. 2, *CB Weapons Today* (Stockholm: Almqvist and Wiksell, 1973), p. 311.

5. Malcolm R. Dando, *The United States National Institute of Allergy and Infectious Diseases (NIAID) Research Programme on Biodefense: A Summary and Review of Varying Assessments,* Science and Technology Report, no. 1 (Bradford, UK: Department of Peace Studies, University of Bradford, July 2004), p. 8, http://www.brad.ac.uk/acad/sbtwc/ST_Reports/ST_Report_No_1.pdf (accessed 7 April 2005).

6. A similar list of "weaponization-related goals" is provided in Raymond Zilinskas and Jonathan Tucker, "Limiting the Contribution of the Open Scientific Literature to the Biological Weapons Threat," *Journal of Homeland Security* (December 2002), http://www.homelandsecurity.org/journal/Articles/Tucker .html#end2 (accessed 5 April 2005).

7. Ronald Mitchell, "Sources of Transparency: Information Systems in International Regimes," *International Studies Quarterly* 42, no. 1 (March 1998): 109–130.

8. Ann Florini, "A New Role for Transparency," in *Arms Control: New Approaches to Theory and Policy,* ed. Nancy Gallagher, 51–72 (London: Cass, 1998).

9. Annette Schaper, *Looking for a Demarcation Between Nuclear Transparency and Nuclear Secrecy,* PRIF Reports, no. 68 (Frankfurt: Peace Research Institute, 2004).

10. Ronald Mitchell, "Sources of Transparency."

11. Lists of signatures for bioweapons related activities are provided in Leitenberg, *Problem of Biological Weapons.*

12. See Judith Miller, Stephen Engelberg, and William Broad, *Germs: Biological Weapons and America's Secret War* (New York: Simon and Schuster, 2002), p. 310.

13. Malcolm R. Dando, "The Need for Transparency in Defence Research on Chemical and Biological Threats," memorandum to the Department of Peace Studies, University of Bradford, UK, 25 February 2003, http://www.publications .parliament.uk/pa/cm200203/cmselect/cmsctech/415/415ap36.htm (accessed 29 March 2005).

14. Roger Roffey, "Biological Weapons and Potential Indicators of Offensive Biological Weapon Activities," in *SIPRI Yearbook 2004: Armaments, Disarmament and International Security* (Oxford: Oxford University Press, 2004), pp. 557–571, p. 562.

15. Eugene B. Skolnikoff, "Research Universities and National Security: Can Traditional Values Survive?" in *Science and Technology in a Vulnerable World: A Special Supplement to the 2003 Yearbook,* ed. Albert H. Teich,

Stephen D. Nelson, Stephen J. Lita, and Amanda E. Hunt (Washington, DC: American Association for the Advancement of Science, 2002), pp. 65–73, p. 66.

16. Ryan Ricks, "Science and Security in the Post-9/11 Environment: 'Sensitive but Unclassified' Information," American Association for the Advancement of Science, July 2004, http://www.aaas.org/spp/post911/sbu/ (accessed 8 April 2005).

17. Leitenberg, *Problem of Biological Weapons*, p. 174.

18. BWC/MSP.2003/MX/WP.13, "Legislation in the Federal Republic of Germany Related to Security and Oversight of Pathogenic Microorganisms and Toxins" (working paper prepared by the Federal Republic of Germany, 28 July 2003), http://www.opbw.org/new_process/mx2003/bwc_msp.2003_mx_wp13.pdf.

19. Ricks, "Science and Security."

20. Julie E. Fischer, *Stewardship or Censorship? Balancing Biosecurity, the Public's Health, and the Benefits of Scientific Openness* (Washington, DC: Henry L. Stimson Center, February 2006), pp. 69–73.

21. Ronald Atlas, "Conducting Research During the War on Terrorism: Balancing Openness and Security," testimony of the American Society for Microbiology before the House of Representatives Committee on Science, 10 October 2002, http://www.house.gov/science/hearings/full02/oct10/atlas.htm (accessed 11 April 2005).

22. Jonathan B. Tucker, *Biosecurity: Limiting Terrorist Access to Deadly Pathogens,* Peaceworks, no. 52 (Washington, DC: United States Institute of Peace, November 2003), pp. 19–21.

23. Ibid., p. 20.

24. Allison Chamberlain, "Science and Security in the Post-9/11 Environment: Foreign Students and Scholars," American Association for the Advancement of Science, July 2004, http://www.aaas.org/spp/post911/visas/ (accessed 8 April 2005).

25. Council of Graduate Schools, "Findings from 2006 CGS International Graduate Admissions Survey, Phase I: Applications," March 2006, http://www.cgsnet.org/portals/0/pdf/R_intlapps06_1.pdf (accessed 15 June 2006).

26. Iris Hunger, *Confidence Building Needs Transparency: A Summary of Data Submitted Under the Bioweapons Convention's Confidence Building Measures, 1987–2003,* Sunshine Project, September 2005, http://www.biological-arms-control.org/download/hunger_CBM (accessed 14 October 2005).

27. Ibid.

28. Mark Wheelis and Malcolm Dando, "Back to Bioweapons?" *Bulletin of the Atomic Scientists* 59, no. 1 (January/February 2003): 40–46.

29. Joan Lowy, "Secret Desert Project on Anthrax," Scripps Howard News Service, 30 October 2001, http://www.anthraxinvestigation.com/shns.html.

30. Judith Miller, Stephen Engelberg, and William Broad, "U.S. Germ Warfare Research Pushes Treaty Limits," *New York Times,* 4 September 2001.

31. Ibid.

32. Ibid.

33. Leitenberg, *Problem of Biological Weapons,* pp. 181–182.

34. DDA/BWC/2000/CBM, "Annual Information Exchange of States Parties on Confidence-Building Measures, as Agreed at the Third Review Conference of

the Parties to the Convention," United Nations Department for Disarmament Affairs, p. 648.

35. Milton Leitenberg, James Leonard, and Richard Spertzel, "Biodefense Crossing the Line," *Politics and the Life Sciences* 22, no. 2 (17 May 2004): 2–3.

36. See "Leading Edge of Biodefense: The National Biodefense Analysis and Countermeasures Center," http://www.cbwtransparency.org/archive/nbacc .pdf (accessed 8 April 2005).

37. Sunshine Project, *US Special Forces Seek Genetically Engineered Bio-weapons*, 12 August 2002, http://www.sunshine-project.org (accessed 11 April 2005).

38. David Ruppe, "United States: Army to Revise Patent amid Treaty Violation Concerns," Global Security Newswire, 28 May 2003, http://www.nti.org/ d_newswire/issues/2003/5/28/1s.html (accessed 11 April 2005).

39. Jonathan B. Tucker, "Biological Threat Assessment: Is the Cure Worse Than the Disease?" *Arms Control Today* 34, no. 8 (October 2004), http://www .armscontrol.org/act/2004_10/Tucker.asp (accessed 11 April 2005).

40. Sunshine Project, *Some Statistics About the US Biodefense Program and Public Health,* http://www.sunshine-project.org (accessed 8 April 2005).

41. Dando, *United States National Institute of Allergy and Infectious Diseases (NIAID) Research Programme on Biodefense*, p. 5.

42. Sunshine Project, "The Genetic Engineering of Smallpox: WHO's Retreat from the Eradication of Smallpox Virus and Why It Should Be Stopped" (briefing paper, Third World Network/Sunshine Project, April 2005), http:// www.smallpoxbiosafety.org/poxpaper.pdf (accessed 7 April 2005).

43. Edward Hammond and Lim Li Ching, "No WHA Approval for Expanding Smallpox Virus Research," 26 May 2005, http://www.smallpoxbio safety.org/news260505.html (accessed 26 August 2005).

44. Jeffrey K. Taubenberger et al., "Initial Genetic Characterization of the 1918 'Spanish' Influenza Virus," *Science* 275, no. 5307 (21 March 1997): 1793–1796.

45. Terrence M. Tumpey et al., "Existing Antivirals Are Effective Against Influenza Viruses with Genes from the 1918 Pandemic Virus," *PNAS* 99, no. 21 (15 October 2002): 13849–13854, http://www.pnas.org/cgi/content/full/99/21/ 13849 (accessed 26 August 2005). See also Sunshine Project, "Recreating the Spanish Flu?" (briefing paper, 9 October 2003, http://www.sunshine-project.org (accessed 11 April 2005).

46. Debora Mackenzie, "Bird Flu Warning from Replica Virus," *New Scientist* (8 October 2005): 16.

47. Allison Chamberlain, "Science and Security in the Post-9/11 Environment: Federal Grants and Contracts," American Association for the Advancement of Science, August 2004, http://www.aaas.org/spp/post911/grants/ (accessed 8 April 2005).

Part 4

Conclusion

9

Securing Society Against the Risk of Bioterrorism

ANDREAS WENGER

BIOTERRORISM REMAINS AN ELUSIVE THREAT AND A TROUBLING POLICY ISSUE. A shifting problem, it will be on the agenda of policymakers and communities of experts for years to come. Shaped by rapid technological advances in the life sciences, bioterrorism will evolve in a political environment marked by asymmetric conflicts and persistent political violence, and in a social environment characterized by national health infrastructures that are becoming increasingly vulnerable to the risk of a rapid global spread of natural diseases.

This book has shown that bioterrorism, although a potential global threat, is a largely unsubstantiated one. Given the high level of uncertainty about the nature and relevance of the threat, the design of sensible policies that secure our communities against bioterrorism remains an extraordinarily daunting task. The multifaceted nature of the problem demands policy coordination between public, private, and international actors across a wide range of policy fields (including security, public health, and the regulation of research and development) and at all levels of policy (local, national, and international). Today, policy for the successful assessment and management of bioterrorism is made in an increasingly pluralist international system shaped by economic liberalization and privatization, rapid technological advances, persistent political conflict, and increased societal expectations.

Picking up the major themes of this book, this chapter discusses what I deem to be the three major conclusions to be drawn from the authors' findings. First, a good part of the problem of understanding bioterrorism resides in the uncertainties about the potential actors and their potential capabilities. Second, although the threat may be exaggerated and manipulated, it can neither be denied by experts nor ignored by policymakers. But at the same time, there is a real danger of overreaction—potentially with unintended consequences. Third, a key policy challenge to managing this particular threat is the difficulty of striking the right balance between investments in technical security and safety and those in national and international security; and between resources assigned to biodefense and those assigned to the prevention of natural diseases. Securing modern societies against bioterrorism necessitates new governance patterns, because protecting populations against bioterrorism is a responsibility that must be shared by public and private stakeholders at the local, federal, and international levels.

Understanding the Threat: The Complexity of Bioterrorism

Protecting populations against the potential malicious use of microorganisms or toxins by a potentially wide range of malevolent actors is beyond the scope of traditional approaches to threat analysis. Both the intent and capability of potential actors—whether state or nonstate actors—are highly uncertain and not predictable in the same way that the military threats of the Cold War were. Part of the problem is the ambiguous nature of biotechnological processes and products: many are dual use, making it often difficult to separate peaceful from malevolent applications and activities.

In examining the bioterrorism threat, five trends, discussed in the chapters of this book, are of particular relevance to the current debate: First, uncertainty is a key characteristic of bioterrorism. Second, there is insufficient historical data to deduce solid estimates for the future. Third, the rapid development in the biosciences is increasing the knowledge base available to potential malevolent users of bioweapons. Fourth, the general trend toward mass casualty terrorism is heightening the concern of experts that terrorists may become more interested in biowarfare. And fifth, US policy, which is moving toward more secrecy in both the life sciences and in US biodefense programs, is having worldwide repercussions (a result of transnational policy diffusion).

Uncertainty as a Key Characteristic of the Threat

There is widespread agreement among experts that bioterrorism assessments are based on data and information that is marked by a high level of uncertainty. Current security policy for most nations reflects the complexity of—and concomitant uncertainty relating to—ongoing technological developments and the political and social impacts of new technologies and scientific results. The fact that there are clearly limits to our understanding of the threat due to the complexity and unpredictability of bioterrorism has important repercussions for the policy process, where traditional planning assumptions and standard procedures can no longer be applied. As a consequence, the policy process is often perceived as incoherent and as shaped by political rhetoric and media attention rather than by an informed public policy debate based on a realistic definition of the parameters of the problem.

Ambiguity emanates from the diversity of potential agents, targets, effects, and methods of attack and release. There are many agents that could be used as bioweapons. In theory, malevolent actors could use bacteria—including anthrax, plague, and tularemia—or viruses—for example, smallpox, polio, and viral encephalitis. In addition, a range of toxins could also be deliberately released—those mentioned most often include botulinum toxin and ricin toxin, and also fungi and rickettsia.[1] Depending on the type of agents, they can be used against humans, animals, or plants. The impact on humans of attacks on animals and plants—so-called agroterrorism—is largely economic,[2] while the impact of direct attacks on humans ranges from a temporary reduction of physical and psychological abilities to serious illness to life-threatening disease with eventual death. The most important difference between various types of possible bioattacks against humans is that between attacks perpetrated against individuals or specific communities and those perpetrated against the masses. Further, there is a significant difference between contagious viruses and noncontagious bacteria or toxins. Recently, naturally occurring outbreaks of viruses such as SARS (severe acute respiratory syndrome) in humans and foot-and-mouth disease in animals—raising the specter of past pandemics like the Spanish flu—have illustrated the far-reaching consequences of contagious epidemics.[3]

A crucial difference that should be considered in bioterrorism threat assessments is that between malevolent actors who are likely to perpetrate a single attack and those deemed capable of attacking several times in a row or in several locations simultaneously. Equally relevant, especially for crisis management professionals, is the difference between overt and covert attacks.[4] Further, there is a wide range of methods available for delivering a biological weapon to its target, including the contamination of single objects, as was the case in the anthrax letters of 2001; the contamination of foodstuffs, as was the case in the attacks of the Rajneesh group in The Dalles, Oregon, in 1984; and the highly sophisticated aerosol delivery, a technology so far mainly developed in state programs.

Ambiguity in terms of potential agents, targets, effects, and methods of attack and release translates into poor knowledge about the scope and the sophistication of the potential biowarfare programs of both state and nonstate groups. It is extremely complicated to trace biological weapons programs. Moreover, it is often difficult to establish whether biological weapons have been used or not.

A Largely Unsubstantiated Threat: Insufficient Historical Data

In contrast to chemical and nuclear weapons, biological weapons have not been subject to public debate; nor has there been any major precedent for their use in warfare in the twentieth century. Aside from the events related to the Rajneesh group[5] and Amerithrax,[6] bioterrorism is a threat without precedent, too. At the beginning of the twenty-first century, the extremely low incidence of real biological events stands in marked contrast to the amount of political rhetoric and media attention that have accompanied the very large number of hoaxes since Amerithrax in particular. Experts tend to agree that insufficient historical data on bioterrorism events precludes a reliable prediction of future bioterrorism events.

Given the lack of historical data, the few real cases that have occurred are given a disproportionate significance in attempts to gain a better understanding of the threat. Of crucial importance in this regard are the anthrax letters of 2001. Whether the perpetrator, who is still at large, came from within the US government's own biodefense program or was acting independently of it will have important repercussions on the way we assess the entire phenomenon of the future biological threat.

As a result of Amerithrax, twenty-two people fell ill and five died. However, over thirty thousand people were preventively treated with antibiotics.[7] One letter—that sent to US senator Tom Daschle—contained enough pathogens to kill hundreds or even thousands of people. However, warnings with the word "anthrax" on the envelopes suggest that the perpetrator or perpetrators had not intended to cause high lethality. The means of delivery—the postal service—allowed the perpetrators to undertake anonymous, targeted attacks against specific individuals. Nevertheless, the distribution of threatening letters had huge consequences for the economy and the community: the US Postal Service faced billions of dollars in damages, and numerous buildings had to be decontaminated.[8]

The Rapid Development of the
Biosciences and of Biotechnological Applications

Experts agree that the ongoing revolution in the biosciences and the increasing commercial use of biotechnological applications are lowering the technical obstacles to bioweapons research, development, production, testing, and potential use. Much of the new material and processes produced as a result of advancements in the life sciences have dual-use capabilities. Critical expertise, facilities, and skills are increasingly in the hands of private bodies, spreading rapidly around the globe. However, it is unclear how and when the increasingly organized development and diffusion of materials and expertise with potential bioweapons capability will affect the choices of malevolent state or nonstate actors.

Today's bioterrorist threat is predominantly the product of former state offensive bioweapons programs. These state programs generated stocks of weapons-capable pathogens and relevant expertise that, if disseminated—either deliberately or by accident—could allow nonstate actors to use bioweapons.[9] Today, the spread of biotechnological expertise and sensitive material is being accelerated by the expansion of state biodefense research programs. At the same time, the number of actors in the private sector with expertise in dealing with potential bioweapons agents adds considerably to the complexity of the problem.[10]

Advances in the life sciences—for example, in microbiology and gene technology—might greatly ease the acquisition and development of bioweapons. And the decoding of the human genome has paved the way for as yet unpredictable developments.[11] Future efforts might lead to the development of new weapons-capable agents, or they could produce new versions of classical bioweapons agents tailored into near-perfect bioweapons.[12] Gene technology may allow the future manipulation of bacteria to render them resistant to antibiotics. And the range of available hosts might be increased, so that, for example, a virus that affects only animals today might be manipulated in such a way that it crosses over to humans. Finally, scientists may also develop so-called stealth bioweapons, agents that remain inactive after infection and that can be activated at a later stage by a so-called trigger.

The most likely actors to develop such technologies for malevolent purposes are states. Terrorist groups hardly have the resources or opportunities to engage in ambitious research and development activities in the field of molecular genetic modification—even the handling of classical bioweapons is too great a challenge for them. If terrorist groups should decide to work with pathogens, then we can expect their efforts to be limited to classical agents. Nevertheless, we should not discount the fact that the desired effect might well be achieved with relatively simple resources.

Mass Casualty Terrorism and Terrorist Interest in Biowarfare

Although the history of bioterrorism is largely one of nonuse, experts acknowledge that some terrorist groups, most notably Al-Qaida, have shown an interest in acquiring bioweapons. Experts are unsure, however, about whether or not this interest is part of a larger, general trend toward mass casualty terrorism as a result of the increasingly networked ideology of a global jihad. The recent increased lethality of terrorism can be verified in the statistical data, and some experts view this trend as the result of the emergence of a dominant religious component in the motivations of terrorist groups, a trend, they argue, that points toward an increased likelihood of terrorist attacks with weapons of mass destruction.[13]

Yet other experts warn that the political rhetoric surrounding so-called superterrorism obscures the fact that the motivation of most terrorist groups is still basically political and that most terrorist attacks are of a conventional nature, combining the power of explosives with a fully globalized media.[14] There is also controversy about how much technical expertise it takes to acquire bioweapons capabilities. Close analysis of these factors helps explain the differences between the various experts' policy prescriptions—prescriptions that are based mostly on the same original bioterrorism threat assessments.

For many years, noted experts and high-ranking government officials assumed that bioterrorism could be perpetrated with little expertise and limited resources. Government officials propagated the view that university graduates and biologists with average expertise could build bioweapons in improvised laboratories in their cellars, using recipes from the Internet.[15] This view is no longer commonly held and is, in fact, strongly refuted by many experts. The technical obstacles to the acquisition of bioweapons should not be underestimated, as shown by the failed attempts of the Aum Shinrikyo group in the 1990s and by the more recent results of tests of ricin that were found in European Al-Qaida cells.[16]

Nevertheless, attempted and failed bioweapons attacks are still relevant to assessments of the threat. From a security policy perspective, such cases show that certain terrorist actors have, in fact, shown an interest in acquiring such weapons. Of particular concern is the discovery of professional microbiology literature and rudimentary laboratory equipment in Afghanistan and the recruitment by Al-Qaida of individuals with expertise and access to the scientific community. From the perspective of law enforcement, this case and other failed attacks show that it is very difficult to uncover cases where bioweapons have been successfully produced. In the Al-Qaida case, it became evident that the group's program was both more advanced and more sophisticated than US intelligence had expected at the time.

There is little doubt that gaining access to bioweapons capabilities has become, at least in theory, easier as a result of the spread of new technologies and of changes in terrorists' modus operandi. Social and economic developments, like globalization, and technical achievements, like the Internet and mobile telephony, have fundamentally changed terrorism as a method of warfare in the past few decades. Terrorist groups benefit from global news reporting by the mass media, are loosely connected to each other via the Internet, have easier access through electronic media to information and goods, and are able to build up complex financing structures.[17]

However, it is unclear whether there will be changes in terrorists' motivation to use bioweapons in the future, or if such change has not, in fact, already begun.[18] Evaluating the motivation of actors is a huge challenge for intelligence and counterterrorism specialists. When they analyze the intentions of terrorists, they have to take into account a wide range of factors. They have to assess, for example, whether a group might possess a pathogen, whether it has the skills necessary to produce one, the stage of development of a possible weapon, and, in particular, the inclination or willingness of a group to use a pathogen.

A terrorist group's decision to acquire bioweapons may not necessarily represent a rejection of the common motivation of terrorists, outlined by Brian Jenkins: "Terrorists don't want a lot of people to die, but a lot of people to watch."[19] A large number of victims or widespread damage is not necessarily the key attraction of bioweapons. A terrorist group or state actor may contemplate the use of bioterrorism because of the huge psychological, societal, and economic impact of bioweapons use. Such attacks always gain a vast amount of attention, regardless of whether their effects are big or small. Events in 2001 and since are indeed proof of the big amount of media space given even to hoaxes.[20]

The recent terrorist attacks in Iraq, London, Madrid, and Egypt show the continued popularity of conventional attacks, in particular of suicide attacks. The uncertainty from the fact that terrorists have easier access to bioweapons technologies these days and that there is proof that some terrorists are showing an interest in biowarfare is a huge challenge to policymakers attempting to formulate policies to prevent and manage bioterrorism.

US Policy Change: The Integration of National Security and the Life Sciences

Any assessment of the bioterrorism threat should be based on the recognition that the diffusion of bioweapons is directly affected by the policies of Western states in general and of the United States in particular. The integration of national security and the life sciences in US policy has had an important worldwide impact on the dominant threat frame and on the correlative policy response elsewhere. Transnational policy diffusion is not a new phenomenon. However, we should be particularly wary of such diffusion with regard to bioterrorism. The level of uncertainty involved in the assessment of bioterrorism vastly increases the risk of overreaction, leading to both a poor allocation of scarce resources and to missed opportunities to influence worldwide standards and best practices in biological research.

The shift in US policy toward a narrow civil defense approach has coincided with a reduced openness in the US biosciences and increasing secrecy within the rapidly expanding US biodefense program. The rapid growth of the program has the potential to increase the likelihood of a malicious use of microorganisms by individuals or, if such expertise is acquired by extremist groups, by nonstate terrorist actors. At the same time, the expansion of the biodefense program in the United States will affect the decisions of other states regarding their own biodefense programs. The rapid growth of a knowledge base in the area of biodefense research cannot but increase the difficulties in assessing the bioterrorist threat.

Since the attacks of 9/11 and the 2001 anthrax letters, bioterrorism has been perceived as a major national security issue in the United States, and thus it should be seen in the larger context of the current administration's so-called war on terror. The repercussions of the current mix of security policy tactics—including counterterrorism, military preemption, unilateralism, and democracy building—and the impact of these tactics on bioterrorism are as yet unclear. On the one hand, it is possible that the war on terrorism will hinder the access of terrorist groups to bioweapons capabilities. On the other, however, the motivation of such groups to acquire and use bioweapons or other weapons of mass destruction might increase as a result of the additional pressure and repression caused by the war on terror. In short, the way in which policy is written when there is a high level of uncertainty is likely to affect the probability of future bioterrorism events.

Assessing the Threat: The Danger of Overreaction

The high level of uncertainty in any bioterrorism assessment means that the threat may be exaggerated and manipulated. Although the policy prescriptions of various experts differ considerably, the experts tend to agree that the future likelihood of mass casualty bioterrorism is probably low—though the risk cannot be denied or calculated in any precise way. Conversely, policymakers cannot ignore the threat, and although they are often unfamiliar with the technological aspects of the problem, they still have to determine the interests of the state and develop policies for dealing with the problem. When they turn to the experts for technical advice, they are confronted with warnings that overreaction may be part of the problem rather than of the solution.

Likely Scenarios

One of the main reasons why the experts believe that the likelihood of bioterrorism—although it cannot be precluded in terms of technical capabilities—is low is that the process that potential bioterrorists would have to undergo—from the acquisition, to the production, and in particular to the dissemination of a bioagent—in order to carry out an attack is complex and therefore susceptible to failure. Even in medium complexity scenarios—like, for example, the attempted production and dissemination of botulinum toxin by the Japanese Aum Shinrikyo group—acquisition problems have caused attacks to fail.[21] Experience with bioterrorism attacks so far has led experts to conclude that large and complex attacks without the support of a state are unlikely, and the development of bioweapons as a result of the revolution in the life sciences is not to be expected first and foremost from nonstate actors.

The more probable scenarios, at least in the near future, are low-scale attacks that do not involve sophisticated agents. However, even limited attacks that do not cause serious damage in terms of their lethality have significant political, economic, and psychological impacts. Thus, we cannot exclude the possibility that state and nonstate actors might consider a low-scale attack, or even attempt a low-scale attack, as a promising means of terrorist violence.

Likely Perpetrators

Most experts agree that it is rather unlikely that advanced industrial states will resort to bioweapons. International legal and moral norms strongly reject the use of bioweapons, and a major military conflict between the great powers seems unlikely. The most likely states to acquire biological programs are those whose centralized governments, existing military-industrial resources, and perceptions of political threats predispose them to consider the use of unconventional weapons. But even in this group of states, there are no indications of an increasing trend in favor of biowarfare.

Further, there is no official evidence of state assistance to terrorist groups in acquiring biological weapons. Although some terrorist groups have shown an interest in acquiring bioweapons, no terrorist group is known to have successfully cultured a pathogen. It is unclear if this could change as a result of the spread of technology and of a change in the motives of terrorist actors. Since 1980, five people have been killed by bioterrorism attacks—all in 2001 and all presumably involving anthrax spores from US military laboratories. However, the expansion of state biodefense programs has increased the number of individuals familiar with the weaponization and dissemination of agents, thereby increasing the threat posed by insiders and the likelihood that expertise or material could end up in the hands of terrorist actors, as a result of either negligence or the deliberate transfer of such knowledge or material.

A Growing Gap Between the
Policy Community and the Academic Community

Policymakers have a tendency to focus on visible and communicable threats. As a result of several highly publicized simulations of catastrophic scenarios, the gap between the academic community and the policy community seems likely to have grown in recent years, in particular in the United States. The general opinion of the academic community regarding the bioterrorist threat seems to be considerably more cautious than that of the policy community. At the same time, there is no common framework in the academic community, either, that would allow a definition of the parameters of the problem and thus ultimately guide the selection of policy options.

The technical difficulties associated with attempts to spread biological weapons agents as aerosols are considerable. Aerosol methods of delivery have been developed and perfected in various state programs, and the studies available indicate that the use of aerosols could have catastrophic consequences.[22] However, it would be extremely difficult for nonstate actors to implement an aerosol attack. Yet in past years government analysts have concentrated on exactly these types of worst-case scenarios.[23] All large-scale exercise scenarios undertaken in the United States since 2000 have been based on aerosol scenarios in which plague bacteria or smallpox virus are disseminated.[24] Such exercises are justified with the argument that an aerosol cloud attack would be particularly treacherous, because the agents are invisible, odorless, and tasteless; they behave like a gas and can therefore penetrate buildings; and, consequently, large areas and a considerable number of people would be affected.[25]

Policymakers who base their policies on catastrophic scenarios run the risk of overreaction, which may entail unnecessary costs. Overreaction, academic experts warn, may bring about at least three unforeseen consequences: First, it may lead to the exact reverse of what the initial policies aimed to prevent, increasing the interest of terrorist actors in the deliberate use of biological weapons. Second, the creation of large biodefense programs may increase the risk of an accidental transfer and diffusion of such expertise and skills. The anthrax letters of 2001 are a case in point. Third, overreaction may lead to unwarranted policy priorities in terms of the time, expertise, and money invested in biodefense—at the expense of activities undertaken to prevent and manage naturally occurring diseases. While work on agents of bioweapons concern has received an enormous increase in funding in the United States, funding for research into other diseases has been cut considerably.

Managing the Threat: Key Policy Challenges

The uncertainty of the bioterrorism threat makes it extraordinarily difficult for policymakers to design sensible policies for securing modern societies against the risk of bioterrorism. The problem defies traditional approaches to threat analysis and thus constitutes a new policy challenge to both states and societies in defining countermeasures, assigning responsibilities, and providing resources. The measures for securing societies against bioterrorism are remarkably different from those needed to secure a state against the threat of an armed attack by another state. Formulating and implementing policy to protect a population against an ambiguous threat is a multifaceted challenge for policymakers at the local, federal, and international levels.

Key challenges for policymakers lie in (1) the framing of the threat and in defining the trade-offs between various policy-relevant issues, (2) striking the right balance between secrecy and transparency as a precondition of an informed public policy debate, (3) developing standards and procedures for institutional oversight and accountability for the global governance of new technologies, (4) assuring that crisis management structures are built in an open way from the bottom up to allow for the necessary level of communication and coordination among a wide range of actors and across a large number of policy fields, and (5) strengthening the legal and moral norms against the use of biological weapons at the international level.

Policy Coordination: Threat Frames and Trade-Offs

Coordinating policy among a wide range of fields and among a large group of public and private stakeholders is one of the key challenges in addressing the risk of the malicious use of microorganisms or poisonous toxins by state or nonstate actors. At a conceptual level, the key challenges for policymakers are in deciding how best to frame the parameters of the threat, how to define policies, and how to assign responsibilities. Specifically, policymakers have to consider the advantages and disadvantages of a narrow national civil defense approach on the one hand and, on the other, a broad international security approach. While the former tends to set a premium on secrecy, the latter is built on transparency—a trade-off that should be decided upon before policies are set.

At the operational level, a key challenge for policymakers is to achieve the right balance between the time, expertise, and money invested in biodefense and their investment in the prevention and management of natural diseases. Rather than evaluating the costs and benefits of new technologies in relation to biodefense alone, policymakers need to address the broader question of what role these new technologies might play in the management of dangerous naturally occurring diseases. In the absence of a reliable way to establish what level of effort is needed to deal with the biological risk, policymakers have to devote more time and energy to establishing why, and to what degree, investments in biodefense are competing with investments in the prevention of natural diseases; they also need to identify synergies between the two.

The Importance of Transparency

Given the lack of transparency at the operational level of national biodefense efforts, policymakers at both the national and the international levels will find it difficult to agree on policy trade-offs. Transparency is a precondition for an informed public policy debate on an issue that demands a multijurisdictional, multiagency, and multinational approach. Transparency is crucial because the relevant technical expertise is the domain of laboratories and research centers rather than of public policy institutions, and also because the prevention and management of bioterrorism involve public and private actors at the local, national, and international levels.

Several authors in this book emphasize that the increased secrecy in the biosciences in general and in biodefense research in particular can have three types of costs: First, increased secrecy can erode international legal and moral norms and standards against bioweapons. Second, it can increase the risk that organizationally entrenched research programs could produce undesirable results due to a lack of review, evaluation, and oversight. Third, it can impair the ability of a society to successfully react to the spread of a natural disease, because the containment of an epidemic depends heavily on an informed public.

Governing New Technologies: Institutional Oversight and Accountability

The global diffusion of biotechnologies and the spread of a disease, regardless of its origin, cannot be regulated by states alone. Traditional public sector mechanisms and structures have to adapt to this reality. States have to strengthen their regulatory reach by developing new cross-sector patterns of global governance. Institutional oversight and accountability have to start at the level of national biodefense programs. At the same time, public actors have to reach out to a globalizing academic and industrial community, setting standards and facilitating the development of norms and codes of conduct.

From a security policy point of view, the main point is to ensure that potential perpetrators—if they do decide to attempt a bioweapons attack—are not able to see the process through to its end. In order to achieve this, access to potential capabilities should be prevented through improved controls of biological agents and laboratories.[26] In addition, the dissemination of sensitive knowledge and materials should be reduced to a minimum. Securing societies against bioterrorism means extending the reach of security policies into the domestic and private spaces while at the same time limiting the public efforts to the less than extraordinary measures of technical safety and security.[27] The current expansion of biodefense research programs must not lead to a weakening of state control mechanisms.[28] Institutional oversight and organizational accountability must be ensured and standards must be developed under which border-line activities—activities that may have either illegal offensive research objectives or legal defensive research objectives—can be dealt with. The purpose of strengthening biosecurity measures is to prevent the biodefense industry—which is designed to protect society—from itself becoming a risk.

However, while state biodefense programs are expanding, so also is the number of actors in the private sector. This trend is exacerbated by the global diffusion of biotechnological research and by the rapid growth of biotechnological applications in the commercial market. While the means of accessing technology and equipment are becoming increasingly diverse, the control of actors and their activities is becoming ever more difficult, because there are many peaceful and useful applications even for highly dangerous organisms. The expertise and equipment used in an offensive bioweapons program are almost the same as those used for civilian medical or biological purposes. What ultimately determines whether a research project has a defensive or an offensive purpose is the intention of the researcher.

Thus, preventive measures initiated by researchers are just as important as state and international controls: codes of conduct can sensitize biotechnology researchers to the relevant issues and avert misconduct. With the National Science Advisory Board for Biosecurity, managed by the National Institutes of Health, the United States introduced a promising instrument to support and monitor life sciences research that could fall into the dual-use category. This bottom-up approach could very well inspire a similar board or forum in the international arena that would enable discussion of aspects of dual-use research and propagate the development of international guidelines and principles for the safe and ethical conduct of this research.

Crisis Management: The Necessity for Openness and Cooperation

The effects of bioterrorism cannot be immediately distinguished from those of a natural disease outbreak for the simple reason that it takes time before it becomes clear what has caused a particular occurrence. The management of a bioterrorism crisis begins at the local level, and from there it spreads to the national and possibly to the international levels. It involves many different actors with different institutional, professional, and cultural backgrounds, resulting in a complex communication and coordination problem. Openness and cooperation rapidly become key factors in any crisis management situation. The decisionmaking process in a crisis has to be congruent with the problem structure—a fact that should be taken into account at the planning and preparation phase.

The anthrax letters in the United States showed clearly that the management of a crisis begins at the local level. Federal or state forces enter the scene only when local authorities have reached their limits. At all levels, antiterrorist experts, law enforcement experts, biologists, biochemists, and medical practitioners must work together. Security policy experts must work with health specialists; and economists, transport specialists, and environmental experts, all immediately affected, should also be integrated into crisis management procedures. At the operational level, cooperation among the military, the medical services, the fire service, and other first responders is vital.

Time is another critical factor. Typically, bioterrorist events, and especially covert attacks, are discovered only sometime later, as the incubation period of most bioagents is several days or even weeks. Thus, the sooner the authorities react to the spread of a contagious disease, the greater the chances that the situation can be contained. In addition, there is a danger that during the incubation period people already infected will have dispersed widely, thus spreading the disease, and this in turn draws additional forces into the crisis management process.

The medical authorities face other problems: In many states, the medical system is typically overloaded and insufficiently funded. In a crisis, hospital staff members are directly exposed to the danger, and if they themselves fall ill, the entire medical infrastructure is at risk of collapsing. Further, the first cases are likely to appear in hospitals, where staff may expect to encounter, for example, influenza symptoms but not symptoms resulting from a bioterrorism attack. It is debatable how soon an outbreak of an uncommon disease would be noticed by the authorities.[29]

In terms of crisis management, bioterrorism presents itself as a typical interdisciplinary issue. It demands of the political and societal structures a high level of transparency, coordination, and communication.[30] Should governments decide to withhold or distort information about disease outbreaks, they risk delaying diagnosis and allowing the problem to spread. The possibility of an infectious disease outbreak from an unpredictable source demands openness of government toward society at the local, national, and international levels.

The Criminalization of Biological Weapons: Strengthening the BTWC

In the twentieth century, Great Britain and subsequently the United States started to withdraw from their offensive biological warfare programs.

Instead, they began to promote the international criminalization of biological weapons, paving the way to the formulation of the Biological and Toxin Weapons Convention (BTWC). Over time, a robust legal and moral norm against biological weapons has emerged. This, among other things, helps to explain why it is unlikely today that advanced industrial states will resort to biological warfare. The strengthening of the multilateral regime against bioweapons is vital to securing the state infrastructure and to limiting the probability of the diffusion of critical expertise and material to nonstate actors.

In principle, however, we cannot exclude the possibility that research findings, expertise, and serviceable weapons from state laboratories might end up—whether by accident or by design—in the hands of nonstate actors—either discontented individuals or extremist groups. Thus, precisely because of the danger from potential nonstate actors, it is crucial that the further development of bioweapons is prevented at an international level. An effective weapons control regime will indirectly affect nonstate actors, even though terrorists themselves cannot be directly deterred from using bioweapons by international prevention treaties.

The 1972 BTWC prohibits the development, production, storage, and acquisition of biological and toxin weapons. The convention has so far been ratified by 155 states parties; a further 16 signatories have yet to ratify the agreement. But although the BTWC constitutes a far-reaching prohibition, it suffers from structural deficiencies. In comparison to the Chemical Weapons Convention (CWC) and the Nuclear Non-Proliferation Treaty, the BTWC is a relatively weak regime because it lacks an instrument that would allow for its effective implementation. In the recent past, the shortfalls of the BTWC have become evident on several occasions. The basic problem lies in the fact that the BTWC lacks an effective body for verification, one that might deter potential breaches and allow the international community to apply sanctions when the convention is breached. The convention experienced its biggest setback when, at the beginning of the 1990s, it emerged that at least two states—the former Soviet Union and Iraq[31]—had breached it and were running bioweapons programs.

Since 1994, an ad hoc group had been working on a legally binding protocol for strengthening the convention. The group was unable, however, to reach an agreement on its suggestions for controlling biotechnological facilities through declarations, visits, clarification procedures, and investigations. Particular sticking points were the selection of the facilities to be monitored, the rules for surprise visits, and the procedure for triggering an investigation. Major international criticism, most prominently led by the United States, ended this process at the Fifth Review Conference of the states parties to the convention in November 2001. Since then, initiatives to substantially strengthen the regime have stagnated.

Since the Fifth Review Conference, the states parties have held annual meetings in an attempt to make concrete improvements in the convention. The focus has been on (1) measures to implement the convention's prohibition in national legislation; (2) increasing the oversight of pathogenic microorganisms and toxins; (3) enhancing the capabilities for crisis management in an outbreak; (4) increasing the surveillance, detection, diagnosis, and combating of infectious diseases; and (5) adopting codes of conduct for scientists.[32] While the usefulness of this process is a matter of dispute, it enables the continuation of a multilateral process and preserves the network of experts and diplomats.

Even after the Sixth Review Conference in Geneva in 2006, the goal must be to overcome the impasse in the multilateral BTWC process. Advocates of a strengthening of the convention envision a redress of the structural deficiencies through either the creation of a secretariat with responsibilities similar to those of the Organization for the Prohibition of Chemical Weapons in relation to the CWC, or a less ambitious institutional approach involving existing bodies within the UN. Further, the convention has not been revised since 1996 and needs to be adapted in light of recent scientific developments. Also, the BTWC should be developed into a universal agreement that is binding under international law and should then be implemented by all states parties to the convention at the national level.

Reframing the Threat:
Toward a Better Balance in Bioterrorism Policies

The degree to which the debate about bioterrorism since 9/11 and the 2001 Amerithrax events has been shaped by a set of narrow national security policy tactics cannot be overlooked. Political rhetoric in the context of the so-called war on terror has increased the risk of an overreaction, which is particularly troubling given the fact that US policies have worldwide repercussions, and that the potential diffusion of biological weapons is directly affected by the policies of Western states in general and of the United States in particular.

The increasing worldwide concern about the possible—or likely, according to some experts—outbreak of a natural influenza pandemic may provide a window of opportunity for policymakers to reframe the threat in favor of a better balance in bioterrorism policies. Specifically, the political rhetoric of policymakers could be refocused away from catastrophic worst-case scenarios to more realistic, small-scale scenarios on the one hand, and from the malicious use of microorganisms and toxins by malevolent actors to the more probable outbreak of a natural disease on the other. This, in turn, would allow a refocusing of policies away from a narrow national civil defense approach with a premium on secrecy to a broader national and international security approach that emphasizes transparency, oversight, accountability, openness, cooperation, and legal restraint.

While US policymakers may find themselves moving in such a direction by necessity as much as by design in the aftermath of the war in Iraq and that war's regional and global impacts, policymakers in other Western states should step up their efforts and contribute to the strengthening of the national and international regulatory environments in order to successfully deal with the rapid diffusion of new biotechnologies and with the potential malevolent application of bioweapons by state or nonstate actors.

Notes

1. Brad Roberts, *Terrorism with Chemical and Biological Weapons: Calibrating Risks and Responses* (Washington, DC: Chemical and Biological Arms Control Institute, 1997). The diseases that could be used by terrorists are listed by the US Centers for Disease Control and Prevention (CDC) and divided into categories A through C. CDC, *Bioterrorism Agents/Diseases,* http://www.bt.cdc.gov/agent/agentlist-category.asp (accessed 20 September 2005).

2. Roger Breeze, "Agroterrorism: Betting Far More Than the Farm," *Biosecurity and Bioterrorism: Biodefense Strategy, Practice, and Science* 2, no. 4 (2004): 251–264.

3. World Organisation for Animal Health, World Health Organization, and Food and Agriculture Organization of the United Nations, "Report of the WHO/FAO/OIE Joint Consultation on Emerging Zoonotic Diseases," Geneva, Switzerland, 3–5 May 2004, http://whqlibdoc.who.int/hq/2004/WHO_CDS_CPE_ZFK_2004.9.pdf (accessed 20 September 2005).

4. Ron Purver, *Chemical and Biological Terrorism: The Threat According to the Open Literature* (Ottawa, ON: Canadian Security Intelligence Service, 1995).

5. Members of the Bhagwan Shree Rajneesh sect in The Dalles, Oregon, attempted in 1984 to influence a local election by contaminating the salad bars of ten restaurants with salmonella. Over 750 people fell ill, and 45 had to be hospitalized. W. Seth Carus, "The Rajneeshees," in *Toxic Terror: Assessing*

Terrorist Use of Chemical and Biological Weapons, ed. Jonathan B. Tucker, 115–138 (Cambridge, MA: MIT Press, 2000).

6. The US Federal Bureau of Investigation dubbed the anthrax attacks "Amerithrax." It created a special website for the ongoing anthrax investigation, which was given the same name.

7. Centers for Disease Control and Prevention, "Update: Investigation of Bioterrorism-Related Anthrax, 2001," *Morbidity and Mortality Weekly Report* 50, no. 45 (16 November 2001): 1008–1010, http://www.ncbi.nlm.nih.gov/entrez/query.fcgi?cmd=Retrieve&db=PubMed&list_uids=11724158&dopt=Abstract (accessed 12 September 2005).

8. David Heyman, *Lessons from the Anthrax Attacks: Implications for U.S. Bioterrorism Preparedness; A Report on a National Forum on Biodefense* (Federation of American Scientists report based on a daylong forum convened by the Center for Strategic and International Studies under contract to the Defense Threat Reduction Agency, December 2001), p. 4, http://www.fas.org/irp/threat/cbw/dtra02.pdf (accessed 12 September 2005).

9. Milton Leitenberg, *The Problem of Biological Weapons* (Stockholm: Swedish National Defence College, 2004), pp. 55–68.

10. Gregory Koblentz, "Pathogens as Weapons: The International Security Implications of Biological Warfare," *International Security* 28, no. 3 (Winter 2003–2004): 118.

11. Steven M. Block, "Living Nightmares: Biological Threats Enabled by Molecular Biology," in *The New Terror: Facing the Threat of Biological and Chemical Weapons,* ed. Sidney D. Drell, Abraham D. Sofaer, and George D. Wilson (Stanford, CA: Hoover Institution, 1999), p. 56, http://www.stanford.edu/group/blocklab/Block%20New%20Terror%20Chapter%202.pdf (accessed 13 September 2005).

12. Ken Alibek, "Smallpox: A Disease and a Weapon," *International Journal of Infectious Diseases* 8, suppl. 2 (October 2004): 3–8.

13. Bruce Hoffman, "Terrorism Trends and Prospects," in *Countering the New Terrorism,* ed. Ian O. Lesser et al., 7–38 (Santa Monica, CA: Rand Corporation, 1999).

14. Martha Crenshaw, "The Psychology of Terrorism: An Agenda for the 21st Century," *Political Psychology* 21, no. 2 (June 2000): 405–420; Ehud Sprinzak, "The Great Superterrorism Scare," *Foreign Policy* (Fall 1998): 110–124.

15. Milton Leitenberg, "An Assessment of the Biological Weapons Threat to the United States" (white paper prepared for the "Conference on Emerging Threats Assessment, Biological Terrorism," Institute for Security Technology Studies, Dartmouth College, Hanover, NH, 7–9 July 2000), http://academic.udayton.edu/health/syllabi/Bioterrorism/3Bioterror/bioterror05.htm (accessed 12 September 2005). Also see Kathleen Bailey quoted in Jessica Stern, *The Ultimate Terrorists* (Cambridge, MA: Harvard University Press, 1999), p. 50.

16. See Milton Leitenberg's chapter (3) in this book.

17. Gabriel Weimann, *How Modern Terrorism Uses the Internet* (Washington, DC: United States Institute of Peace, 2004), pp. 5–10, http://www.usip.org/pubs/specialreports/sr116.pdf (accessed 20 September 2005).

18. Brad Roberts, ed., *Hype or Reality? The "New Terrorism" and Mass*

Casualty Attacks (Alexandria, VA: Chemical and Biological Arms Control Institute, 2000).

19. Brian Michael Jenkins, *Will Terrorists Go Nuclear?* Rand Paper P-5541 (Santa Monica, CA: Rand Corporation, 1975).

20. In Switzerland, over a thousand unsubstantiated anthrax scares in fall 2001 led to massive attention in the media. Over a hundred post offices and mail distribution centers were temporarily closed, and parts of Zurich airport came to a temporary standstill. See Michael Guery, "Biologischer Terrorismus in Bezug auf die Schweiz: Unter besonderer Berücksichtigung rechtlicher Aspekte" [Biological terrorism and Switzerland: With a focus on legal aspects], *Zürcher Beiträge für Sicherheitspolitik,* no. 74, p. 11; available in German and French at http://www.isn.ethz.ch/crn/publications/publications_crn.cfm?pubid =380 (accessed 20 September 2005).

21. David E. Kaplan, "Aum Shinrikyo (1995)," in Tucker, *Toxic Terror,* p. 213.

22. Ken Alibek, "Biological Weapons/Bioterrorism Threat and Defense: Past, Present and Future" (paper presented at the conference "Meeting the Challenges of Bioterrorism: Assessing the Threat and Designing Biodefense Strategies," Fürigen, Switzerland, 22–23 April 2005), http://www.isn.ethz.ch/ crn/publications/publications_crn.cfm?pubid=414 (accessed 15 September 2005); Richard Danzig, *Catastrophic Bioterrorism: What Is to Be Done?* (Washington, DC: Center for Technology and National Security Policy, 2003), p. 5.

23. For example, the dissemination of bioweapons as aerosols appears in a recent scenario catalog of the US Department of Homeland Security. One of these scenarios includes the spraying of bioweapons from a truck whose deadly freight is driven through five cities and spread to 350,000 people, of whom 13,000 die. Department of Homeland Security, *Planning Scenarios* (Washington, DC: Homeland Security Council, July 2004); "Federal Officials Catalogue Possible Terror Attacks," Associated Press, 16 March 2005, http://www.tkb.org/ NewsStory.jsp?storyID=60169.

24. The exercises are based on the following scenarios: Top Off I, May 2000: Aerosolized plague; July 2000: Aerosolized plague; Dark Winter, June 2001: Aerosolized smallpox; Top Off II, May 2003: Aerosolized plague; Atlantic Storm, January 2005: Aerosolized dry powder smallpox. See, for example, Tara O'Toole, Michael Mair, and Thomas Inglesby, "Shining Light on Dark Winter," *Clinical Infectious Diseases* 34, no. 2 (2002), http://www .journals.uchicago.edu/CID/journal/issues/v34n7/020165/020165.html (accessed 12 September 2005).

25. Experts from the Center for Biosecurity at the University of Pittsburgh Medical Center have focused on the smallpox virus and anthrax bacterium because these two agents are believed to be most effectively disseminated through aerosols. See Donald A. Henderson, *Bioterrorism: Testimony Before Congress of the United States,* US Senate Veteran's Affairs Committee and the Appropriations Committee on Labor, Health, and Human Services, Education and Related Services, 16 March 1999, http://www.upmc-biosecurity.org/pages/

resources/hearings/da_01.html (accessed 20 September 2005).

26. Biosafety measures are designed to ensure the safe handling of biological agents and to prevent accidents in laboratories, while biosecurity measures are designed to ensure the safety and containment of biological substances by preventing unauthorized access to them and by monitoring and running checks on laboratory staff. See Reynolds M. Salerno and Daniel P. Estes, "Biosecurity: Protecting High Consequence Pathogens and Toxins Against Theft and Diversion," in *Encyclopedia of Bioterrorism Defense,* ed. Richard F. Pilch and Raymond A. Zilinskas (Hoboken, NJ: Wiley, 2005), pp. 57–62; World Health Organization, *Laboratory Biosafety Manual,* WHO/CDS/CSR/LYO/2003.4, rev. ed. (Geneva: WHO, 2003), pp. 1–3, http://www.who.int/csr/resources/publications/biosafety/who_cds_csr_lyo_20034/en/print.html (accessed 19 September 2005).

27. I am indebted to Myriam Dunn with regard to this point: Myriam Dunn, "Cyber-Security and Threats Politics: US Efforts to Secure the Information Age" (New York: Routledge, forthcoming).

28. Koblentz, "Pathogens as Weapons," p. 118.

29. Eric K. Noji, "Mass Casualty Care and Medical Countermeasures: Surge Capacity, Patient Tracking, and Decontamination" (paper presented at the conference "Meeting the Challenges of Bioterrorism: Assessing the Threat and Designing Biodefense Strategies," Fürigen, Switzerland, 22–23 April 2005), http://www.isn.ethz.ch/crn/publications/publications_crn.cfm?pubid=427 (accessed 15 September 2005).

30. Center for Counterproliferative Research, *Toward a National Biodefense Strategy: Challenges and Opportunities* (Washington, DC: National Defense University, April 2003), pp. 5–11.

31. *Iraq: The UNSCOM Experience,* SIPRI Fact Sheet, October 1998, http://editors.sipri.se/pubs/Factsheet/unscom.html (accessed 16 September 2005).

32. *United Nations Biological and Toxin Weapons Convention Report of the Meeting of Experts,* "Meeting of the States Parties to the Convention on the Prohibition of the Development, Production and Stockpiling of Bacteriological (Biological) and Toxin Weapons and on Their Destruction," Geneva, 5 August 2005, http://www.opbw.org/new_process/mx2005/bwc_msp.2005_mx_3_E.pdf (accessed 16 September 2005).

Acronyms

ACDA	Arms Control and Disarmament Agency
AIDS	acquired immunodeficiency syndrome
BTWC	Biological and Toxin Weapons Convention
CBACI	Chemical and Biological Arms Control Institute
CBW	chemical and biological weapons
CDC	Centers for Disease Control and Prevention
CIA	Central Intelligence Agency
CSS	Center for Security Studies
CWC	Chemical Weapons Convention
DDRS	Declassified Documents Reference System
DHS	Department of Homeland Security
DIA	Defense Intelligence Agency
DNI	Director of National Intelligence
DNSA	Digital National Security Archives
EU	European Union
FAO	Food and Agriculture Organization
FARC	Revolutionary Armed Forces of Colombia
FBI	Federal Bureau of Investigation
GAO	Government Accountability Office
HGP	Human Genome Project
HIV	human immunodeficiency virus
HUMINT	human intelligence
IAEA	International Atomic Energy Agency
IRA	Irish Republican Army
ISG	Iraq Survey Group
MASINT	measurement and signals intelligence
NATO	North Atlantic Treaty Organization

NGO	nongovernmental organization
NIAID	National Institute of Allergy and Infectious Diseases
NIC	National Intelligence Council
NIE	National Intelligence Estimate
NSC	National Security Council
OIF	Operation Iraqi Freedom
OTA	Office of Technology Assessment
SARS	severe acute respiratory syndrome
SIPRI	Stockholm International Peace Research Institute
SPICE	smallpox inhibitor of complement enzymes
UNMOVIC	United Nations Monitoring, Verification and Inspection Commission
UNSCOM	United Nations Special Commission
USAMRIID	United States Army Medical Research Institute for Infectious Diseases
VCP	vaccinia virus complement control protein
WHO	World Health Organization
WMD	Weapons of Mass Destruction

Bibliography

Alibek, Ken, with Stephen Handelman. *Biohazard: The Chilling True Story of the Largest Covert Biological Weapons Program in the World—Told from Inside by the Man Who Ran It*. New York: Random House, 1999.

Beck, Ulrich. *Risk Society: Towards a New Modernity*. Translated by M. Ritter. London: Sage, 1992.

Carus, W. Seth. *Bioterrorism and Biocrimes: The Illicit Use of Biological Agents Since 1990*. Washington, DC: National Defense University, 2002.

Chevrier, Marie Isabelle et al., eds. *The Implementation of Legally Binding Measures to Strengthen the Biological and Toxin Weapons Convention*. Dordrecht: Kluwer Academic, 2004.

Dando, Malcolm R., V. Nathanson, and M. Darrel. *Biotechnology, Weapons and Humanity*. London: Harwood Academic, 1999.

———. *Biotechnology, Weapons and Humanity II*. London: British Medical Association, 2004.

———. *Bioterrorism: What Is the Real Threat?* Science and Technology Report, no. 3. Bradford, UK: Department of Peace Studies, University of Bradford, March 2005.

———. *Biowar and Bioterror: A Beginner's Guide*. Oxford: Oneworld, 2006.

———. *The New Biological Weapons: Threats, Proliferation, and Control*. Boulder, CO: Lynne Rienner, 2001.

Dando, Malcolm R., and Mark Wheelis. "Back to Bioweapons?" *Bulletin of the Atomic Scientists* 59, no. 1 (January/February 2003): 41–46.

———. "New Technology and Future Developments in Biological Warfare." *MilitaryTechnology* 27 (May 2003): 52–56.

Drell, Sidney D., Abraham D. Sofaer, and George D. Wilson, eds. *The New Terror: Facing the Threat of Biological and Chemical Weapons*. Stanford, CA: Hoover Institution, 1999.

Falkenrath, Richard A., Robert D. Newman, and Bradley A. Thayer. *America's Achilles' Heel: Nuclear, Biological, and Chemical Terrorism and Covert Attack*. BCSIA Studies in International Security. Cambridge, MA: MIT Press, 1998.

Geissler, Erhard, and John Ellis van Courtland Moon, eds. *Biological and Toxin Weapons: Research, Development, and Use from the Middle Ages to 1945.* New York: Oxford University Press, 1999.

Guillemin, Jeanne. *Biological Weapons: From the Invention of State-Sponsored Programs to Contemporary Bioterrorism.* New York: Columbia University Press, 2005.

Jensen, K. M., and David Wurmser, eds. *Is It Feasible to Negotiate Chemical and Biological Weapons Control?* Washington, DC: United States Institute of Peace, 1990.

Koblentz, Gregory. "Pathogens as Weapons: The International Security Implications of Biological Warfare." *International Security* 28, no. 3 (Winter 2003–2004): 84–122.

Leitenberg, Milton. *Deaths in Wars and Conflicts Between 1945 and 2000.* Occasional Paper, no. 29. Ithaca, NY: Peace Studies Program, Cornell University, 2003.

———. "Distinguishing Offensive from Defensive Biological Weapons Research." *Critical Reviews in Microbiology* 29, no. 3 (2003): 223–257.

———. *The Problem of Biological Weapons.* Stockholm: Swedish National Defence College, 2004.

Lesser, Ian O., et al., eds. *Countering the New Terrorism.* Santa Monica, CA: Rand Corporation, 1999.

McBride, David. *Bioterrorism: The History of a Crisis in American Society.* New York: Routledge, 2003.

O'Toole, Tara, Michael Mair, and Thomas V. Inglesby. "Shining Light on Dark Winter." *Clinical Infectious Diseases* 34 (2002): 972–983.

Parachini, John. "Putting WMD Terrorism into Perspective." *Washington Quarterly* 26, no. 4 (Autumn 2003): 37–50.

Petro, James, Theodore R. Plasse, and Jack A. McNulty. "Biotechnology: Impact on Biological Warfare and Biodefense." *Biosecurity and Bioterrorism: Biodefense Strategy, Practice, and Science* 1, no. 3 (September 2003): 161–168.

Pilch, Richard F., and Raymond A. Zilinskas, eds. *Encyclopedia of Bioterrorism Defense.* Hoboken, NJ: Wiley, 2005.

Purver, Ron. *Chemical and Biological Terrorism: The Threat According to the Open Literature.* Ottawa, ON: Canadian Security Intelligence Service, June 1995.

Rasco, Barbara A., and Gleyn E. Bledsoe. *Bioterrorism and Food Safety.* Boca Raton, FL: CRC Press, 2005.

Rifkin, Jeremy. *The Biotech Century.* London: Phoenix, 1999.

Roberts, Brad, ed. *Hype or Reality? The "New Terrorism" and Mass Casualty Attacks.* Alexandria, VA: Chemical and Biological Arms Control Institute, 2000.

———, ed. *Terrorism with Chemical and Biological Weapons: Calibrating Risks and Responses.* Washington, DC: Chemical and Biological Arms Control Institute, 1997.

Salerno, Reynolds M., Jennifer Gaudioso, Rebecca L. Frerichs, and Daniel Estes. "A BW Risk Assessment: Historical and Technical Perspectives." *Nonproliferation Review* 11, no. 3 (Fall/Winter 2004): 25–55.

Simon, Jeffrey D. *Terrorists and the Potential Use of Biological Weapons: A Discussion of Possibilities.* Rand Paper R-3771-AFMIC. Santa Monica, CA: Rand Corporation, 1989.

Stockholm International Peace Research Institute. *The Problem of Chemical and Biological Warfare: A Study of the Historical, Technical, Military, Legal and Political Aspects of CBW, and Possible Disarmament Measures.* Vol. 2, *CB Weapons Today.* Stockholm: Almqvist and Wiksell, 1973.

Thompson, K. M., et al. *Bayes, Bugs, and Bioterrorists: Lessons Learned from the Anthrax Attacks.* Defense and Technology Papers 14. Washington, DC: Center for Technology and National Security Policy, National Defense University, April 2005.

Tucker, Jonathan B., ed. *Toxic Terror: Assessing Terrorist Use of Chemical and Biological Weapons.* Cambridge, MA: MIT Press, 2000.

Wheelis, Mark, Lajos Rózsa, and Malcolm Dando, eds. *Deadly Cultures: Biological Weapons Since 1945.* Cambridge, MA: Harvard University Press, 2006.

Zilinskas, Raymond, ed. *Biological Warfare: Modern Offense and Defense.* Boulder, CO: Lynne Rienner, 1999.

Zilinskas, Raymond, and Jonathan Tucker. "Limiting the Contribution of the Open Scientific Literature to the Biological Weapons Threat." *Journal of Homeland Security,* December 2002.

The Contributors

Marie Isabelle Chevrier is associate professor of public policy and political economy at the University of Texas at Dallas. She serves as the chair of the Scientists Working Group on Chemical and Biological Weapons at the Center for Arms Control and Non-Proliferation in Washington, DC. She is a member of the board of directors of the Bioweapons Prevention Project and has written extensively on biological weapons arms control.

Anthony H. Cordesman holds the Arleigh A. Burke Chair in Strategy at the Center for Strategic and International Studies in Washington, DC. He has worked in a wide range of national security positions, including in the Office of the Secretary of Defense, and is a former director of the Defense Intelligence Assessment. In 2001, he published *The Challenges of Biological Terrorism* and *Terrorism, Asymmetric Warfare, and Weapons of Mass Destruction: Defending the US Homeland*.

Malcolm Dando is professor of international security in the Department of Peace Studies at the University of Bradford, UK. He trained originally as a biologist and his research interests center on preventing the hostile misuse of modern biology. Together with Mark Wheelis and Lajos Rózsa, he edited *Deadly Cultures: Biological Weapons Since 1945*.

Jeanne Guillemin is a senior adviser in the Security Studies Program at the Massachusetts Institute of Technology. Her most recent book is *Biological Weapons: From the Invention of State-Sponsored Programs to Contemporary Bioterrorism*. As a senior fellow at the Carr Center for Human Rights Policy, Harvard University, she is currently researching the 1932–1945 Japanese biological warfare program and how its chief scientists evaded prosecution at the postwar Tokyo war crimes tribunal.

Iris Hunger is the head of the Research Group for Biological Arms Control at Hamburg University and the author of *Bioweapons Control in a Multipolar World* (in German).

Peter R. Lavoy directs the Center for Contemporary Conflict and is a senior lecturer in the National Security Affairs Department at the Naval Postgraduate School, Monterey, California. His main research interests are in weapons proliferation and South Asian politics and security. He coedited *Planning the Unthinkable: How New Powers Will Use Nuclear, Biological, and Chemical Weapons* and served as director for counter-proliferation policy in the Office of the Secretary of Defense from 1998 to 2000.

Milton Leitenberg is a senior research scholar at the Center for International and Security Studies, School of Public Policy, University of Maryland. Trained as a biochemist, he entered the field of arms control in January 1968 at the Stockholm International Peace Research Institute. Recent publications include *The Problem of Biological Weapons* and *Assessing the Biological Weapons and Bioterrorism Threat.*

Andreas Wenger is professor of international security policy and the director of the Center for Security Studies at ETH Zürich (Swiss Federal Institute of Technology). His main research interests are in security and strategic studies and in the history of international relations. His publications include *Conflict Prevention: The Untapped Potential of the Business Sector* (coauthor) and *How States Fight Terrorism: Policy Dynamics in the West* (coeditor).

Reto Wollenmann was, until 2005, a research fellow at the Center for Security Studies (CSS) at ETH Zürich (Swiss Federal Institute of Technology), where he analyzed new security policy risks and initiated the forthcoming CSS publication *International Handbook on Biodefense Policies.* He is now a policy adviser on arms control and disarmament at the Swiss Federal Department of Defence. He is the author of *Zwischen Atomwaffe und Atomsperrvertrag,* a book on Switzerland's nuclear ambitions in the Cold War.

Index

229

About the Book

ESPECIALLY SINCE THE 2001 ANTHRAX ATTACKS IN THE UNITED STATES, THE issue of bioterrorism has been controversial: Are governments underestimating the potential hazard of biological toxins, as some claim, or is the danger in fact exaggerated? What are the policy options for dealing with such a complex threat? The authors of this book offer a reasoned assessment of the issues at the core of the debates.

Identifying a high level of uncertainty as a key characteristic of the bioterrorism threat, the authors examine the legacies of the secret state biowarfare programs of the previous century, analyze academic and political controversies about current dangers, and consider the impact of rapid scientific and technological change on the development of future threats. In the process, they provide new insights into the broader question of risk management and the role of public and private actors in international security relations.

Andreas Wenger is a professor of international security policy and the director of the Center for Security Studies at the Swiss Federal Institute of Technology (ETH Zürich). **Reto Wollenmann** is a policy adviser on arms control and disarmament in the Directorate for Security Policy of the Swiss Federal Department of Defence.